T0368047

JUST LIKE THE DAYS OF NOAH

Matthew 24

JAN DARNELL

WESTBOW
PRESS®
A DIVISION OF THOMAS NELSON
& ZONDERVAN

WestBow Press books may be ordered through booksellers or by contacting:

WestBow Press
A Division of Thomas Nelson & Zondervan
1663 Liberty Drive
Bloomington, IN 47403
www.westbowpress.com
844-714-3454

Cover image by Bryan Abeling

Scripture quotations taken from the (NASB®) New American Standard Bible®, Copyright © 1960, 1971, 1977, 1995, 2020 by The Lockman Foundation. Used by permission. All rights reserved. www.lockman.org

ISBN: 979-8-3850-3730-8 (sc)
ISBN: 979-8-3850-3731-5 (e)

Library of Congress Control Number: 2024922847

Print information available on the last page.

WestBow Press rev. date: 02/13/2025

To my blessing of a husband, Barry Darnell, who has endured patiently through the years required to complete this study. His sacrifices and counsel made *Just Like the Days of Noah* possible. To the friends, family, and pastoral counselors who contributed their editing services and theological reviews and participated in the abundant revisions necessary to accomplish the task. God knows you each by name and so do I.

You all have a distinguished place in my heart, especially my faithful "mighty comrades" who have co-labored with me as prayer warriors through every edition of this study. To my birth mother, Sue Coursey, who taught me the value of hard work. To my spiritual mother, Kay Arthur, who taught me how to study the Bible and pray fervently.

Above all,
"To Him who is able to do far more abundantly beyond all that we ask or think, according to the power that works within us. To Him *be* the glory in the church and in Christ Jesus to all generations forever and ever. Amen" (Ephesians 3:20–21).

Elizabeth Elliot wrote,
"I keep feeling my own inadequacy in perceiving the truth and in actually formulating it on paper. One wonders if one's soul is really big enough for the task. I keep thinking of old John [the apostle], seeing that tremendous vision, and being told, "Write what you see." None of us can do anything else in honesty—we must write what we see, not what someone else sees, not what we may think we ought to see, not what we wish to see."

Contents

Preface

For more than a century, the pre-tribulation church rapture has been presented as a dependable biblical axiom. Consequently, many believe the saints will be whisked away before the great tribulation. I was counted among them until July of 2013 when Matthew 24 shook me from my unintended stupor. Jesus, the one who promised that He would return, left us with an informative timeline regarding the signs of His coming. It stunned and gripped me. From that pivotal moment forward, I began trekking through the related Scriptures, becoming more and more convinced that Christ's timeline is vital to our interpretation of God's remaining prophecies. This unplanned journey has been enlightening and encouraging—beyond imagination. Outside sources were also referenced but only after allowing the Word of God to speak first. By His Spirit, my attempt with this study has been to bring you a condensed version of my library and litany of notes. I pray you will benefit as I have and, as a result, be better prepared and equipped for the day of the Lord.

Just Like the Days of Noah is a study of Matthew 24—Christ's timeline of "signs" that will predicate His return. Could He be coming soon? Tuck that blessed hope in your heart and let it swell with anticipation for the answer is absolutely yes! While there have been previous eras of unsettling history and apprehension over the future of humanity, the events we see unfolding today speak not only to the credibility of Scripture but also to the imminent fulfillment of God's final prophecies. If there is a God—and there is—then we are currently receiving merciful wake-up calls to repent and prepare for the Lord's return as the Judge of heaven and earth (Acts 17:30–31, Jude 6).

Matthew 24:6–10 reveals wars and natural disasters as visible signs of His coming. Though these have been occurring for centuries, they have increased in intensity and frequency in recent years. Earthquakes, tornadoes, hurricanes, fires, floods, avalanches, and erratic weather are becoming the norm. At present, the war in the Middle East between Israel and Hamas has destabilized not only that region but also the entire world with its effects. Jesus refers to signs such as these as merely "the beginning of birth pangs." In verses 15 and 29, the more prominent signs we should expect to see are (1) the abomination of desolation and (2) the shaking of the heavens. Then Jesus says, "When you see all these things, recognize that He is near, right at the door" (Matthew 24:33). Jesus gave us the signs that signal His returning. Yet the majority within the body of Jesus Christ know little about them because they expect to be raptured beforehand.

After more than two decades of researching the timeline of Christ, I have concluded that the dispensational church age pre-tribulation theory is notably flawed. It is elaborately crafted but biblically undocumented as a sound doctrine we should invest in. Rather, it should be understood as a theological hypothesis. Certainly not a certainty. The timeline of Christ is not only the clear certainty we can depend on but a formidable spine of prophecy capable of simplifying all other eschatological studies. Matthew 24 is a brilliant beacon of light provided for the elect in these final days but currently hidden beneath the rubble of theoretical boulders.

When Jesus returns, He will be revealed as the one and only Savior who redeemed one assembly of saints. While the final prophecies regarding Israel as a nation do unfold in the Middle East primarily, we find no reference by Old Testament prophets, New Testament writers, the apostles, or Jesus that the saints living elsewhere will be removed in a pre-tribulation rapture. Instead, the Scriptures present one resurrection of the righteous, one rapture rescue, and one return of Christ for His prepared bride in the day of the Lord.

Introduction

What if you had seen God part the waters of the Red Sea? Or witnessed just one of Christ's miracles? I often ponder the blessing of those privileged to watch our Savior cure diseases, reinstate failed senses, raise the dead, and exercise authority over demons. Those divine interventions were propelled by God's incredible grace. To behold such mercy flowing through His incarnate Son would have been to observe the Father's affection for us—His redemptive heart reaching out with restorative, eternal benefits. Though you and I were not privy to the first coming of Jesus Christ, we might very well be the generation to behold His second. Allow me to add that this grand event will be unmatched by any other supernatural event heaven has disclosed thus far, including the parting of the Red Sea and astonishing miracles of Jesus.

If we are the generation to glimpse His return, then we will be the ones to witness unparalleled majesty splitting open the heavens. We will be the privileged generation because the return of Jesus Christ will revolutionize what the earth knows of the supernatural. All of God's saints who have died from the time of Adam will descend with Jesus in masse. Can you imagine such a sight? According to Scripture, bodies are then raised from their graves across the world and instantly transformed (1 Cor. 15:52). As Jesus is, so shall we be (1 Jo. 3:2). The elect who remain on earth at that time are "caught up" with Him and reunited with loved ones (1 Thess. 4:13–17). Hallelujah!

Jesus compared His second coming to the days of Noah, "For the coming of the Son of Man will be just like the days of Noah" (Matthew 24:37). This study of Matthew 24, *Just Like the Days of Noah*, will explore the meaning of that statement, along with His unique timeline that cuts straight through the theoretical proposals of our day.

Is today comparable to the days of Noah, a time that grieved God enough to intervene with a global judgment against worldly, sinful deceptions? Consider this: we are living in an age of apostasy, abuse, and applauded violence. Greed and idolatry are pursuits that our world aspires to rather than humbling ourselves before the righteous ways of the Almighty. Many today even refuse to acknowledge Jesus as our Creator, much less our judge. In terms of anticipating the return of Jesus Christ, how many would you say are consciously preparing for this significant event, not fearfully worrying but prayerfully preparing with confidence of what His return entails?

> For as in those days which were before the flood they were eating and drinking,
> they were marrying and giving in marriage, until the day that Noah entered the
> ark, and they did not understand until the flood came and took them all away;
> so shall the coming of the Son of Man be (Matthew 24:38–39).

Noah and his family were warned to prepare for a calamitous flood. They did. They built an ark according to God's specifications, waiting for the fulfillment of His Word. It is my prayer that this study of Matthew 24 will help prepare you as we wait for God to accomplish His Word when

Jesus returns. Should you build an ark? No, but we should all know how to read the signs of a crimson sky forecasting an approaching storm that is coming. Jesus Christ, the King of kings, is our ark, so God's provision of safety has already been accomplished. Are you in the ark? Are you protected by the righteousness of Jesus Christ, by the same blood of the Lamb that protected the Israelites when they were delivered from Egypt?

Be aware that a Bible study of prophecy is more difficult than others, yet it is beneficial and rewarding. Shrouded by mystery, prophecies provide us with an acute sense of God's oversight regarding past, present, and future events, authenticating Scripture in their fulfillment. Since hundreds of prophecies have already transpired exactly as predicted regarding the first coming of Christ, we can be confident that the remainder will be as well when He returns.

In *Just Like the Days of Noah*, we examine the timeline of events Christ shared in Matthew 24. His disciples asked, "What will be the sign of Your coming and of the end of the age?" Jesus divulged a series of notable signs. Many of us today know very little of the events to unfold because the task of navigating the maze of opinions regarding Christ's return is enormous. How many of us know enough Scripture to decipher this vast sea of presentations? Very few. Thus, we hope that our pastors and teachers have interpreted them rightly. But not all have. Who can we believe? Jesus.

Jesus simplified the signs of His return for us when He answered the disciple's questions, providing a brilliant beacon of light. Begin with the timeline of Jesus, and you have a dependable framework on which to build further study. Jesus is coming back! That was and still is His promise. Who should we listen to? "This is My Son, My Chosen One; listen to Him" (Luke 9:35). (Acts 3:22)

I ask, for your benefit, that you consider the high probability that the church of Jesus Christ will indeed endure the great tribulation period. This assertion is rejected by the Christian community at large, but at what cost? Christ's assembly of saints have been chosen as one for eternity—from all nations. One congregation. One Father. One Redeemer. One faith. We are one, brought into the covenant promises together by Christ and blessed by His Spirit as a union of believers. Our calling may also be to endure the fires of this period as His church body, emerging as one unified bride.

First Thessalonians 4:13–17 is the only passage within the writ of Scripture (other than perhaps Daniel 12:1-2) alluding to believers being "caught up" when Jesus returns as a reunion of the dead and the living. It describes the return of Christ as a spectacular event rather than a secret rescue. "For the LORD Himself will descend from heaven with a shout, with the voice of the archangel, and with the trumpet of God" (1 Thessalonians 4:17). Jesus testified that "every eye" will see Him when He returns, not just those raptured (Rev. 1:7). Graves break open across the world. Bodies emerge, ashes reintegrate, as the righteous are resurrected. Then, those who remain will be caught up. Some think God's wrath is poured out during the great tribulation period; therefore, the church should be removed beforehand (1 Thess. 1:10). Yet the Scriptures reveal God's elect are on earth during the great tribulation (Matt. 24:21–22; Rev. 7:14, 12:17, 13:10; Dan. 7:21). Thus, God's wrath will come afterwards. Revelation 11:15-18 designates it to be after the seventh trumpet. Others try to divide the kingdom or "Israel of God," extracting

Gentile believers and leaving their Jewish brethren to endure the great tribulation alone. Do we divide what God has united (Gal. 3:7, 6:16; Rom. 9:6)?

I have made this study as easy as possible without compromising the integrity of the Scriptures, concentrating on what Jesus reveals as clear certainties. These certainties are trustworthy pillars of truth. It is a mistake to invest our faith in a rapture rescue to the detriment of studying both the significance of Christ's return and the great tribulation preceding it. Those who do may find themselves at a disadvantage in the days ahead. Let's look at God's Word together regarding the timeline of Christ and His return. That is the purpose of this study. Awareness. Preparation. Faith.

> Maranatha! O Lord come! May the grace of our Lord Jesus be with you. My love be with all of you in Christ Jesus. (1 Corinthians 16:23–24)

Layout of Just Like the Days of Noah

Welcome to *Just Like the Days of Noah*! This writing has been like the gestation of a child, requiring labor, interminable adjustments, and repeated intervals of waiting in prayerful solitude and surrender. Throughout the process, it has been necessary to rely on God not only for strength but, most importantly, His guidance. The Spirit initiated this project one afternoon as I read through Matthew and came upon chapter 24. Since that day, He has faithfully directed me through more than twenty years of research in the study of Christ's timeline. For all that our Heavenly Father has allowed me to accomplish for the sake of His elect, I offer unreserved blessing to Him. Without His relentless pursuit of this project, it would not be in your hands.

Allow me a brief explanation of the format. There are four days of study each week for seven weeks (the last week has five days). I purposely designed less than five days of homework per week to allow you ample time to enhance what you are studying with cross-references. These are provided in the margins of study Bibles. If you do not own a study Bible, then access an internet site like OpenBible.info and enter the passage address for cross-references. Those that I provide in the study are abbreviated such as (Gen. 3:15) and included in case you want to examine the commentary. You are not required to look these up at any point. When Scripture is directly quoted, the reference is not abbreviated, but spelled out such as "And the Lord was sorry that He had made man on the earth, and He was grieved in His heart" (Genesis 6:6).

If you are in a group with scheduled meetings, please don't forfeit the opportunity for cross-referencing by attempting last-minute study right before class. That, of course, is your decision, and it is better to do a little than nothing at all. However, I do recommend spreading it out—again, for your benefit. The Spirit leads us through His inspired text, providing incredible insights when we lend ourselves to the opportunity and enter His presence in pursuit of truth (Ps. 32:8–9).

Please avoid searching the internet, going to commentaries, or even reading the interpretative helps in your Bibles until Week Six. Allow the Scriptures to speak on their own merit, and you will be surprised how freely they flow when uninterrupted by the multiplicity of different opinions.

Most of the questions asked as we move through this study are simple observation questions. They are not difficult and will help you to see and receive truths with ease. A right knowledge of truth is critical to the process of healthy, fruitful application. Humbling ourselves before the authority of God's Word is the goal. Honoring Him with our lives will be the end result.

Thank you so much for doing this study with me! I love you and pray that God will prepare us all for the "latter" days seen on the horizon as quickly approaching. May the church (Jew and Gentile) stand firmly together, united by the Holy Spirit, with one mind, striving together for the faith of the Gospel (Phil. 1:27). To Him be the glory, great things He has done! Amen, my friends. And may the ransomed bride of the Lord Jesus Christ be found ready when her bridegroom comes (Rev. 19:7)!

> Now may the God of peace Himself sanctify you entirely; and may your spirit and soul and body be preserved complete, without blame at the coming of our LORD Jesus Christ. (1 Thessalonians. 5:23)

Matthew 24 (New American Standard [1995])

Signs of Christ's Return

Jesus came out from the temple and was going away when His disciples came up to point out the temple buildings to Him. And He said to them, "Do you not see all these things? Truly I say to you, not one stone here will be left upon another, which will not be torn down." As He was sitting on the Mount of Olives, the disciples came to Him privately, saying, "Tell us, when will these things happen, and what will be the sign of Your coming, and of the end of the age?" And Jesus answered and said to them, "See to it that no one misleads you. For many will come in My name, saying, 'I am the Christ,' and will mislead many. You will be hearing of wars and rumors of wars. See that you are not frightened, for those things must take place, but that is not yet the end."

"For nation will rise against nation, and kingdom against kingdom, and in various places there will be famines and earthquakes. But all these things are merely the beginning of birth pangs. Then they will deliver you to tribulation, and will kill you, and you will be hated by all nations because of My name. At that time many will fall away and will betray one another and hate one another. Many false prophets will arise and will mislead many. Because lawlessness is increased, most people's love will grow cold. But the one who endures to the end, he will be saved. This gospel of the kingdom shall be preached in the whole world as a testimony to all the nations, and then the end will come."

Perilous Times

"Therefore when you see the abomination of desolation which was spoken of through Daniel the prophet, standing in the holy place [let the reader understand], then those who are in Judea must flee to the mountains. Whoever is on the housetop must not go down to get the things out that are in his house."

"Whoever is in the field must not turn back to get his cloak. But woe to those who are pregnant and to those who are nursing babies in those days! But pray that your flight will not be in the winter, or on a Sabbath. For then there will be a great tribulation, such as has not occurred since the beginning of the world until now, nor ever will. Unless those days had been cut short, no life would have been saved; but for the sake of the elect those days will be cut short. Then if anyone says to you, 'Behold, here is the Christ,' or 'There He is,' do not believe him. For false Christs and false prophets will arise and will show great signs and wonders, so as to mislead, if possible, even the elect. Behold, I have told you in advance. So if they say to you, 'Behold, He is in the wilderness,' do not go out, or, 'Behold, He is in the inner rooms,' do not believe them. For just as the lightning comes from the east and flashes even to the west, so will the coming of the Son of Man be. Wherever the corpse is, there the vultures will gather."

The Glorious Return

"But immediately after the tribulation of those days the sun will be darkened, and the moon will not give its light, and the stars will fall from the sky, and the powers of the heavens will be shaken. And then the sign of the Son of Man will appear in the sky, and then all the tribes of the earth will mourn, and they will see the Son of Man coming on the clouds of the sky with power and great glory. And He will send forth His angels with a great trumpet and they will gather together His elect from the four winds, from one end of the sky to the other."

Parable of the Fig Tree

"Now learn the parable from the fig tree: when its branch has already become tender and puts forth its leaves, you know that summer is near; so, you too, when you see all these things, recognize that He is near, right at the door. Truly I say to you, this generation will not pass away until all these things take place. Heaven and earth will pass away, but My words will not pass away. But of that day and hour no one knows, not even the angels of heaven, nor the Son, but the Father alone."

"For the coming of the Son of Man will be just like the days of Noah. For as in those days before the flood they were eating and drinking, marrying and giving in marriage, until the day that Noah entered the ark, and they did not understand until the flood came and took them all away; so will the coming of the Son of Man be. Then there will be two men in the field; one will be taken and one will be left. Two women will be grinding at the mill; one will be taken and one will be left."

Be Ready for His Coming

"Therefore be on the alert, for you do not know which day your Lord is coming. But be sure of this, that if the head of the house had known at what time of the night the thief was coming, he would have been on the alert and would not have allowed his house to be broken into. For this reason you also must be ready; for the Son of Man is coming at an hour when you do not think He will."

"Who then is the faithful and sensible slave whom his master put in charge of his household to give them their food at the proper time? Blessed is that slave whom his master finds so doing when he comes. Truly I say to you that he will put him in charge of all his possessions. But if that evil slave says in his heart, 'My master is not coming for a long time,' and begins to beat his fellow slaves and eat and drink with drunkards; the master of that slave will come on a day when he does not expect him and at an hour which he does not know, and will cut him in pieces and assign him a place with the hypocrites; in that place there will be weeping and gnashing of teeth."

Prologue

Jesus compared the time of His return to the days of Noah in Matthew 24:37–39. What were those days like? "Then the LORD saw that the wickedness of man was great on the earth, and that every intent of the thoughts of his heart was only evil continually. And the LORD was sorry that He had made man on the earth, and He was grieved in His heart" (Genesis 6:5–6). Additionally, Genesis 6:11–12 says, "Now the earth was corrupt, in the sight of God, and the earth was filled with violence. And God looked on the earth, and behold, it was corrupt; for all flesh had corrupted their way upon the earth." *All flesh had corrupted their way upon the earth.*

Do corruption and violence characterize our day? Is the wickedness of man great and the hearts of humanity bent toward evil? God is the judge of all that, and He knows the true desires of "our hearts." One thing is for sure: "peace on earth" currently eludes us. Wisdom and discernment are being snuffed out by a swelling tide of deception emerging even from the communities of faith, confusing God's truth with satanic lies that appeal to our fallen flesh—lies that ultimately corrupt lifestyles, steal our peace, and separate us from heaven's blessings.

What did the people experience who were unable to enter Noah's ark after the one and only door was closed? They physically endured torrential rain for forty successive days and nights as floodwaters reconfigured land terrain and buried even aquatic life with massive layers of earth. It would have been impossible to find a source of refuge. Even more overwhelming would have been the spiritual sense of hopelessness, terror, and finality. Matthew 24:39 says, "They did not understand until the flood waters came and took them all away." Then, they understood. God judges against sin and evil. But the door of the ark had closed. The opportunity for salvation had passed. If we choose to sidestep the righteousness of our Creator, we are ignoring the very essence of who God is. Yes, He is loving, but His mercy does not negate the righteous foundation of His throne (Ps. 89:14). God's love provided the ark; His righteousness covered the earth with a flood.

Jesus ultimately judges against all who are unrighteous in the day of the Lord, but this Savior, who sacrificed Himself for our sin, has provided a way of escape (2 Pet. 3:9). All who choose the sanctity of Christ as their ark of salvation will be saved. Those who reject Him will not survive.

When Jesus comes again, He descends upon the same Mount of Olives He ascended from, into heaven. The same Mount of Olives He delivered the sermon we are about to study in Matthew 24 (Luke 24:50–53, Zech. 14:1–4). For thousands of years, generations have anticipated His coming. "I will watch expectantly for the Lord; I will wait for the God of my salvation (Micah 7:7). Genesis 3:15 is God's first messianic promise—the Adamic covenant, a promise that initiated a blood-soaked thread of redemption we see woven throughout the entire fabric of holy Scripture. Book by book, chapter by chapter, God unveils Jesus Christ to be the promised Messiah. His first coming as the Lamb of God was for the sinner. His second coming as the majestic Son of God will be for His saints (Heb. 9:28). When He returns, it will be a time "just like the days of Noah," when a void of understanding requires divine intervention for the sake of His elect. Jesus provided that parallel for us and so much more to be aware of—so are you ready? I am. Let's go!

Week One

MATTHEW 24:1–14

Day One: Overview

Greetings! You have chosen a Bible study that will challenge your thinking and change your life. Not that I have anything to offer you, but God certainly does. His Word renews our minds and transforms our hearts every time we receive His truth. Faith, my friend, engages the Word of God by the Holy Spirit for the glory of God. I encourage you to stick with *Just Like the Days of Noah* for the full seven weeks, fortifying your life with a knowledge of future events. We do not know how close these events are, but we should prepare as if they could unfold soon. Jesus taught His disciples more than two thousand years ago to watch for His return. His message to us today remains the same.

The first coming of Jesus Christ initiated an era of gospel grace that transitioned us into the "last days" (Heb. 1:2, 1 Pet. 1:20). Before ascending back into heaven, Jesus said, "Do not let your heart be troubled; believe in God, believe also in Me. In My Father's house are many dwelling places; if it were not so, I would have told you. For I go to prepare a place for you. If I go and prepare a place for you, **I will come again and receive you to Myself**, that where I am, there you may be also" (John 14:1–3). Are you ready for the return of our Savior? I pray that these next seven weeks in *Just Like the Days of Noah* will help you with that. May God greatly bless and enrich your faith in His Word and Spirit because Jesus is coming again!

Please begin by reading Matthew 24 provided prior to the prologue. This will give you an overview of Christ's sermon before we begin breaking it down into sections. If you highlight the repeated words and phrases, it helps to catch the emphasis of the writing. You might want to underline any statements that stick out to you. Then, observe verses 1–14 on the Week One Worksheet at the end of this week's lesson, completing the observations on the right-hand side of the page. The Scriptures utilized in this study are from the New American Standard Bible (NASB) (1995). You are welcome to use a different version in independent study, but for the sake of class continuity, let's use the NASB. It is a reliable and literal translation of the original Hebrew, Aramaic, and Greek texts.

I highly recommend giving the Scriptures the opportunity to speak without interference from outside sources or any internet research until week six. Let the Holy Spirit be your primary teacher first. Then, you're better equipped to navigate the vast sea of conflicting interpretations (John 16:13).

Note any questions you have after reading Matthew 24. As we move through this study, your questions should be answered. Come back after we finish and see!

Matthew 24 Chapter Summary

Matthew, one of the twelve disciples and a former tax collector, recorded Christ's timeline with the precision of an accountant. (It is also recorded in Mark 13 and Luke 17:22–37 and 21:5–36 and provided in the appendix.) Jesus simplified a very complex topic for all of us, both students and scholars.

➢ In verses 1–14, Christ provided an overview in His answer to the disciple's question, "What will be the sign of your coming and of the end of the age?" Jesus described wars, famines, and earthquakes as merely "the beginning of birth pangs" (v. 8). "But that is not yet the end." There will be a rise in false teaching and deception, which gives way to apostasy, persecution, and even martyrdom. Jesus concluded with "But the one who endures to the end, he will be saved" (v. 13). "This gospel of the kingdom shall be preached in the whole world as a testimony to all the nations, and then the end will come" (v. 14). The first fourteen verses summarize the signs of Christ returning and the end of the age.

➢ In verses 15–28, Jesus pointed specifically to the abomination of desolation referred to by the prophet Daniel as the unmistakable sign of His coming. Those in Judea are to flee because the great tribulation will be a time of unparalleled distress. False prophets and Christs deceive through miraculous signs and wonders, targeting even the elect. For the sake of His elect, the great tribulation will be shortened.

➢ Verses 29–31 relate the heavens shaken and luminaries darkened immediately after the great tribulation period. "And then the sign of the Son of Man will appear in the sky." He will come on the clouds with power and great glory (v. 30) and gather His elect at the sound of a great trumpet (v. 31). Jesus has highlighted two major events we should expect to see, also foretold by Old Testament prophets: (1) the abomination of desolation and (2) the heavens being shaken—sun, moon, and stars darkened.

➢ In verses 32–41, Jesus said, "When you see all these things, recognize that He is near, right at the door." At that point, His coming will be imminent. Yet only the Father knows the exact "day and hour." Jesus described the time of His coming to be "just like the days of Noah." People had lost a right understanding until the flood came and took them all away. The same will be true when Jesus returns. Then, one will be taken and one left.

➢ Verses 42–51 speak to the anticipation of His return. The parable of the faithful servant teaches us to be alert, steadfast, and faithful. Two more parables follow this one in Matthew 25, the parable of ten virgins and the parable of the talents, with compatible themes.

Day Two: False Christs

Begin by reading verses 1–14 again on your worksheet. Matthew 24 opens with Jesus and His disciples leaving the temple in Jerusalem. They referenced the Jewish sanctuary as extraordinary, only to find out that Jesus didn't share their enthusiasm. Later, on the Mount of Olives, four of the disciples (Peter, James, John, and Andrew) seek further clarification; and we are the beneficiaries of their questioning. His reply provides us with the only New Testament timeline we have regarding the return of Christ—the only one. It is from Jesus Himself. The other gospel accounts of His Mount Olivet sermon are found in Mark 13 and Luke 17 and 21. Mark 13:3 is where we find the names of the four disciples who questioned Jesus privately.

1. What did Jesus predict in verses 1–2?

2. Afterward, what two questions did the disciples ask (v. 3)?

-

-

The disciples must have assumed the destruction of the temple would signal the end of the age and Christ's return. But it didn't. In AD 70, General Titus led an assault against Jerusalem after years of Jewish resistance (Luke 21:20). Roman soldiers and their allies seized the city and destroyed the temple against the general's direct orders. It was estimated that six hundred thousand Jewish people, residents, and visitors were slaughtered in this siege. Survivors of the massacre were scattered and sent into foreign exile, enslaved to work in Egyptian mines, and utilized as gladiators for games and entertainment in Roman arenas.

Herod's temple, famous for its impressive artisan design of white stones inlaid with gold, reflected the sun like a beacon of light. It was the glory and pride of the Jewish community in Jerusalem. But just as Jesus predicted, the Roman army left no stone unturned. Why? After burning the temple, the soldiers tore the stones apart to retrieve the gold inlay (*Chuck Smith Bible Commentary*). "Truly I say to you, not one stone here will be left upon another, which will not be torn down" (Matthew 24:2). The words of Jesus were fulfilled precisely.

Destruction of the Temple, AD 70

The only first-hand account of the Roman assault on the temple is recorded by the Jewish historian Josephus:

The rebels shortly after attacked the Romans again, and a clash followed between the guards of the sanctuary and the troops who were putting out the fire inside the inner court; the latter routed the Jews and followed in hot pursuit right up to the Temple itself. Then one of the soldiers, without awaiting any orders and with no dread of so momentous a deed, but urged on by some supernatural force, snatched a blazing piece of wood and, climbing on another soldier's back, hurled the flaming brand through a low golden window that gave access, on the north side, to the rooms that surrounded the sanctuary. As the flames shot up, the Jews let out a shout of dismay that matched the tragedy; they flocked to the rescue, with no thought of sparing their lives or husbanding their strength; for the sacred structure that they had constantly guarded with such devotion was vanishing before their very eyes.

No exhortation or threat could now restrain the impetuosity of the legions; for passion was in supreme command. Crowded together around the entrances, many were trampled down by their companions; others, stumbling on the smoldering and smoked-filled ruins of the porticoes, died as miserably as the defeated. As they drew closer to the Temple, they pretended not even to hear Caesar's orders, but urged the men in front to throw in more firebrands. The rebels were powerless to help; carnage and flight spread throughout.

Most of the slain were peaceful citizens, weak and unarmed, and they were butchered where they were caught. The heap of corpses mounted higher and higher about the altar; a stream of blood flowed down the Temple's steps, and the bodies of those slain at the top slipped to the bottom.

When Caesar failed to restrain the fury of his frenzied soldiers, and the fire could not be checked, he entered the building with his generals and looked at the holy place of the sanctuary and all its furnishings, which exceeded by far the accounts current in foreign lands and fully justified their splendid repute in our own.

As the flames had not yet penetrated to the inner sanctum, but were consuming the chambers that surrounded the sanctuary, Titus assumed correctly that there was still time to save the structure; he ran out and by personal appeals he endeavored to persuade his men to put out the fire, instructing Liberalius, a centurion of his bodyguard of lancers, to club any of the men who disobeyed his orders. But their respect for Caesar and their fear of the centurion's staff who was trying to check them were overpowered by their rage, their detestation of the Jews, and an utterly uncontrolled lust for battle.

Most of them were spurred on, moreover, by the expectation of loot, convinced that the interior was full of money and dazzled by observing that everything around them was made of gold. But they were forestalled by one of those who had entered into the building, and who, when Caesar dashed out to restrain the troops, pushed a firebrand, in the darkness, into the hinges of the gate Then, when the flames suddenly shot up from the interior, Caesar and his generals withdrew, and no one was left to prevent those outside from kindling the blaze. Thus, in defiance of Caesar's wishes, the Temple was set on fire.

While the Temple was ablaze, the attackers plundered it, and countless people who were caught by them were slaughtered. There was no pity for age and no regard was accorded rank; children and old men, laymen and priests, alike were butchered; every class was pursued and crushed in the grip of war, whether they cried out for mercy or offered resistance. Through the roar of the flames streaming far and wide, the groans of the falling victims were heard; such was the height of the hill and the magnitude of the blazing pile that the entire city seemed to be ablaze; and the noise—nothing more deafening and frightening could be imagined.

There were the war cries of the Roman legions as they swept onward en masse, the yells of the rebels encircled by fire and sword, the panic of the people who, cut off above, fled into the arms of the enemy, and their shrieks as they met their fate. The cries on the hill blended with those of the multitudes in the city below; and now many people who were exhausted and tongue-tied as a result of hunger, when they beheld the Temple on fire, found strength once more to lament and wail. Peraea and the surrounding hills, added their echoes to the deafening din. But more horrifying than the din were the sufferings.

The Temple Mount, everywhere enveloped in flames, seemed to be boiling over from its base; yet the blood seemed more abundant than the flames and the numbers of the slain greater than those of the slayers. The soldiers climbed over heaps of bodies as they chased the fugitives. (Cornfield 1883)

While the Jews marveled over King Herod's temple of glimmering stones, the majestic, incarnate temple of God walked the streets of Jerusalem, rejected by the same priesthood appointed to proclaim Him. They, along with Herod, mocked and treated Jesus with contempt (Luke 23:11, Acts 4:26–28). He was betrayed, accused, and relinquished to Roman authorities who beat and crucified Him. Ironically, the Jews prophesied against their own nation, shouting, "His blood be upon us and on our children!" (Matthew 27:25). There should be no doubt as to why God allowed Herod's temple to be destroyed and the Jewish people taken into captivity by Rome. God's firstborn nation had rejected His firstborn Son.

3. **After the disciples' questions, Jesus began His Mount Olivet sermon with two warnings or instructions. What were they (vv. 4, 6)?**

   •

   •

5

Application

God's instructions are directives that we all need because "there is a way which seems right to a man, but its end is the way of death" (Proverbs 14:12). Our sense of direction is woefully messed up. Our hearts are morally fickle and inclined toward wickedness (Jer. 17:9). We are sinners (Rom. 3:10, 23). This applies to every man, to every woman, and to every child. Everyone. God's commands are designed to steer us away from the sins we naturally gravitate toward so we can be blessed with His grace, goodness, and salvation instead. These two commands in Matthew 24:4–6 not only serve as preparation for the turbulent days ahead but also fortify us through the navigation of everyday trials.

4. **What is Jesus preparing us for when He says, "See to it that no one misleads you" (Matt. 24:4–5)?**

Think About It

Jesus prioritizes false Christs before false prophets. Recognizing that demographic first makes it easier to discern those who promote false doctrines. Ultimately, both are advancing world kingdoms in opposition to the kingdom of God. "Who is the liar but the one who denies that Jesus is the Christ? This is the antichrist, the one who denies the Father and the Son" (1 John 2:22). False Christs propagate false prophets. False prophets promote false Christs.

Religions such as Islam, Taoism, Buddhism, and Hinduism denounce Jesus Christ as the Son of God. Be willing to recognize these blatant anti-Christ platforms for what they are: against God. Then, you are more apt to identify the false prophets and teachers who attempt to integrate their philosophies and doctrines into Christianity. Jesus asked His disciples, "Who do you say that I am?" (Luke 9:18–20). How would you answer? Is Jesus Christ God's Son, born of a virgin by the Holy Spirit (Matt. 1:18–23)? Is He the world's only Savior (John 14:6)? **How would you answer Jesus if He asked you, "Who do you say that I am?"**

We have been desensitized to recognizing false messiahs because of the global effort to unify all faiths. Yet any religion, leader, pastor, or teacher who denies Jesus to be the Christ is not on the side of truth. Even those who confess Christ but teach false doctrines are promoting error. These "adulterate" the Word of God (2 Cor. 4:2). False teachers and prophets can typically be identified by their lifestyles (Matt. 7:15–23). Yet we aren't always privy to the lifestyles of our teachers and pastors. So take time, as you are now, to study the Word of God. Then, examine their teaching, not to be critical but to grow in wisdom and discernment. If there is cause for debate, ask humbly for a time to share your concerns and always in love. Always (2 Tim. 2:24–25).

5. **How does 2 Peter 2:1–3 depict false prophets and teachers?**

- They secretly introduce …

- Even denying …

- Many will follow their …

- Because of them …

- In their greed, they exploit

- Their judgment from long ago is …

Think About It

The list you just read from 2 Peter sounds like a description of those who should stand out as obvious deceivers. Yet deception is much stealthier than that. False prophets and teachers do not present themselves as offensive people, advertising their wares with blatant lies. Deception hunkers itself down in a Trojan-like horse, saddled with an attractive rider who will solicit allegiance with empty promises. Always alluring. Always appealing. Seemingly harmless. Yet not.

Destructive heresies are opinions or beliefs that contradict truth. Scripture might even be extracted to appear supportive. For instance, "God is love" is often utilized as a permission slip for sin (1 John 4:8). Some are saying, "God's love is greater than our sin, so we can do whatever we want. Sin is no longer an issue. It doesn't matter." That teaching twists truth into a palatable lie for the sake of popularity and profit (2 Cor. 2:17). It is a false doctrine that appeals to our flesh. Yes, God is love. But His love provides a way of escape from sin, not to sin (Rom. 6, 1 John 3:10).

Our culture forbids making distinctions between good and evil, truth and error. This schema is being driven by the spirit of the Antichrist, whose intent is to compromise God's saints and weaken His church. The weight of conformity can be seen across denominational lines from an increasing number of pulpits avoiding the topic of sin altogether. The Holy Spirit will not bless sin. Don't expect it. Jesus admonished the church in Pergamum in Revelation 2:14–15 for tolerating teaching that integrated unholy practices into the holy assembly of God. These put "stumbling blocks" before the people (Rev. 2:14). Stumbling blocks.

> "Give me one hundred preachers who fear nothing but sin and desire nothing but God, and I care not a straw whether they be clergymen or laymen, such alone will shake the gates of hell and set up the kingdom of heaven on Earth" (John Wesley).

6. In Malachi 2:6, what is God's priest or preacher tasked with?

7. What does 2 Timothy 4:3–4 reveal? Is this true today?

If we walk in the flesh rather than the Holy Spirit, we will find ourselves gravitating toward sermons that "tickle" our ears instead of those addressing sin (Gal. 5:16–17). Timothy advised us to stick with the "sacred writings which are able to give you wisdom" (2 Timothy 3:14–15). The best way to avoid becoming a victim of deception is to study and meditate on the Word of God, comparing the Scriptures with what you are hearing and seeing on display. "See to it that no one misleads you" is a personal command. God charged Joshua before entering Canaan with "This book of the law shall not depart from your mouth, but you shall meditate on it day and night, so that you may be careful to do according to all that is written in it; for then you will make your way prosperous, and then you will have success" (Joshua 1:8). Then, you will have success! How do we experience victory? By carefully (rightly interpreting) and observing (acting on) God's precepts. Stay connected to the Word of God every day. Meditate on what you read, digest the truth, and obey His commands every day. Yes, it's that important (Ps. 1:1–3). To believe otherwise is to be deceived by a lie.

Application

Perhaps you are already involved in Bible study. I mean, you're doing this one, right? But are you willing to apply God's Word? Listen, we can attend church and multiple Bible studies for years without truth ever infiltrating our lives. Why is that? We hesitate to adjust our thinking. It's much easier to live the world's broad way than to trust the radical ways of God and His narrow path (Matt. 7:13–14). We're more comfortable with familiar settings than trusting Him with the unknown. Jesus asked, "Why do you call me 'Lord, Lord,' and do not do what I say?"
If Jesus Christ is not your king and you are not investing in His kingdom, then you have cause to pause and examine your faith.

Take time to study the messages you're hearing. Cross-reference Scripture with Scripture and pray for the Holy Spirit to direct you. In addition, establish the context. Who is the author and audience? What is the purpose of the writing? Make sure the overall counsel of God's Word agrees with your analysis. Most importantly, remain humble before God and one another. These guidelines will protect the integrity of Scripture and the direction of your heart. "See to it that no one misleads you." Are you willing? Circle your answer.

YES   NO

Day Two Summary

Jesus began His Mt. Olivet teaching with two warnings: (1) see to it that no one misleads you, and (2) see that you are not frightened. In a two-toned capsule, Jesus prescribed exactly what we need for today and for the turbulence of the latter days. We covered the first part of His warning today: "See to it that no one misleads you." Learn to recognize the deceivers and study the Word of God as if your life depends upon it because it does.

Day Three: Fear

Yesterday, we covered Christ's first command, "See to it that no one misleads you," which is difficult to accomplish if we are more centered on following our dreams than following Jesus—dreams being differentiated from gifted callings sanctioned by the Holy Spirit (Matt. 16:24; 2 Cor. 5:15). Fleshly dreams incite us to gravitate toward sermons promoting personal success rather than those challenging fleshly lusts. Yet recognizing and forsaking sin is the crust and crux of holy living (1 Pet. 1:13–16). Please don't be offended. Just think about your pursuits. Are they sanctioned by God?

Today, let's look at Christ's second command: "See that you are not frightened." Lessons today and tomorrow may delve into an uncomfortable subject for some, but it is necessary and oh-so-Biblical. Get yourself a cup of tea or coffee and settle in with humble, teachable hearts. "O taste and see that the LORD is good; how blessed is the man who takes refuge in Him!" (Psalm 34:8).

1. Why would Jesus say, "See that you are not frightened" (Matt. 24:6–7)?

Wars, famines, and earthquakes have been occurring for ages. However, these in Matthew 24 increase in prolificity like labor pains, unsettling global economies, and food supplies. The same difficulties are revealed by the first four scroll seals in Revelation 6. No one can open that sealed scroll except for the Lamb, Jesus (Rev. 5:4–5). When He begins to break the seals, four apocalyptic riders are unveiled: (1) on a white horse, Antichrist(s); (2) on a red horse, wars; (3) on a black horse, famine; and (4) on an ashen horse, death. In Matthew 24:8, Jesus refers to these plights as merely the "beginning" of birth pangs. In Matthew 24:9, Jesus also references martyrdom, which is disclosed by the fifth scroll seal. Essentially, Jesus describes the same events regarding His return in Matthew 24:1–14, as He discloses in the first five seals on the scroll. What would be the significance of that? Just like Matthew 24:1–14, the seals reveal an overview of signs prior to Christ returning: Antichrist(s), wars, famine, death, and martyrdom. They characterize the contents of the scroll. At the end of His timeline, Jesus denotes the heavens being shaken as the climactic sign—the same sign disclosed by the sixth scroll seal. The seals basically replicate Christ's timeline (see appendix "The Sixth Seal").

9

2. **Whether or not you've participated in the birth of a child, how would you expect the onset of birth pangs to compare with their progression?**

Think About It

After Adam sinned, the Lord decreed that Eve's labor in childbirth would be "greatly" increased (Gen. 3:16). Sin always exacts painful consequences. But perhaps there is a deeper meaning to be realized here. Apparently, Eve would have experienced birth pangs before her sin, just not as egregious. So let's consider the real purpose of contractions and labor. Contractions signal an approaching birth and a new family era. They herald the pending arrival of a greatly anticipated event after months and months of waiting. Get ready! Get ready! A new life is coming! When God uses the analogy of birth pangs as signals leading up to Christ's return, get ready! New life is coming! When the infant arrives, everything will change—dramatically.

We shouldn't ignore the beginning of birth pangs, such as wars, famine, earthquakes, and deception, because they have been occurring for eons of time. This waiting period simply means (1) God is exercising divine patience (2 Pet. 3:9), and (2) every generation is meant to live in anticipation of Christ returning (Rom. 8:18, 1 Pet. 1:3–4). God's calendar will eventually flip to the year, month, day, and hour for Jesus Christ to come in indescribable glory. When that finally happens, know this: a brand-new era for the family of God will suddenly, eternally commence—one that we cannot possibly fathom.

First Corinthians 2:9 says, "Things which eye has not seen and ear has not heard, and which have not entered the heart of man, all that God has prepared for those who love Him." Romans 8:20–22 tells us that creation has been groaning with birth pangs since the fall of man. That's a long time, my friend, and those birth pangs will escalate in intensity as the return of Christ draws near. Yet a new era is coming! What we cherish today (apart from our affection for Christ) will dissipate in the wake of an inexpressible joy we have only begun to experience (Ps. 34:8, 1 Pet. 1:8).

3. **In Matthew 24:9–10, what causes the birth pangs to escalate?**

4. **What is the outcome of persecution according to Luke 21:12–13 and 2 Corinthians 4:7–12?**

Think About It

Continuing with the illustration of childbirth, what might happen if you went into labor unprepared? You would be at the complete mercy of others without the opportunity to check the credibility of their counsel. Fear would enjoy a real tactical advantage. Listen, God gives us nine months to get ready for the birth of a child. If we don't prepare for his or her arrival, then we won't be equipped for the labor or the change. The child will still come but without a proper reception. Our Heavenly Father has given His saints over two thousand years to prepare for the return of His Son. Don't panic. Prepare. "See that you are not frightened."

5. **Persecution escalates the birth pangs just as pain increases in childbirth. Look at Matthew 24:9–11 more closely:**

Then they will deliver you to _____ and _____ you, and

you will be _____ by all _____ because of My name. At that

time, many will _____ and will _____ one another and

_____ one another. _____ false prophets will arise and _____

many.

Application

Jesus did not advocate stockpiling or wilderness camping. He advised us to fortify our lives spiritually, just as He advised the congregants of seven churches in Revelation 2–3. Preparation is our best recourse and a preemptive strike against fear. Have you ever considered what your response might be if and when persecuted? Would it make a difference in your commitment to Christ to discover that you will be hated, betrayed, imprisoned, or even killed for following Him? "Many" will "fall away" on that day when faced with persecution. Many. Your peers, career associates, and family members might betray you to save themselves (Mk. 13:12, Mic. 7:5–7). As you ponder that warning, consider your close associations and evaluate whether you should be more selective in the friends you depend upon. Again, please don't be offended. Just think through your choices and where they are taking you. Choices do have consequences.

> I am a companion of all those who fear You, and of those who keep Your precepts.
> (Psalm 119:63)

The primary reason for this study is the fortification of our faith so we aren't blindsided by the persecution and betrayal Jesus predicts as a certainty. What are your friends pursuing? If not Christ or eternal truth, then find better friends. Walking with Jesus means to travel in His direction by the might of the Holy Spirit (Rom. 8:14, Gal. 5:16, Eph. 3:16). Which direction do your friends walk, live, speak, and travel? Ungodly friends are, at best—a distraction; at

11

worst—they will throttle your faith with a barrage of crippling compromises. If we truly desire to be faithful to the risen Savior, we should find "faith pilgrims" who encourage and support rather than sabotage our journey with Jesus (1 Chron. 29:15; Heb. 11:10, 16; Phil. 3:20).

6. Who are the friends supporting and encouraging your walk with Christ?

> But realize this, that in the last days difficult times will come. For men will be lovers of self, lovers of money, boastful, arrogant, revilers, disobedient to parents, ungrateful, unholy, unloving, irreconcilable, malicious gossips, without self-control, brutal, haters of good, treacherous, reckless, conceited, lovers of pleasure rather than lovers of God, holding to a form of godliness, although they have denied its power; and avoid such men as these. (2 Timothy 3:1–5)

Timothy describes people in love with themselves rather than God. Some even "hold to a form of godliness," meaning that if you ask them if they believe in Jesus Christ, they will say, "Yes, of course." But does their lifestyle support or contradict their confession? Lovers of self, money, and pleasure exhibit dominant fleshly traits rather than a spiritual walk with God. The Scriptures teach us to pursue God and His kingdom with all our heart, strength, soul, and mind (Matt. 6:33, 22:37), putting to death the deeds of the flesh (Rom. 8:13, Gal. 5:19–25). For "no one can serve two masters; for either he will hate the one and love the other, or he will be devoted to one and despise the other" (Matthew 6:24). Ungodly living distinguishes the ungodly, not the godly.

Think About It

You need not list your friends or family members who fall into the 2 Timothy 3:1–5 category. Take this opportunity to make sure you are not in it yourself (Matt. 7:3–5). Then, if you have friends entrenched in your life who are a hindrance rather than a strength to your pursuit of Christ, consider reducing the amount of time spent with them. Just like healthier eating becomes more beneficial and your tastes adapt, so will healthy fellowships. You can find friends in Bible studies or Christian circles who do more than talk the talk; they actually walk the walk. Find committed, dedicated, devoted lights who seek truth. Avoid those who merely "hold to a form of godliness." Pray for God to assist you in this, and He will. Jesus would never instruct you to prepare for difficult days ahead and then forsake you willy-nilly in that effort. You are never on your own when you walk with Jesus (Deut. 31:8, Heb. 13:5). Never. Even when we do not sense or "feel" His presence, He is with us every minute of every day.

Application

Both directives—"See to it that no one misleads you" and "See that you are not frightened"—are commands, not suggestions. "See to it" holds each of us personally accountable to prepare. The days we live in are getting darker and more difficult to navigate, with respect for human life waning and persecution, escalating (2 Tim. 3:12). There is no better time than now to consider living by Christ's mandates that He has set before us. We can choose to disregard these directives and regard them as trivial pursuits, but is that wise? Jesus wouldn't waste our time with insignificant, irrelevant instructions. Will you commit to responding affirmatively to "see to it that no one misleads you" and "see that you are not frightened"? Circle your answer.

YES   NO

Day Three Summary

"See that you are not frightened" can be accomplished right now by trusting and following our Savior every day through the present challenges, whether thick or thin. Instead of following dreams or living in the shadows of corruptible influences, follow Jesus Christ with a formidable, unwavering commitment. He will prove Himself faithful against the fear factors of today and, yes, even those of tomorrow.

Day Four: Endurance

Are the laws of God being disregarded in our day? Absolutely, they are, and being rewritten to advance the schematics of lawlessness. As this trend continues, we should expect peace and civility to diminish because it is God's laws that keep human depravity in check (Rom. 7:7, Gal. 3:24). Without them, our hearts consistently pump contaminants throughout our lives like diseased chambers dumping sewage into the bloodstream (Jer. 17:9). Have you ever smelled the stench of a sewer? Sewage stinks. In contrast, God's redemptive mercies revive and restore hearts to become capable of compassion, forgiveness, and mercy. The sewage is replaced by the sweet aroma of God (2 Cor. 2:14–16). His Spirit circumcises our hearts and circulates eternal life through our veins, sanctifying and removing sinful desires (Rom. 6:22, 2 Cor. 5:17). "Moreover, I will give you a new heart and put a new spirit within you; and I will remove the heart of stone from your flesh and give you a heart of flesh" (Ezekiel 36:26). This "new heart" miracle is not cardiac surgery; Ezekiel is speaking of a heart transplant! Stone to flesh signifies God replacing a cold, hard, indifferent heart with a soft, tender receptor instead, capable of receiving and extending eternal life. It is a heart that bears the imprint of the Holy Spirit (2 Cor. 3:3).

1. **Why did Jesus say people's love would grow cold (v. 12)?**

2. **Then what does Matthew 24:13 say?**

> "Endure" *hupomeno* means "to remain under, endure, or sustain a load of miseries, adversities, persecutions, or provocations in faith and patience."

3. **Look at the Greek meaning of *hupomeno* in the box. What is the opposite of enduring?**

4. **In 2 Timothy 2:10, who benefits from our endurance besides us?**

Jesus commissioned and empowered His disciples to share the Gospel—God's message of good news (Matt. 28:19, 2 Cor. 5:18–21)! Why wouldn't we want to share it? God's redemptive work is for all who seek forgiveness and freedom from their sins (Gal. 5:1). If you and I have seen the hopelessness of our sin as the terminal plague that it is, then the Gospel of good news is a welcome proclamation worthy of unrestrained celebration. Do you celebrate your exodus and freedom from sin? Israel annually celebrates a Passover feast to commemorate their deliverance from Egypt. We celebrate birthdays. How about celebrating the day we were born again and delivered from sin?

The Gospel message is a healing balm for every fractured heart wounded by the curse of sin. Jesus removed our iniquities with His blood so that we can be forgiven, allowing us to stand before God as if we never sinned at all (2 Cor. 5:19). By His stripes, we are healed (Isa. 53:5)! That is the best news we could possibly hear, receive, or share! "Sing to the LORD, all the earth; proclaim good tidings of His salvation from day to day" (1 Chronicles 16:23). Did you notice in verse 14 of Matthew 24 that the Gospel will be proclaimed throughout the earth to all nations before the end of the age? This is why we must endure to the end—to proclaim the Gospel of salvation.

Jesus also warned that those who believe and deliver the Gospel will be like sheep surrounded by wolves—wolves who devour His sheep (Matt. 10:16). Why? Wolves aren't interested in the good news of the Gospel. That's so strange, isn't it? But those unwilling to forsake sin are blinded by it, clinging to the acceptance of their howling communal packs (2 Cor. 4:4). They prefer to die in their sin rather than accept God's sacrifice and freedom. Are we willing to endure the rejection and hostility of the world's wolves? Will we pray for those who persecute and bite us, forgiving them and sharing the life of Christ with them? "For we who live are constantly being delivered over to death for Jesus' sake, so that the life of Jesus also may be manifested in our mortal flesh" (2 Corinthians 4:11).

5. Do you remember who shared the Gospel with you? Who was it?

Think About It

What did that person endure to share the Gospel with you? You might never know of the adversity they encountered. Pastors, Bible teachers, and evangelists expend years in study, prayer, and outreach, enduring huge obstacles every day. Your neighbor or friend might have battled demonic fears of rejection to share Jesus with you. The Bible itself has survived a millennium of attempted delineations, preserved by Jewish priests and saints who suffered persecution, even martyrdom in their efforts. In 1536, William Tyndale was burned at the stake for translating the Bible into English just so you and I could read it for ourselves. The Bible you hold in your hands is a priceless, formidable sword forged by the Spirit and elect of God who were willing to endure intense flames. Don't take their sacrifices for granted. Neither should we underestimate what someone else endured to share the Gospel with us and what might be necessary for us to do the same.

We are called to love a world that rarely reciprocates. Accept that certainty with eyes wide open and with affections set upon your calling and heavenly home (Heb. 11:16, Eph. 2:6). Choosing to pick up the cross of Christ is a choice to follow the Christ of the cross through adversity into those deep valleys and scary lions' dens. That, my friend, requires an exercise of spiritual endurance as if training for a marathon or achieving excellence in any task (1 Cor. 9:24–25, 1 Tim. 6:12, Phil. 3:14).

6. How does Hebrews 12:1–3 tell us to run our race?

7. What can we learn from Moses in Hebrews 11:24–26?

Jesus was honest regarding the difficulties that His followers would encounter. "A slave is not greater than his master. If they persecuted Me, they will also persecute you; if they kept My word, they will keep yours also" (John 15:20). Peter warned us not to be surprised at the fiery ordeals, as though some strange thing were happening. "To the degree that you share the sufferings of Christ, keep on rejoicing, so that also at the revelation of His glory you may rejoice with exultation. If you are reviled for the name of Christ, you are blessed, because the Spirit of glory and of God rests upon you" (1 Pet. 4:13–14). In other words, when Jesus returns and is revealed, we will rejoice with the Savior because we endured by the might of His Spirit (2 Cor. 4:7–10).

Examine your willingness to accept this calling and challenge for Christ's sake—the same one He accepted for you. Christians who live by faith in the Son of God will be persecuted because they are holy (separated) people living in an unholy world of wolves and wickedness.

8. Read Mark 13:11. Who helps the elect when persecuted?

Visiting a popular park in Atlanta years ago, I saw a bearded guru speaking to a gathering of people underneath the branches of a giant southern oak. Behind him, a guitarist sang soft, meditative choruses. God urged me to move closer, which I did, then found myself praying for someone to share the Gospel in contrast to the guru's pensive message. After a few minutes, I realized God meant for me to be the one to speak. It was an unsettling moment. I quickly asked for an alternative, but as I looked around, everyone was either listening or singing along with the guitarist. Plus, it was Sunday, and any viable alternative who could have shared with the group was attending church. A life lesson.

Stepping forward, I asked the guru for permission to speak. To my surprise, he granted the request. I proceeded to share the gospel of God's mercy and His provision of escape from a righteous judgment that must take place against our sins. John 14:6 was quoted regarding Jesus Christ as the way, the truth, and the life. Only a sinless sacrifice could remove our sin, which is why God's sinless Son is the one choice for redemption. I further explained that their guru might relieve stress through his reflective exercises and songs, but no one other than Jesus Christ could reconcile them to God and bring lasting peace to their lives.

The crowd laughed and ridiculed me as I shared. Yet I felt what can only be described as a protective barrier between myself and the crowd. The Holy Spirit enveloped me. His immersing presence provided an internal fortitude that further defined my words with boldness and conviction. I became acutely aware that the words coming from my mouth were not mine and that I was merely a conduit. Afterward, one young man in his twenties came from the back of the crowd and said, "Thanks for sharing the truth with us today." We connected eye to eye, and I still remember replying, "Truth comes only from God. It was my honor to share it with you." What an incredible experience provided by the protection, power, and presence of the Holy Spirit!

Who knows, maybe others heard and received God's Gospel that day. I know of at least one who did. When we share the Word and our testimonies, some will respond positively, while others won't. It depends solely upon the working of God the Father. John 6:37 and 44 reveal that no one can come to Christ unless the Father draws them. Our job is to share the good news. The Father is the one who draws and calls. But know this—God does support those who are His. He is faithful! We should be too.

Application

"Therefore, those also who suffer according to the will of God shall entrust their souls to a faithful Creator in doing what is right" (1 Peter 4:19). If you're trusting God to save you from your sins, then you can trust Him when persecuted too. Salvation is not a "Wocket in Your Pocket" Dr. Seuss ticket of admission into heaven for future use. Eternal life begins the moment you receive Jesus Christ as your Redeemer. Not later. You will grow in Christ every day. "Behold, I stand at the door and knock; if anyone hears My voice and opens the door, I will come in to him and will dine with him, and he with Me" (Revelation 3:20). He is the Bread of Life (John 6:35). His Spirit provides living water (John 7:37–39). Even through persecutions and suffering, Jesus sustains and satisfies us for our benefit and the sake of others (2 Cor. 1:3–7). Crucibles of suffering are never about just you or just me. God's vision and purpose are much bigger than that. Turn loose of any shortsighted perceptions and trust His eternal plan. Entrust your soul "to a faithful Creator in doing what is right."

9. Look at Hebrews 2:17–18. What kind of priest is Jesus?

10. In verse 18, why can He adequately assist us?

Application

Hebrews 12:2 tells us that Jesus is "the author and perfecter of faith, who for the joy set before Him endured the cross, despising the shame, and has sat down at the right hand of the throne of God." Jesus is our High Priest who presently intercedes for us and has made Himself always available (Rom. 8:34). Jesus suffered without sinning. He is in a position to comfort us because He understands the rejection, persecution, betrayal, and heartaches we face too. He knows how to navigate suffering. "Blessed be the God and Father of our LORD Jesus Christ, the Father of mercies and God of all comfort, who comforts us in all our affliction so that we will be able to comfort those who are in any affliction with the comfort with which we ourselves are comforted by God" (2 Corinthians 1:3–4).

Has God spoken to you through this week's lessons? If so, write it down and plan to act upon it (Matt. 7:24–27).

Day Four Summary

As lawlessness increases, love for one another will decrease and persecution escalate. How do we prepare and respond? By the guidance and strength of the Holy Spirit. We should exercise muscles of endurance today and trust the provisions of salvation we are blessed to enjoy this very hour, running the race for the joy set before us. That joy is Jesus!

Week One Synopsis

See to it that neither deception or fear defines you.

Encourage each other as you see the day drawing near.
(Hebrews 10:25)

WEEK ONE WORKSHEET

Matthew 24:1–14

Jesus came out from the temple and was going away when His disciples came up to point out the temple buildings to Him. And He said to them, "Do you not see all these things? Truly I say to you, not one stone here will be left upon another, which will not be torn down."

As He was sitting on the Mount of Olives, the disciples came to Him privately, saying, "Tell us, when will these things happen, and what will be the sign of Your coming, and of the end of the age?

And Jesus answered and said to them,

"See to it that no one misleads you. For many will come in My name, saying, 'I am the Christ,' and will mislead many. You will be hearing of wars and rumors of wars. See that you are not frightened, for those things must take place, but that is not yet the end. For nation will rise against nation, and kingdom against kingdom, and in various places there will be famines and earthquakes. But all these things are merely the beginning of birth pangs.

Then they will deliver you to tribulation, and will kill you, and you will be hated by all nations because of My name. At that time many will fall away and will betray one another and hate one another. Many false prophets will arise and will mislead many.

Because lawlessness is increased, most people's love will grow cold. But the one who endures to the end, he will be saved.

This gospel of the kingdom shall be preached in the whole world as a testimony to all the nations, and then the end shall come."

Observations

The disciples asked two questions:

1. When _____

2. What _____

Jesus answered with two commands:

1. See to it that _____

2. See that _____

The beginning of birth pangs:

- Many will be misled

- Wars and rumors of wars

- Famines and earthquakes

Then:

- They will deliver you to _____

- And will _____

- You will be hated by all nations because of _____

Many is repeated five times:

- Many *will come* in My name, saying, "I am the Christ."

- Many *will be misled* as a result.

- Many *will fall away, betray,* and *hate* one another.

- Many false prophets *will arise* and *mislead* many.

Most people's love *will grow cold.*

The end will come after the Gospel of the kingdom is:

_____

Week Two

THOSE WHO ENDURE TILL
THE END WILL BE SAVED

Day One: Our Rescue

Last week, we touched on the topic of endurance (*hupomeno*). Before proceeding with the next section of Christ's sermon in verses 15–28, let's dig deeper into what must be endured. Look again at your Week One Worksheet. In verses 4–8, we are told to expect Antichrists, wars, rumors of wars, famines, and earthquakes. Jesus said these are the "beginning of birth pangs." Then, in verse 9, the birth pangs intensify with persecution and martyrdom. False prophets will be prolific; consequently, many are misled.

1. **According to Matthew 24:10, what will *many* do when persecuted?**

2. **What does 1 Timothy 4:1 tell us?**

Application

How would such pervasive apostasy affect you personally? Some of these "many" may even include leaders we have trusted—Christian authors, teachers, and singers. Think about that. Not fearfully but with a prayerful sobriety of what Jesus is predicting. Stop and pray for God to fortify your faith, your mind, and your heart. Express your petition briefly in the space below. Our prayers don't have to be eloquent or lengthy for God to hear them—just sincere.

Should we interpret this "falling away" from the faith to mean God's redeemed can lose their salvation? If saints are sealed by the Holy Spirit as a pledge of our redemption and resurrection, then salvation is a **guarantee** (Eph. 1:13–14, 2 Cor. 5:2–5). Would God renege on His faithful promise to save His redeemed? No way. "God is not a man that He should lie" (Numbers 23:19). Plus, salvation is a gift—eternal life is a gift—the Holy Spirit is a gift. Gifts are not earned, won, or lost; gifts are freely given. Christ in us is the hope and **guarantee** of His glory yet to come (Col. 1:27)!

Also, Jesus defined salvation as a rebirth. "Truly, truly, I say to you, unless one is born again he cannot see the kingdom of God" (John 3:3). Once born, can we be unborn? Peter wrote that we are "born again" of an "imperishable seed," no longer perishable (1 Pet. 1:23). Some might argue that if we lose our salvation, it is not God who defects but the sinner instead. So let me ask you this: Is our salvation accomplished by our works or the redemptive work of Christ? In other words, is our salvation dependent upon what we do or dependent upon what Jesus did?

3. What does Ephesians 2:8–9 say?

Jesus stated, "All that the Father gives Me will come to Me, and the one who comes to Me I will certainly not cast out. For I have come down from heaven, not to do My own will, but the will of Him who sent Me. And this is the will of Him who sent Me, that of all that He has given Me I lose nothing, but raise it up on the last day" (John 6:37–39). Those who receive Jesus Christ will be resurrected by Him. Saved. Preserved for the resurrection of the saints on the last day.

Falling away would not be referring to a loss of salvation but a disclosure of the unsaved (Heb. 3:14). They consider themselves to be Christians but have zero interest in suffering for Christ. No desire to be set apart for Him and live as a holy vessel, rejected by the world. No intentions of walking in the Holy Spirit rather than fleshly lusts. When the hay hits the fan, so to speak, those who fall away are turning the fan off, picking up their hay, and leaving the premises, refusing to *hupomeno.*

4. Let's read 2 Thessalonians 2:1–4. What precedes the return of Jesus (v. 3)?

•

•

In 2 Thessalonians 2:1–2, Paul links the day of the Lord directly to the return of Jesus. Old Testament prophets describe the day of the Lord as the time when God removes all unrighteousness and establishes His Kingdom. However, before this new era begins, "the apostasy" or "falling away" occurs and "the man of lawlessness" is revealed. Because of increased persecution, many will fall away. Because the world accepts and embraces lawlessness, the man of lawlessness ascends to power. He will "take his seat in the temple of God" and display himself as God. This insidious event is the abomination of desolation, which Jesus highlights in Matthew 24:15 as the distinctive sign of His coming.

Jesus quantified the abomination of desolation to be the "sign" when He answered, "What will be the sign of Your coming and of the end of the age?" Paul reiterated the same sign in 2 Thessalonians 2:1–4. When we allow the Word of God to speak without human interference or reconstruction—then, clearly the abomination of desolation must transpire prior to the return of Jesus Christ and the day of the Lord.

Application

Enduring the fallout of Christ's predicted apostasy and the abomination of desolation requires a readiness under the leadership of the Holy Spirit today. We cannot expect our sinful, fallen flesh to sustain us during a period of such unique and heightened testing. Get that first. Make your decision now to saturate yourself with God's Word of promises and His provisionary Spirit. Regardless of the rejection. Regardless of the betrayal. Regardless of the persecution. Are you willing to be a light during this time of penetrating darkness? Are you a light presently? If we cannot confess Jesus Christ amid today's oppositional forces, how can we expect to proclaim His name in the days ahead? Jeremiah warned, "If you have run with footmen and they have tired you out, then how can you compete with horses? If you fall down in a land of peace, how will you do in the thicket of the Jordan?" (Jeremiah 12:5).

5. **Look again at Matthew 24:13. What does it say?**

6. **What about Matthew 24:14?**

7. **What do you think Jesus meant by *the end* in Matthew 24:13–14? (Consider the context of His sermon and questions He answered.)**

Jesus utilized a timeline to answer the disciple's questions regarding His coming and end of the age. He first provided an overview that concluded with a promise: "The one who endures **to**

the end, he will be saved." At a glance, that verse might seem to be saying salvation is predicated upon enduring, yet we are saved by Christ alone, not on our own merit. Try looking at it through an unbiased lens if you can. Remember, endurance (*hupomeno*) means "to remain under, endure or sustain a load of miseries, adversities, persecutions or provocations in faith and patience."

Those who endure to the end by pressing through tribulations will distinguish themselves as true believers with a saving faith in Jesus Christ. Thus, kept in its proper context, Jesus is assuring those who endure the difficulties of the latter days—they will be saved. Rescued. Luke 21:28 adds, "But when these things begin to take place, straighten up and lift up your heads, because **your redemption is drawing near.**"

The apostle Peter wrote, "In this you greatly rejoice, even though now for a little while, if necessary, you have been distressed by various trials, so that the proof of your faith, *being* more precious than gold which is perishable, even though tested by fire, may be found to result in praise, glory, and honor at the revelation of Jesus Christ" (1 Peter 1:6–7).

8. Look at James 1:2–5. What is the benefit of various trials?

We are kidding ourselves with these appetizing "donut gospels" currently circulating in America: dipping the cross of Christ with sugary sprinkles to entice patrons. These messages project a tantalizing, sweet aroma but prove detrimental to Christ's body as individuals and congregations (1 Cor. 12:27). Sugar provides quick energy. That's a fact. Yet sugar fails to build strong, durable mass—also a fact. Picking up the rugged cross of Jesus Christ and confronting turbulent wind shears is God's strategy for developing durable, spiritual muscles. Facing adversity, despite the fickle feelings and insidious cravings, is, without a doubt, the best faith-building exercise for learning endurance.

James speaks of "various trials" or all trials as valuable, not just those entailing persecution. Being rejected by someone you love is a trial. Losing a job, facing a health crisis, marital stress, dealing with political differences—these are arduous afflictions of body, spirit, and soul that test us every day! When we face such trials patiently and seek God in them, we will find Him. In fact, verse 5 of that same James passage says, "If any of you lacks wisdom, let him ask of God, who gives to all generously and without reproach [meaning that God will not rebuke us], and it will be given to him." Just ask.

If you have time, read Paul's description of his pilgrimage in 2 Corinthians 6. Note in verse 7 that he mentions weapons of righteousness provided for both our right and left hands. We are fully equipped to meet all challenges coming at us from any direction (Eph. 6:13–17).

America today revels in the conveniences of her "instant gratification" culture. Not taking the time to pray, save financial resources or even consider that our desires might be frivolous—exhibits and establishes a habitual pattern for decision-making that often sidesteps trials of self-denial. Just as we make purchases without blinking, we might also walk away from difficulties without thinking.

Self-denial is a crucible of fire. Jesus advised the lukewarm church of Laodicea to "buy from Me gold refined by fire so that you may become rich, and white garments so that you may clothe yourself, and that the shame of your nakedness may not be revealed; and eye salve to anoint your eyes so that you may see" (Revelation 3:18). Though these refining fires are often exhausting, we grow spiritually in Christ when we walk with Him through them rather than around them without Him (Isa. 43:1–2).

Application

Exercising your faith in trials today will fortify your mind and heart for those tomorrow (James 1:4). Allow your faith to be tested. Don't run from trials. Pray for Christ to meet you in them. "Be anxious for nothing, but in everything by prayer and supplication with thanksgiving let your requests be made known to God. And the peace of God, which surpasses all comprehension, will guard your hearts and your minds in Christ Jesus" (Philippians 4:6–7). Take a moment to ask God for strength and wisdom in whatever you are going through presently. Shelter your mind and heart in the secret place of His presence (Ps. 31:20)! "Seek the Lord and His strength; seek His face continually" (Psalm 105:4).

Day One Summary

After describing the birth pangs that precede His return, Jesus makes a promise to those who endure to the end of the age—you will be saved. How do we learn endurance? By persevering through today's trials, placing our faith in the Faithful One. We will be refined as we walk through these trials, not around them.

Day Two: Our Rapture

"The one who endures to the end, he will be saved." Scriptures such as Isaiah 25:9 state, "And it will be said in that day, 'Behold, this is our God for whom we have waited that He might save us. This is the Lord for whom we have waited; let us rejoice and be glad in His salvation.'" God's saints, revealed by their endurance to the end, will be saved. Rescued. In both the Old and New Testaments, God repeatedly promised to save and rescue the redeemed from His forthcoming wrath against all unrighteousness.

> Say to those with anxious heart, "Take courage, fear not. Behold, your God will come with vengeance; the recompense of God will come, But He will save you." (Isaiah 35:4)

> For they themselves report about us what kind of a reception we had with you, and how you turned to God from idols to serve a living and true God, and to wait for His Son from heaven, whom He raised from the dead, that is Jesus, who rescues us from the wrath to come. (1 Thessalonians 1:9–10)

1. What is God saving or rescuing His people from?

When religious leaders approached John the Baptist for baptism, he responded with, "You brood of vipers, who warned you to flee **from the wrath to come**?" (Matthew 3:7) A final, comprehensive wrath has been declared and on the books. Romans 5:9 says, "Much more then, having now been justified by His blood, we shall be saved from the wrath *of God* through Him." John 3:36 says, "He who believes in the Son has eternal life; but he who does not obey the Son shall not see life, but the wrath of God abides on him." Those who are not sealed by the Holy Spirit for salvation are marked for God's wrath instead. Since humanity is born into sin, we are also born under the penalty of sin. But when born again, we become righteous in Christ and are preserved in the day of God's wrath (2 Cor. 5:21).

First Thessalonians 4:13–17 is the rapture or rescue passage of modern eschatology. The English word "rapture" is not in the text; it's a derivative of the Latin word *raptus*. The Greek word *harpazo* translates as "caught up" in English and technically means "to seize and carry off by force," like the angels "seizing" the hands of Lot and his family when they were removed from Sodom (Gen. 19:16). This Thessalonians passage is the only Scripture revealing God's saints being caught up when Jesus returns. There are many New Testament passages referring to His return and the resurrection of the righteous but none besides this one revealing a rapture rescue. Just stop and think about that for a minute. A single minor mention has been awarded major platforms of attention in seminaries, sermons, songs, apocalyptic-themed conferences, evangelistic literature, fictional novels, movies, and twentieth-century commentaries. Since the rapture or being "caught up" has been granted such a significant mantle of importance, let's look at it.

> But we do not want you to be uninformed, brethren, about those who are asleep, so that you will not grieve as do the rest who have no hope. For if we believe that Jesus died and rose again, even so God will bring with Him those who have fallen asleep in Jesus. For this we say to you by the word of the LORD, that we who are alive and remain until the coming of the LORD, will not precede those who have fallen asleep. For the LORD Himself will descend from heaven with a shout, with the voice of the archangel and with the trumpet of God, and the dead in Christ will rise first. Then we who are alive and remain will be caught up together with them in the clouds to meet the LORD in the air, and so we shall always be with the LORD. (1 Thessalonians 4:13–17)

In that passage, *harpazo* is used in conjunction with the return of Christ. The same Greek word is also found in Acts 8:39 and 2 Corinthians 12:2–4, where a person is caught up and transferred from one place to another. Additionally, *harpazo* is used in Revelation 12:5: "And she [Israel] gave birth to a son [Jesus], a male *child*, who is to rule all the nations with a rod of iron; and her child was caught up *harpazo* to God and to His throne." In 1 Thessalonians 4:13–17, the people of God who remain on earth at the time of Christ's return will be caught up *harpazo* just as He was caught up *harpazo* and transferred from the earth to meet Him in the air. Hallelujah!

2. **Look at verse 13 from 1 Thessalonians 4:13–17 above. What problem was Paul addressing? This helps establish context.**

3. **In verse 14, who comes with Jesus when He comes?**

4. **What precedes those who endure being caught up?**

5. **How will Jesus be announced when He returns?**

According to Paul in 1 Thessalonians 4:13–17, Jesus descends from heaven with **a shout**, the **voice of an archangel** (perhaps Michael; see Dan. 12:1, Jude 1:9), and the **trumpet of God**. The Greek word for "shout" literally means "a cry of command," like that of Jesus when He "cried out with a loud voice, 'Lazarus, come forth'" (John 11:43). When Jesus returns, He brings the saints already in heaven. Remnants of their decayed bodies will be raised from graves, caves, mountains, fields, rivers, lakes, and oceans across the world—instantly transformed. Instantly! Then those "who are alive and remain" on earth will suddenly be "caught up together with them in the clouds." Rescued.

Note the timing of the rapture to be **after** the righteous are resurrected. Did you see that? "The dead in Christ will rise first," a miracle testifying to God's victory over death, sin, and Satan. The earth supernaturally releases all bodies of Christ's redeemed to their resurrected King. Unlike His first humble appearing with meager beginnings in a manger, the return of Jesus will be a spectacular event, drawing the attention of the world toward the living Word of God from heaven (Rev. 1:7).

> And I saw heaven opened, and behold, a white horse, and He who sat on it is called Faithful and True, and in righteousness He judges and wages war. His eyes *are* a flame of fire, and on His head are many diadems; and He has a name written *on Him* which no one knows except Himself. *He is* clothed with a robe dipped in blood, and His name is called The Word of God. (Revelation 19:11–13)

When Jesus returns, His saints are reunited with their lost loved ones (2 Thess. 2:1). Paul's emphasis on the rapture passage in 1 Thessalonians 4:13–17 is on this anticipated gathering and reunion, not a tribulation escape plan. And the timing of it all? Being caught up with Christ takes place after the resurrection of the righteous. Now, let's begin looking at the Scriptures on the timing of that.

6. When does 1 Corinthians 15:20–24 say the righteous are resurrected?

7. What happens after the resurrection of the righteous?

Paul provides a specific order to the resurrection of the righteous. Christ was raised as the "first fruits of those asleep," a different resurrection from those raised by prophets, apostles, and even Jesus Himself. Their bodies were reinstated but not transformed as they will be at the righteous resurrection. Secondly, those in Christ will be resurrected at His coming. Just like that of Christ, the resurrection of the righteous is a permanent transformation. Eternal. At that very moment, all who are Christ's will be "clothed with our dwelling from heaven" (2 Corinthians 5:2). "Then comes the end, when He hands over the kingdom to the God and Father, when He has abolished all rule and all authority and power" (1 Corinthians 15:24). Tomorrow, we look at additional Scriptures regarding the specifics and timing of the righteous resurrection.

The **rapture** of the saints has commandeered a spotlight within Christian circles for over a century, eclipsing the Bible's emphasis on the **resurrection** as the hope of our faith (see appendix "Rapture"). Most of us don't realize that the pre-tribulation rapture is merely hypothetical mystery, requiring a dissection and assemblage of Scripture for its presentation. The context of verses, phrases and words are being disregarded and interpretations forced. In 1 Thessalonians 4:13–17 (the rapture passage) Paul taught that when Jesus returns, the righteous will be resurrected first, and then those who are remain alive will be caught up. He is writing to encourage a suffering church at the time who is enduring persecution and losing loved ones. That is the context.

The pre-tribulation rapture contradicts Christ's timeline and conflicts with the overall counsel of God's Word regarding His return and righteous resurrection. Wouldn't it be more prudent to stick to clear revelation rather than invest in speculation? Jesus was resurrected. When He returns, the dead in Christ will be resurrected, and those who have endured will be caught up to meet their loved ones in the air. Thus, "the one who endures to the end, he will be saved" (Matthew 24:13).

I pray that we can discuss the resurrection and rapture of the righteous without hostile arguments or dishonoring the Christ we now wait and watch for. Corrie Ten Boom, a legendary Jewish Holocaust survivor, said, "God's Word is to be savored, not debated." I agree, don't you? The Bible is a precious provision. If we become contentious while enjoying this sacred sustenance, then our fellowship in and with the Spirit suffers. You might wonder, "Why does it even matter when the church is caught up or raptured?" I've been asked that multiple times. So here it is: what we believe regarding the timing of the rapture determines what we prepare for, which is either (1) the Lord's imminent return, which could happen any moment, or (2) the great tribulation that must be endured prior to His imminent return. Do you see the difference? Stay open to the leading of the Holy Spirit as we proceed, and let the Word of God speak freely! Are you willing?

YES   NO

When Jesus descends from heaven, He is announced with **a shout**, the **voice of the archangel**, and the **trumpet of God**. He has a name written on Him that no one else knows until He returns on a brilliant white horse of victory. The world has seen Jesus as the Lamb of God, the Faithful, and True Word of God but not as the majestic Son of God and King of kings. His return will be the full revelation of His glory, set aside in order to become our atoning sacrifice (Phil. 2:5–11). When He returns, the day of the Lord begins, and His blood-bought kingdom is revealed. It will be a spectacular moment for the people of God, especially for those who have endured to the end!

A.W. Tozer wrote, "I confess that I would have liked to have seen the baby Jesus. But the glorified Jesus yonder at the right hand of the Majesty on high, was the baby Jesus once cradled in the manger straw. Taking a body of humiliation, He was still the Creator who made the wood of that manger, made the straw, and was the Creator of all the beasts who were there. In truth He made the little town of Bethlehem and all that it was. He also made the star that lingered over the scene that night. He had come into His own world, His Father's world. (*The Word Made Flesh*)

8. What does Psalm 31:19-20 say to those who take refuge in God?

Day Two Summary

In 1 Thessalonians 4:13–17, Paul reminds the church that those who are alive will be reunited with deceased loved ones when Jesus returns—resurrecting their bodies before those who remain are caught up. In 1 Corinthians 15:20–24, Paul also said the righteous will be resurrected when Jesus returns, which Christ designates on His timeline to be after the great tribulation, not before.

Day Three: Our Resurrection

The resurrection of the righteous is God's promise and guarantee for the family of faith (Isa. 26:19; 1 Pet. 1:3; Rom. 6:8, 8:11; 1 Cor. 6:14; 2 Cor. 5:1–5). "I am the resurrection and the life; he who believes in Me shall live even if he dies" (John 11:25). All who are in Christ will be raised, and our bodies will be completely restored! Hallelujah! Yesterday, we read in 1 Thessalonians 4:13–17 that when Jesus returns, the righteous are resurrected before those who remain are caught up. It makes sense then to delve into the timing of this resurrection if we want to establish the timing of the rapture, right? Let's begin with the Old Testament. Highlight time phrases that specify when the righteous resurrection occurs. Job, the oldest Bible book, is the first to mention this resurrection and its timing.

> So man lies down and does not rise. Until the heavens are no longer, he will not awake nor be aroused out of his sleep. (Job 14:12)

1. When does Job say the resurrection occurs?

When the heavens are no longer! Look again at Matthew 24:29–31. The heavens are shaken, and luminaries darkened—**after** the great tribulation period. This is the sign that Old Testament prophets predicted would predicate the day of the Lord. It was also the same sign revealed by the sixth scroll seal in Revelation 6:12–17. In Week One, Lesson Three, we discussed Christ's timeline paralleling the scroll seals. The  seals disclose the scroll's contents of the scroll: (1) Antichrist(s), (2) war, (3) famine, (4) death, and (5) martyrdom. Then, the sixth seal reveals the heavens being shaken and are "no longer," as Job describes it. This occurs **after** the great tribulation according to the timeline of Christ. Don't miss that. There is another Old Testament passage providing insight into the great tribulation period and resurrection or rescue of the righteous. Most, if not all, New Testament teachings have roots of origin in the Old Testament canon. Think about Paul's reference to the rapture in 1 Thessalonians 4:13–17 as you read this from Daniel:

> Now at that time Michael, the great prince who stands guard over the sons of your people, will arise. And there will be a time of distress such as never occurred since there was a nation until that time; and at that time your people, everyone who is found written in the book, will be rescued. Many of those who sleep in the dust of the ground will awake, these to everlasting life, but the others to disgrace and everlasting contempt. (Daniel 12:1–2)

2. What is happening when Daniel says the righteous are resurrected or rescued?

This "time of distress," referred to in earlier chapters by Daniel, is the great tribulation that comes after the abomination of desolation (Matt. 24:21). In Daniel 12:1–2, "everyone who is found written in the book, will be rescued," and "those who sleep in the dust of the ground will awake." John wrote about this resurrection, "Do not marvel at this; for an hour is coming, in which all who are in the tombs will hear His voice and will come forth; those who did the good *deeds* to a resurrection of life and those who committed the evil *deeds* to a resurrection of judgment" (John 5:28–29). John was teaching from Daniel 12:1–2. In 1 Thessalonians 4:16, from the rapture passage, Jesus descends from heaven with a shout to resurrect, rescue, and rapture His saints— "Come forth!"

Jesus is the judge of both the living and the dead (Acts 10:42). Everyone has a future resurrection forthcoming, the righteous exonerated with eternal life, and the unrighteous condemned by their sin (Acts 24:15). However, these two resurrections are not simultaneous. Revelation 20:4–6 reveals the righteous are raised in "the *first* resurrection" before the one-thousand-year reign of Christ. His millennial reign begins after He returns and initiates the day of the Lord (Rev. 20:2–7; Isa. 2:4, 9:6, 11:1–9, 42:1). "For He must reign until He has put all His enemies under His feet" (1 Corinthians 15:25). Then, in verses 11–15, we see the unrighteous are raised afterward to face the Great White Throne of judgment.

In the Old Testament, God speaks directly to Israel because, at that time, they were designated as His chosen people. Yet the New Testament reveals all believers to be the chosen of God. We will discuss this more next week, but for now, consider this: "There is neither Jew nor Greek, there is neither slave nor free man, there is neither male nor female; for you are all one in Christ Jesus. And if you belong to Christ, then you are Abraham's offspring, heirs according to the promise" (Galatians 3:28–29). Originally, God spoke to and through prophets and priests from one nation but now speaks to and through believers from all nations. He began with one man and one nation for the sake of all.

3. Was Paul in 1 Thessalonians 4:13–17 drawing from Daniel 12:1–2 when he wrote of a future resurrection and rapture? What are your thoughts?

God's Word presents one resurrection of the righteous, therefore, only one rapture or rescue. Multiple resurrections or rescues of the righteous are not substantiated or taught in Scripture. When allowed to speak freely without dissection, the Word of God presents one return of Christ for His saints and one resurrection of the righteous when He reunites the saints—the dead with the living.

4. **Look at these New Testament Scriptures regarding the righteous resurrection and when it occurs. Highlight the time phrases with a yellow marker.**

    This is the will of Him who sent Me, that of all that He has given Me I lose nothing, but raise it up on the last day. (John 6:39)

    For this is the will of My Father, that everyone who beholds the Son and believes in Him will have eternal life, and I Myself will raise him up on the last day. (John 6:40)

    No one can come to Me unless the Father who sent Me draws him; and I will raise him up on the last day. (John 6:44)

    He who eats My flesh and drinks My blood has eternal life, and I will raise him up on the last day. (John 6:54)

    Jesus said to her, "Your brother [Lazarus] will rise again." Martha said to Him, "I know that he will rise again in the resurrection on the last day." (John 11:23–24)

5. **According to those Scriptures, when does Jesus resurrect His righteous?**

Let's read 1 Corinthians 15:20–24 again:

    But now Christ has been raised from the dead, the first fruits of those who are asleep. For since by a man came death, by a man also came the resurrection of the dead. For as in Adam all die, so also in Christ all will be made alive. But each in his own order: Christ the firstfruits, after that those who are Christ's at His coming, then comes the end, when He hands over the kingdom to the God and Father, when He has abolished all rule and all authority and power.

6. **What is the order of the resurrection of the righteous?**

7. **How many resurrections of the righteous should we expect?**

8. In Hebrews 9:28, how many comings of Christ are there and why?

Hebrews 9:28 reveals two comings of Christ, both in regards to salvation: (1) for sinners and (2) for His saints who "eagerly await Him." Very specific. Very clear. God has not made His plan difficult to understand. It is man's timelines that deviate from the timeline of Jesus Christ and the overall revelation of His Word that are confusing.

Sozo is the Greek word for "saved," meaning "to save, deliver, protect." Saved from sin, we are first rescued from its power and penalty, transferred from Satan's dungeon of slavery into the freeing kingdom of God. "For He rescued us from the domain of darkness, and transferred us to the kingdom of His beloved Son, in whom we have redemption, the forgiveness of sins" (Colossians 1:13–14). Additionally, the saints of God are "saved, delivered, protected" from His wrath against all unrighteousness in the day of the Lord (1 Pet. 1:5). Those who endure to the end will be saved.

9. Back to 1 Corinthians 15:24, note what else happens at the end?

In the end, Jesus delivers the kingdom to His Father. We will see tomorrow that Jesus acquires this kingdom at the seventh and last trumpet of Revelation 11:15. Paul taught in 1 Corinthians 15:51–52 that the dead will be resurrected at the *last* trumpet. Some say that the seventh trumpet in Revelation 11 could not be Paul's last trumpet because his letters were written prior to John's apocalyptic vision on Patmos. Is God that shortsighted? That limited? He created our world and galaxy in six days. He is from everlasting, the Alpha and Omega (Ps. 90:2, Isa. 44:6, Rev. 21:6–7). "He is before all things, and in Him all things hold together" (Colossians 1:17). Couldn't this omniscient, eternal, revelatory God apprise Paul of a last trumpet before disclosing through John that there will be seven in totality? Of course, He could.

From the earliest book of Scripture (Job) to the last (Revelation), God's redeemed are promised victory over death and a personal resurrection from the grave. David said, "I shall not die, but live" (Psalm 118:17). This miraculous emergence from the grave is the destiny of every believer. It is the hope of our faith. "For if the dead are not raised, not even Christ has been raised; and if Christ has not been raised, your faith is worthless; you are still in your sins" (1 Corinthians 15:16–17).

Because of Jesus Christ, death can no longer claim you—even your abandoned, decomposed body! When forgiven, we are exonerated and reconciled to God, forever set free from the power and puppeteer of our sin—Satan, as well as the consequences of our sin—death. We are made righteous in Christ and will live forever with Him. Believers are received into heaven when they die: "Absent from the body, present with the Lᴏʀᴅ" (2 Cor. 5:8). It is these believers who come with Jesus when He returns for those who have endured to the end (1 Thess. 4:13–17, Matt. 24:13). Deserted bodies will be resurrected and renewed (1 Cor. 15:52, 1 John 3:2). Can I hear a hallelujah? New bodies! Every blemish, handicap, and defect forever removed! We will breathe again. Move again. Be able to think again. Hear clearly and see perfectly while enjoying the glory and freedom of God that we were created to enjoy. Amen! Come back, Lord Jesus, soon!

> For our citizenship is in heaven, from which also we eagerly wait for a Savior, the Lᴏʀᴅ Jesus Christ; who will transform the body of our humble state into conformity with the body of His glory, by the exertion of the power that He has even to subject all things to Himself. (Philippians 3:20–21)

Application

In my introduction to this study, I promised to stick to what is clear in Scripture: the certainties. Hebrews 9:28 is one of those clear certainties: "So Christ also, having been offered **once** to bear the sins of many, will appear **a second time** for salvation without *reference to* sin, to those who eagerly await Him." The Bible only reveals two comings of Christ. First, He comes on behalf of sinners; and then, He comes for His saints. Multiple resurrections and returns to rescue or save the saints at different junctures for assorted reasons are the byproduct proposals of theological theories—not supported by Scripture. Does that surprise and trouble you? If so, why?

Day Three Summary

According to the Word of God, the resurrection of the righteous occurs when the heavens are "no longer"—on the "last day," at the "last trumpet," at "the end," when Jesus acquires His kingdom. These time phrases clearly place the righteous resurrection, rescue, and reunion of the saints at the end of the age, after the great tribulation which agrees with the timeline of Christ. In addition, Hebrews 9:28 states there are two comings of Christ regarding salvation: (1) to save sinners and (2) to save His saints. The Scriptures never speak of multiple returns for multiple reasons—anywhere.

Day Four: The Last Trumpet

In 1 Thessalonians 4:13–17, Paul referenced the rapture because the saints in Thessalonica were suffering, mourning deceased loved ones, and needed reassurance of their reunion. That is the context and backdrop of the rapture passage—a reunion, not a tribulation escape plan, delivered to a church experiencing persecution at the time (1 Thess.

1:6 and 2:14–15). Paul wrote to encourage them in their tribulations, not promise them that an imminent end was in sight. Think about it.

God's Word highlights a future resurrection of the righteous in both the Old and New Testaments that Christ confirmed (John 11:23-25). Peter wrote that we have been "born again to a living hope through the resurrection of Jesus Christ from the dead" (1 Peter 1:3). "But if the Spirit of Him who raised Jesus from the dead dwells in you, He who raised Christ Jesus from the dead will also give life to your mortal bodies through His Spirit who dwells in you" (Romans 8:11). The resurrection of God's crucified Christ is proof that we too will be resurrected. This proclamation is the central hope of our faith, not a rapture rescue (1 Cor. 15:14–19). The rapture is the vehicle for reuniting the living who remain on earth when Christ returns with their deceased loved ones.

Yesterday, we read, "This is the will of Him who sent Me, that of all that He has given Me I lose nothing, but raise it up on the last day" (John 6:39). **On the last day** is repeated four times in that one chapter alone (John 6:39, 40, 44, and 54). Later, when Jesus told Martha that Lazarus would "rise again," she replied, "I know that he will rise again in the resurrection **on the last day**" (John 11:24). Jesus said, "The one who endures to the end, he shall be saved" (Matthew 24:13). Wouldn't the end and the last day be referring to the culmination of this present age (Eph. 1:21)? Let's also consider Paul's teaching on the "last trumpet."

> Behold, I tell you a mystery; we will not all sleep, but we will all be changed, in a moment, in the twinkling of an eye, at the last trumpet; for the trumpet will sound, and the dead will be raised imperishable, and we will be changed. (1 Corinthians 15:51–52)

1. **When are the saints resurrected and their bodies changed?**

2. **How does "we will not all sleep" agree with 1 Thessalonians 4:17?**

We've already looked at Paul teaching the Thessalonians that the rapture happens after the resurrection of the righteous. To the Corinthians, he added that this resurrection occurs at the last trumpet. Those alive when Jesus returns will be changed in the "twinkling of an eye" as they are caught up to meet Him in the air. That's quicker than a millisecond. Faster than we can blink, the saints who endure to the end will be physically transformed as the bodies of all deceased saints are resurrected. At that juncture, there is no time for debating Christ's return in an interactive chatroom. When God's Word is fulfilled, it just is, independent of committee meetings or emergency conference calls; the enactment was authorized when the promise was made.

3. In 1 Thessalonians 4:16, how is Jesus announced?

In the rapture passage, Paul wrote to the Thessalonians that with a shout, the voice of an archangel, and the trumpet of God, the coming of Christ would be proclaimed. Writing to the Corinthians, he clarified that trumpet to be the last, inferring there are other trumpets before it. Do we know anything about a final trumpet within a sequence? Not unless we consider the seven trumpets Christ revealed to John (Rev. 1:1). The first six are found in Revelation 8 and the seventh in 11:15–19. The first six trumpets sound alarms through disasters designated to humble humanity and extend opportunities for salvation. That opportunity as well as repentance ceases by the sixth trumpet (Rev. 9:20–21). Remember that Jesus said the Gospel message will be declared in the whole world for a witness to all nations, and then the end will come (Matt. 24:14 and 28:20).

Don't miss the significance of the seventh trumpet, as notably unique from the previous six trumpet warnings. The last trumpet makes an announcement, "The seventh angel sounded; and there were loud voices in heaven, saying, 'The kingdom of the world has become the kingdom of our LORD and of His Christ; and He will reign forever and ever'" (Revelation 11:15). This final trumpet is an earth-shattering proclamation, a divine period at the end of a dramatic six-trumpet sentence. No more wake-up calls. No further opportunity to be saved. Just like in the days of Noah and Lot, judgment is at hand.

Some teach that the trumpets in Revelation dispense God's wrath. No. Revelation 11:15–18 reveals the wrath of God succeeding the seventh trumpet in "bowls of wrath." Plus, Scripture reveals that the elect endure the great tribulation prior to Christ's return, which wouldn't be the case if God's wrath were in play. For further confirmation, consider the prophetic foreshadowing built into the Jewish feasts (see Appendix "Seven Jewish Feasts"). The Feast of Trumpets commemorates a period of reflective repentance prior to Yom Kippur (Judgment Day). The first six trumpets in Revelation 8 magnify God's sovereignty over the earth, similar to the plagues in Egypt (Exod. 7:5; Micah 7:15). With each plague, both Egyptians and Israelites were extended opportunities to recognize the hand of God and repent. In the final plague, those who responded were protected by the Lamb's blood and delivered, just as those marked by the blood of Jesus Christ will also be delivered at the seventh and last trumpet.

> *He is* clothed with a robe dipped in blood, and His name is called The Word of God. (Revelation 19:13)

Consider additional points supporting John's seventh trumpet as Paul's "last." First, when this seventh trumpet sounds, Jesus acquires His kingdom. "The kingdom of the world has become the kingdom of our LORD and of His Christ; and He will reign forever and ever" (Revelation 11:15). We already read this in 1 Corinthians 15:23–24: "Each in his own order: Christ the firstfruits, after that those who are Christ's at His coming, **then comes the end**, when He hands over the kingdom to the God and Father, when He has abolished all rule and all authority and power." Jesus acquires His kingdom and submits it to His Father at the seventh and last trumpet (John 6:38).

Second, in the wake of the seventh trumpet, Revelation 11:18 says, "And the nations were enraged, and **Your wrath came**, and the time *came* for the dead to be judged, and *the time* to reward Your bond-servants the prophets and the saints and those who fear Your name, the small and the great, and to destroy those who destroy the earth." The wrath of God follows the seventh trumpet. Since the righteous will be saved from God's wrath, it follows that the righteous are raptured, rescued, and reunited at the seventh and last trumpet (1 Thess. 1:10).

4. Revelation 11:18 lists four events succeeding the seventh trumpet. Fill in the blanks.

- Nations were enraged and God's _____ came

- Time for the _____ to be judged

- Time to _____ God's bond-servants, prophets, and saints

- Time to _____ those who destroy the earth

The seventh trumpet initiates God's wrath, His judgment of the dead, and distribution of rewards. God's saints have been exonerated from His wrath against sin. They will be rescued beforehand, just like in the days of Noah and Lot. But if we are not found to be in Christ and Christ in us, then no saving grace remains (Col. 1:27, Rom. 5:9). The door of the ark will be securely shut. The seventh trumpet will sound, and bowls of wrath will be emptied out against all who have rejected God's provision for salvation—standing outside of the ark, unprotected (John 3:36).

Third, Revelation 11:18 also states that with the seventh trumpet, it is time for the dead to be judged and saints rewarded—components of the day of the Lord. When does the day of the Lord begin? When Jesus returns (2 Thess. 2:1–2). The Scriptures reveal that the righteous will be resurrected first and the House of God judged. "For *it is* time for judgment to begin with the household of God; and if *it begins* with us first, what *will be* the outcome for those who do not obey the gospel of God?" (1 Peter 4:17). The saints will not be condemned; instead, they are rewarded according to their faithfulness (Rom. 8:1, 2 Tim. 4:8, 1 Cor. 4:5). Crowns will be distributed and perhaps a loss of crowns suffered (Rom. 14:10–12, 2 Cor. 5:10). Then, after Christ's one-thousand-year reign, the unrighteous will be resurrected to face the Great White Throne, judgment, and death (Rom. 6:23, Rev. 20:14–15). Woe to those who have rejected the Way, the Truth, and the Life (John 14:6), for "I am the LORD, and there is no other" (Isaiah 45:5).

Fourth, Revelation 10:7 reveals a unique accomplishment with this last trumpet: "In the days of the voice of the seventh angel, when he is about to sound, then the mystery of God is finished, as He preached to His servants the prophets." This mystery of the Gospel and God's kingdom began to emerge through Noah and Abraham long before it was achieved in Christ (Gen. 9:26–27,

12:1–3; Gal. 3:8). "*To be specific*, that the Gentiles are fellow heirs and fellow members of the body, and fellow partakers of the promise in Christ Jesus through the gospel" (Ephesians 3:6). "The mystery which has been hidden from the past ages and generations, but has now been manifested to His saints" (Colossians 1:26). God's kingdom is His assemblage of saints redeemed by heaven's Lamb sacrifice, whether Jew or Gentile, male or female (Rom. 1:16, 16:25–26; Mark 4:11; Eph. 3:8–9; Col. 1:25–26). At the seventh and last trumpet, this mystery is finished, not before.

In conclusion, John's seventh trumpet is verifiably Paul's last trumpet in 1 Corinthians 15:51–52, when the dead are raised imperishable, and God's saints are forever changed. At this trumpet, the day of the Lord begins when Jesus returns to resurrect and rescue His redeemed, acquire His kingdom, and begin His spectacular millennial reign. In tandem, this is reality presented by Scripture.

5. **Fill in the blanks from the Scriptures we looked at this week regarding the resurrection of the righteous:**

   • The resurrection occurs _____(John 6:39, 40, 44, 54; 11:23–24).

   • The resurrection occurs prior to _____(1 Thess. 4:15–17).

   • The resurrection occurs at His _____(1 Thess. 4:15).

   • The resurrection occurs at the last _____(1 Cor. 15:51–52).

   • The resurrection occurs prior to the _____reign of Christ (Rev. 20:4–6).

   • The resurrection occurs when _____are no more (Job 14:12).

In 1 Thessalonians 4:13–17, the rapture follows the resurrection of the righteous. Since the Bible reveals the resurrection of the righteous to be on the last day, at the last trumpet, when the heavens are no more, and prior to Christ's one-thousand-year reign, we have a compelling Scriptural consensus, as well as evidentiary proof of a post-tribulation rapture that agrees with Christ's timeline. This study was not conceived to argue against a pre-tribulation rapture. It was intended as a study of Christ's timeline regarding His return. Yet in so doing, the amount of Scriptural evidence revealing a post-tribulation rapture became compelling and could not be ignored. Nor should it be.

Jesus did not highlight His rapture rescue in the visions of Revelation, a book written to and for the churches (Rev. 1:4–7, 22:16). Those snippets of future events were shared to prepare His overcomers for the great tribulation, as well as His Second Coming. The rapture is not highlighted on Christ's timeline either unless Matthew 24:40–41 is the reference, which we will examine in week seven. My point is this: Jesus did not put an emphasis on the rapture of the saints, so why are we?

Application

Second Corinthians 5:4–5 says, "For indeed while we are in this tent, we groan, being burdened, because we do not want to be unclothed, but to be clothed, so that what is mortal will be swallowed up by life. Now He who prepared us for this very purpose is God, who gave to us the Spirit as a pledge." Is the hope of your faith centered on the assurance of your resurrection or the hope of a pre-tribulation rapture rescue?

RESURRECTION   RAPTURE

That may sound like a silly question, maybe even impertinent. But just think about it. Where should our faith be centered and concentrated? Jesus Christ, yes. But why? He overcame sin and death for us! Because He lives, we too will live forever with Him (2 Cor. 4:14). Second Corinthians 1:9 says we do not trust in ourselves, "but in God who raises the dead." My friends, do not fear the future. Do not fear persecution or the tribulations of today and tomorrow. "For we know that if the earthly tent which is our house is torn down, we have a building from God, a house not made with hands, eternal in the heavens. For indeed in this *house* we groan, longing to be clothed with our dwelling from heaven" (2 Corinthians 5:1–2). Amen. Are you afraid of death? Explain why or why not.

> Your dead will live, their corpses will rise. You who lie in the dust, awake and shout for joy, for your dew is as the dew of the dawn, and the earth will give birth to the departed spirits. (Isaiah 26:19)

Day Four Summary

First Corinthians 15:51–52 says that the resurrection of the righteous and Christ's return will occur at the last trumpet when He also acquires His kingdom. This coincides with the account of the seventh trumpet in Revelation 11:15. The time phrases regarding the return of Christ and resurrection of the righteous designate the rapture rescue of the church to be on the last day after the great tribulation at the seventh and last trumpet.

Week Two Synopsis

The righteous are resurrected and raptured at the seventh and last trumpet.

Encourage each other as you see the day drawing near.
(Hebrews 10:25)

Week Three

MATTHEW 24:15–28

 **Day One: The Sign**

After His disciples asked, "What will be the sign of Your coming and of the end of the age?" Jesus answered with an overview of what to expect in Matthew 24:5–14. Then, He highlighted specific events in verses 15 and 29. His overview is also disclosed by the scroll seals in Revelation 6. Go back to Week One, Day Four, if you need a refresher. What were the first five seals?

1-

2-

3-

4-

5-

Read verses 15–28 printed on the Week Three Worksheet at the end of this week's lesson. Then, complete the observations on the right side of your worksheet, noting the timeline at the bottom for when the abomination of desolation occurs. Next week, we go to Daniel 9:24–27 as the source of this seven-year timeline. Stay tuned for that. You don't want to miss it!

In the study of Scripture, it helps to read slowly while observing the text. Speed reading through God's Word is like running through a magnificent garden yet missing the beauty and details of existing flora. God's Word contains multidimensional layers of truth. Asking questions about what you're reading facilitates an unimaginable journey beneath the surface of those layers. Who is writing and to whom? What is going on at the time? These questions help to establish context. Then, note repeated words and phrases because repetition reveals the purpose and emphasis of the writing. One question we should ask when coming to a word of conclusion such as "therefore" in Matthew 24:15 is "What is the word "therefore" there for?"

1. **What is the word *therefore* there for? (What question is Christ addressing?)**

2. In verse 15, what did Jesus say we would see?

3. How should Judeans respond?

When the abomination of desolation occurs, the inhabitants of Judea are directed to flee to the mountains. Why? The Antichrist will rise to a position of power, seizing the Jewish temple and claiming the authority of God. Caves already exist in the mountains of Galilee, previously designed to shelter Israelites in seasons of war. Some even survived the Roman invasion in AD 70 by escaping to these places of refuge. Will God take care of them? Absolutely. Revelation 12:6 reveals His provision: "Then the woman [Israel] fled into the wilderness where she had a place prepared by God, so that there she would be nourished for one thousand two hundred and sixty days" (Revelation 12:6).

It will be a horrific time for those in Judea. Jesus said, "Woe to those who are pregnant and to those who are nursing babies in those days!" (Matthew 24:19). He instructed them to pray that their flight not be in the winter or on a Sabbath (Matt. 24:20). Winters in Israel extend from late October to mid-March with nights especially cold. It is their rainy season when the lowlands and dry streambeds flood. Thus, fleeing would be more challenging in the "wet season" or on a Sabbath when physical exertion is limited. Such attention to detail reveals Christ's heart for the specifics of our difficult situations. Deuteronomy 32:10 says, "He found him in a desert land, and in the howling waste of a wilderness; He encircled him, He cared for him, He guarded him as the pupil of His eye."

4. What type of tribulation does the abomination of desolation initiate (v. 21)?

Perhaps you have noticed the repetitive use of the word "great," such as a "great" tribulation or false Christs and prophets performing "great" signs and wonders. The Greek word for "great," *megas*, is also used in verse 31 when speaking of a "great" trumpet. According to the definition of *megas*, these events "powerfully affect the senses as violent, mighty, strong in intensity and degree." Ask any woman who has experienced childbirth, "Were you able to ignore the contractions? Would you describe them as strong and intense, even violent?" I have birthed seven children myself, and not one of those deliveries could be described as anything but *megas* in intensity, affecting all sensory receptors. How about you?

Application

Jesus describes the great tribulation as a distinctively unique time in human history. He also said that for the sake of the elect, those days will be cut short (Matt. 24:22). This tells us two things: (1) the elect are on earth during the great tribulation, and (2) we should give thought to preparation. Will you trust Jesus to encircle, care for, and guard you as the pupil of His eye (Deut. 32:10)?

YES   NO

After looking at verses 15–28 more closely, do you have additional questions about Christ's timeline? **Record them here and see if they are answered as we continue to study together.**

Day One Summary

In verses 15–28, Jesus pointed specifically to the abomination of desolation as the unmistakable sign of His coming. Those in Judea should flee because of the great tribulation that ensues. But for the sake of His elect, this difficult time will be cut short.

Day Two: God's Elect

"Unless those days had been cut short, no life would have been saved; but for the sake of the elect those days will be cut short" (Matthew 24:22). Let that sink in. Here, we read a clear and undeniable truth: God's elect remain on earth during the great tribulation. Theologians struggle with this disclosure and the reign of the Antichrist, disagreeing with how to interpret and disseminate the information. It is like trying to handle a flaming hot potato, so the majority cast it aside. The dispensational approach (see appendix "Rapture") is to assert that Jesus was referring to the Jews rather than the Gentiles or the church. Yet Scripture never elucidates a division of Jew and Gentile once united. In fact, the opposite is true. The Bible reveals God's elect to be a union of Jews and Gentiles without distinction. And once united, we never read of being separated for any reason. Israel was the first nation to be entrusted with the oracles of God (Rom. 2:2). But all nations have been invited to join His Kingdom and proclaim God's Gospel together (Matt. 28:19–20, Acts 1:7–8).

The Greek word for "elect" *eklektos* means "chosen, selected, saints of God." The Hebrew word for "elect," *bahir*, also means "chosen ones."

1. **Highlight or underline who the *eklektos* (chosen) are in the following:**

For you are all sons *and daughters* of God through faith in Christ Jesus. For all of you who were baptized into Christ have clothed yourselves with Christ. There is neither Jew nor Greek, there is neither slave nor free man, there is neither male nor female; for you are all one in Christ Jesus. And if you belong to Christ, then you are Abraham's descendants, heirs according to promise. (Galatians 3:26–29)

For he is not a Jew who is one outwardly, nor is circumcision that which is outward in the flesh. But he is a Jew who is one inwardly; and circumcision is that which is of the heart, by the Spirit, not by the letter; and his praise is not from men, but from God. (Romans 2:28–29)

Do not lie to one another, since you laid aside the old self with its *evil* practices, and have put on the new self who is being renewed to a true knowledge according to the image of the One who created him—*a renewal* in which there is no *distinction between* Greek and Jew, circumcised and uncircumcised, barbarian, Scythian, slave and freeman, but Christ is all, and in all. (Colossians 3:9–11)

2. **Who are the descendants of Abraham?**

3. **Which circumcision identifies the true Jew?**

4. **The best interpreter of Scripture is the Scriptures themselves, so who are the elect of God?**

The Bible abounds with Scripture revealing the elect to be a union of Jew and Gentile believers as the church of Jesus Christ, an assemblage embroiled within God's covenant to Abraham. "I have made you the father of a multitude of nations" (Genesis 17:4). Before that, Noah even prophesied, "Blessed be the LORD, the God of Shem; and let Canaan be his servant. May God enlarge Japheth, and let him dwell in the tents of Shem; and let Canaan be his servant" (Genesis 9:26–27). Noah prophesied that Japheth's lineage (Gentiles) would join the lineage of Shem (Jews), and they would dwell together. The descendants of Canaan (unbelievers) would not.

Christ and His church was a mystery in the Old Testament even though a number of Gentiles joined the nation of Israel (Lev. 24:22; Num. 9:14, 15:15–16; Isa. 56:3–6). In the genealogy of Christ, Gentile women such as Tamar, Rahab, and Ruth can be found. God incorporated Gentile believers in the Old Testament, just as Jewish believers were included in the New Testament. He has never restricted the choosing of His elect to only one demographic either before or after Christ.

5. In Exodus 12:48–49, how were Gentile converts assimilated into Israel?

The church of Jesus Christ is "the mystery which has been kept secret for long ages past, but now is manifested" (Romans 16:25–26). Abraham, one individual, has fathered descendants who are appointed to share the Messiah with the whole world (Rom. 4:16–17). This mystery has always been God's plan, a union of believers, empowered and commissioned at Pentecost by the Holy Spirit to "go ye" together as a royal priesthood and proclaim His excellencies (1 Pet. 2:9–10). Together, we have been redeemed by the precious blood of Jesus; and together, we will be gathered in His holy land when He returns. "For He Himself is our peace, who made both *groups into* one … so that in Himself He might make the two into one new man, thus establishing peace" (Ephesians 2:14–15). When we become one, we are no longer two.

> Gentiles are fellow heirs and fellow members of the body, and fellow partakers of the promise in Christ Jesus through the Gospel. (Ephesians 3:6)

> For even as the body is one and yet has many members, and all the members of the body, though they are many, are one body, so also is Christ. For by one Spirit we were all baptized into one body, whether Jews or Greeks, whether slaves or free, and we were all made to drink of one Spirit. (1 Corinthians 12:12–13)

When we fully grasp the mystery of our eternal union in Christ, then the canon of Scripture we know as the Holy Bible becomes a covenant book of assurance for all believers, not just Israel (John 3:16; Rom. 4:16). This is not "replacement" theology but a "redemption" song, clearly revealed in God's covenant to Abraham. I'm not sure why some continue to separate the body of Christ into Jew and Gentile other than they are looking at the rite of passage rather than the end result. We are all baptized into one body by one Spirit through the sacrifice of one Redeemer as descendants of one man, Abraham. All his descendants are the elect and destined to inherit the earth—together!

Jesus carried the mystery forward in His prayer. Fill in the blanks:

> For their sakes I sanctify Myself, that they themselves also may be sanctified in truth. I do not ask on behalf of these alone [His disciples], but for those also who believe in Me through their word; that they may all be_____; even as You, Father, are in Me and I in You, that they also may be in Us; so that the world may believe that You sent Me. The glory which You have given Me I have given to them, that they may be _____, just as We are _____; I in them, and You in Me, that they may be perfected in _____, so that the world may know that You sent Me, and loved them, even as You have loved Me. (John 17:19–23)

> *Ekklesia* is the Greek word for "church" in the NT, a combination of *ek*, meaning "out of or away from," and *kaleo*, meaning "a called-out assembly or congregation." It is akin to *eklektos*, the Greek word for "elect."

The Septuagint, which is the Koine Greek translation of the Old Testament, often translates the Hebrew word *qahal*—meaning "assembly, congregation, or gathering"—as *ekklesia* or "church" (Gen. 48:4, Ps. 149:1). Essentially, *qahal* is the Old Testament word for "church." Everyone called out and chosen by the Father, redeemed by the Lamb, are His elect—one called-out assembly, one flock with one Shepherd (John 10:14–16), Christ's church (Heb. 2:12, 12:23).

Think About It

Theologians who remove Gentiles prior to the great tribulation or exclude the church of Jesus Christ depend heavily upon Romans 11:25 as a foundational tenet. They contend that when "the fullness of the Gentiles has come in," God will be finished with everyone but Israel. Is that a possibility? Anything is possible, but we don't see that tenet taught in Scripture. Please keep an open mind as we continue. In the pursuit of truth, we all must remain humble before the Word of God with a willingness to let the Holy Spirit speak.

In Romans 11, Paul speaks of this "fullness," using a vine analogy to illustrate the uniting of Jew and Gentile in Christ. He also reprimands Gentile converts for assuming God was finished with Israel, "For I do not want you, brethren, to be uninformed of this mystery, so that you will not be wise in your own estimation, that a partial hardening has happened to Israel until the fullness of the Gentiles has come in" (Romans 11:25). God's focus will return to the nation of Israel in the latter days (Hosea 3:5, 6:1; Rom. 11:23; Zech. 12:10). But does that mean the Gentiles are removed and no longer relevant? According to Revelation 10:7, the "mystery of God" (His church) is not finished until the seventh trumpet sounds.

Yes, anything is possible, but not everything is probable. Scripture reveals that "the elect" remain on earth during the great tribulation (Matt. 24:22; Rev. 7:14, 13:7; Dan. 7:21). Scripture also teaches the composition of God's elect is both Jew and Gentile. Those two points are undeniably clear. Romans 10:12 says, "For there is no distinction between Jew and Greek; for the same Lord is Lord of all, abounding in riches for all who call on Him." So the question is—if all believers are descendants of Abraham and one in Christ, why would God separate them (Gal. 3:7)? Can Christ be divided (1 Cor. 1:13)?

Some dispensationalists propose that a "church age" began with the apostle Peter after Pentecost because Christ said, "You are Peter [*petros* or *stone*], and upon this rock I will build My church; and the gates of Hades will not overpower it" (Matthew 16:18). Before Peter's devastating triad of denials, Jesus changed his name from Simon to Peter, prophetically promising that his future would be greater than his failures. He would be instrumental as a builder. But Jesus is the cornerstone of the New Testament church and rock of her foundation, not Peter. Jesus was also the Old Testament rock who supplied Israel with water in the wilderness (Deut. 32:4, 1 Cor. 10:4)!

Another point to consider: Peter was sent to the Jews, not the Gentiles; Paul was the apostle called to preach to the Gentiles (Rom. 11:13, Gal. 2:7, 16). Both had significant roles in bringing Christ's Gospel to the New Testament church (Jew and Gentile), but neither was responsible for her conception or ushering in a church age. The church is an assembly of saints that began with the descendants of Adam and extends through the spiritual seed of Abraham. This congregation or church, according to Hebrews 12:23, was disclosed by the Christ who shed His own blood, sweat, and tears for her. Our individual contributions merely testify to the greatness and glory of the church He is building (1 Pet. 2:4–5)!

> So then you are no longer strangers and aliens, but you are fellow citizens with the saints, and are of God's household, having been built on the foundation of the apostles and prophets, Christ Jesus Himself being the corner *stone*, in whom the whole building, being fitted together, is growing into a holy temple in the LORD, in whom you also are being built together into a dwelling of God in the Spirit. (Ephesians 2:19–22)

The Holy Spirit descended upon those who gathered at Pentecost, fulfilling Joel's prophecy: "I will pour forth of My Spirit upon all mankind" (Acts 2:17). Since that time, all believers have been anointed to operate as a united force of emissaries for Christ, both Jew and Gentile, with access to one Father by one Spirit (Eph. 2:18, 2 Cor. 5:20, Gal. 3:14). Was Pentecost the beginning of a Gentile church age or simply the ratification of the Abrahamic covenant, God's oath that Abraham would be the "father of a multitude of nations" (Gen. 17:4–5, Gal. 3:7–8, 29, 3:14)? Scripture supports the latter.

Together, believers are being placed into the house of God as "living stones" with Jesus as the cornerstone (1 Pet. 2:5). John the Baptist preached this message to a Jewish audience, "Bring forth fruits in keeping with repentance, and do not begin to say to yourselves, 'We have Abraham for our father,' for I say to you that from these stones, God is able to raise up children to Abraham" (Luke 3:8). All believers are God's elect and descendants of Abraham—His chosen—and the "Israel of God" (Gal. 6:15–16, Rom. 9:6).

Unity, despite our profound *diversity*, is undoubtedly a miracle only God can accomplish. How will God unite us? By the Holy Spirit who transforms our hearts and minds (Eph. 4:1–6, 13). It may take a blazing inferno to fuse our divided interests and pursuits, but God beckons us to walk together through such flames in order to accomplish just that. Are Gentile believers willing to go with their Jewish brethren through the great tribulation? Are we willing to trust God in the preparation process as we wait for the return of Jesus? The fires of persecution refine and challenge us (1 Pet. 1:7, Rev. 3:18). They have a purpose. With the courage of Christ Himself, we should trust our Heavenly Father and watch the Holy Spirit work in response to the Lord's prayer: "That they may all be one; even as You, Father, *are* in Me and I in You, that they also may be in Us" (John 17:21). Amen.

6. **Before we close today, please look at Revelation 1:4–8.**

- Who received letters from John?

- According to Revelation 22:16, who is the book written for?

Think About It

In Revelation 22:16, we read that the entire book of Revelation was written to and **for the churches** without any distinction being made between Jewish or Gentile believers. The church, whom the book of Revelation addresses both in its opening and closing pages, is a holy congregation of all saints. Jesus sent visions to John for the purpose of divulging components of the great tribulation and its associated forces of wickedness. The disclosure of the saints as overcomers, Jesus returning to reign and make all things new—is the outcome! In Revelation 7:9–14, a great multitude that no one could count is standing around the throne of God—**people from every nation, tribe, people, and tongue**. They are clothed in white robes, worshipping the Lamb of God. "These are the ones who come out of the great tribulation, and they have washed their robes and made them white in the blood of the Lamb" (Revelation 7:14). The Church of Jesus Christ.

Jesus reveals saints coming out of the great tribulation from all nations. Matthew 24:14 tells us that all nations will hear the Gospel until the end. Matthew 28:19–20" says, "Go therefore and make disciples of all the nations, baptizing them in the name of the Father and the Son and the Holy Spirit, teaching them to observe all that I commanded you; and lo, I am with you always, even to the end of the age." Revelation 14:6 even depicts an angel "flying in midheaven, having an eternal gospel to preach to those who live on the earth and to **every nation and tribe and tongue and people**." Throughout the tribulation period, the Gospel is being proclaimed to all nations, not just the nation of Israel. Until the end of the age.

> Note: So what might the "fullness" of the Gentiles mean? The Greek word *pleroma* means "filled up" or "complete." When we are interpreting a difficult passage, it helps to find the same word utilized elsewhere by the same author. In Galatians 4:4, Paul also used *pleroma*: "But when the fullness of the time came, God sent forth His Son, born of a woman, born under the Law." He used it again in Ephesians 1:10: "With a view to an administration suitable to the fullness of the times, that is, the summing up of all things in Christ, things in the heavens and things on the earth." In both cases, *pleroma* emphasizes a time shift. At the right time, God sent forth His Son. At the right time, things in heaven and on earth will come together in Christ. As we look at how the word *pleroma* was used by Paul in these other instances, the "fullness" of the Gentiles could simply mean that when all Gentile nations have heard the Gospel, it will be time for the Holy Spirit to bring it to Israel. Remember Matthew 24:14? Jesus said, "This gospel of the kingdom shall be preached in the whole world as a testimony to all the nations, and then the end will come."

Application

Do you think it is equitable for Gentile believers to inherit God's promises alongside the Jews yet not share in their sufferings—or the afflictions of Christ (2 Cor. 1:5)? The prophet Habakkuk wrote, "Though the fig tree should not blossom and there be no fruit on the vines, *though* the yield of the olive should fail and the fields produce no food, though the flock should be cut off from the fold and there be no cattle in the stalls, yet I will exult in the Lord, I will rejoice in the God of my salvation. The Lord God is my strength, and He has made my feet like hinds' *feet*, and makes me walk on my high places (Habakkuk 3:17-19). Are we in it as one kingdom to the glory of God? One family of faith? How about you?

YES   NO

Day Two Summary

Jew and Gentile are one in Christ—His elect and the true descendants of Abraham. The dispensational phrase *church age* is not found in Scripture. Nor does the Bible teach that once united, Jews and Gentiles are ever separated for any reason. All of Revelation was written to encourage and prepare the church of Jesus Christ for the great tribulation and His return.

Day Three: Signs and Wonders

In Matthew 24:23–26, Jesus reiterates His warning regarding false Christs and prophets, preparing us for a massive proliferation of deceptive error. He is not trying to scare us. His purpose is to prepare us. "See to it that no one misleads you. See that you are not frightened" (Matthew 24:4, 6). When lawlessness increases, love will decrease (Matt. 24:12). Why? Lawlessness creates chaos and encourages corrupt desperate behavior.

What was society like in the days of Noah and Lot prior to God's wrath? It was "business as usual," according to Matthew 24:38; however, lifestyles were apparently deviant enough for God to intervene. Satan is the source of deviant thinking, deception, and lawlessness. And yes, he does exist.

> Be of sober *spirit*, be on the alert. Your adversary, the devil, prowls around like a roaring lion, seeking someone to devour. (1 Peter 5:8)

> He [Satan] was a murderer from the beginning, and does not stand in the truth because there is no truth in him. Whenever he speaks a lie, he speaks from his own *nature*, for he is a liar and the father of lies. (John 8:44)

Satan "deceives" the entire world and "accuses" the brethren of God (Rev. 12:9–10). My friend, we are in a fight for truth against a nasty, formidable opponent. It is a battle that will only intensify as the day of the Lord draws near, with many being deceived and confused by a weighty blanket of error. Jeremiah 14:14 says, "The prophets are prophesying falsehood in My name. **I have neither sent them nor commanded them nor spoken to them**; they are prophesying to you a false vision, divination, futility and the deception of their own minds."

False prophets propagate the same deception that they have believed, maybe unintentionally, but the outcome is the same. They "lead the people astray; and those who are guided by them are brought to confusion" (Isaiah 9:16). Truth matters.

1. **Define "deception" and share an example of being deceived at some point in your life by a salesperson, friend, or foe. What was the result?**

2. **What do we learn in Matthew 24:24 about the abilities of false Christs and prophets during the great tribulation?**

God performs miracles. So does Satan. We are talking about exceptional phenomena from the realm of the supernatural, where both angels and demons have fluid passage. Little is known about this traffic of angelic activity, but one thing is certain—supernatural signs have supernatural origins. When Jesus said, "For false Christs and false prophets will arise and show great signs and wonders, so as to mislead, if possible, even the elect," He was alluding to a rising tide of deceptive abilities that will challenge even the saints.

Is it possible to deceive the elect? Anyone can be deceived, and we all have been. To think otherwise is deception itself. Eve, created in the image of God and living in a perfect garden, was deceived. How did that happen? She exchanged the truth of God for a lie (Rom. 1:25). Jesus was tempted by Satan as well but could not be deceived. He is the Truth, the infallible, incorruptible, eternal Word of God. Though we may fail, He will not. Though we may stumble, He always stands. The Word of God is truth. God the Father, Son, and Holy Spirit are independently and collectively faithfully true. Satan attempts to cast doubt on their integrity, hoping to see our defection for his own depraved, hateful pleasure. "Woe to the earth and the sea, because the devil has come down to you, having great wrath, knowing that he has *only* a short time" (Revelation 12:12). This is why Jesus warned us in advance, "See to it that no one misleads you" (Matthew 24:4).

Let's discuss these signs and wonders. Luke describes them as "terrors and great signs from heaven" (Luke 21:11). "Sign" (*semeion*) means "extraordinary in character, apt to be observed and kept in the memory." The word "wonder" (*teras*) means "a miracle with an ethical end and

49

purpose." "These words combined do not refer to different classes of miracles but to different qualities of the same miracle" (Zodhiates, p. 961).

The great signs and wonders Jesus refers to are not phony magic tricks or optical illusions. Jesus is referring to authentic miracles that will rock our world, originating from either God or Satan. We should be aware of what's coming, why, and when in order to discern the difference.

3. Look at 2 Thessalonians 2:8–12. What is the man of lawlessness able to do?

4. God allows this for higher purposes. What is it (vv. 11–12)?

God authorizes this deluding influence as a judgment against those who have consistently and persistently rejected salvation—those who have rejected His grace and in effect solicited justice against themselves (Nah. 1:2). Is it fair for God to allow deceptive influences to prevail? Listen, we have no way of knowing what God tolerated before His judicious gavel declares this verdict. Neither do we know how many times Jesus stood knocking at the door with salvation but was turned away (Rev. 3:20). Do you recall that before the seventh trumpet sounds, repentance on earth will have ceased? Six trumpet warnings provide opportunities for the world to repent and receive Christ. Israel should be able to recognize those trumpet signals as reminiscent of the signs and wonders seen in Egypt, signs that Moses (a type of Christ) utilized to prepare them for deliverance (Micah 7:15). Revelation 7:1–8 also discloses 144,000 Jewish witnesses appointed to proclaim the Gospel during the great tribulation period, perhaps even during the trumpet judgments. Revelation 11:1–11 reveals two specific witnesses, supernaturally protected for 1,260 days, preaching and performing miraculous signs and wonders. All of this is God's final invitation for salvation. Those with ears to hear will receive the Gospel. Others will "believe the deluding influence" (2 Thess. 2:11).

Regarding the two protected witnesses, Revelation 11:5–6 adds, "And if anyone desires to harm them, fire proceeds out of their mouth and devours their enemies; and if anyone would desire to harm them, in this manner he must be killed. These have the power to shut up the sky, in order that rain may not fall during the days of their prophesying, and they have power over the waters to turn them into blood, and to smite the earth with every plague, as often as they desire." "Signs and wonders" are displayed for the primary purpose of reaching His "first-born" nation of Israel for Christ (Exod. 4:22). Just as the signs in Egypt were literal miracles, these will be as well.

The book of Revelation is full of robust angelic activity, images of evil authorities, enthroned Satanic forces, intense battles and projections of Christ and His saints overcoming. John's vision has always been difficult to fully comprehend because of its dense supernatural composition. But if the return of Jesus Christ is a literal event, then the events surrounding His return will be literal as well. Both Jesus and Paul predicted deceptive signs and wonders coming through false Christs, false prophets, and the man of lawlessness—all literal actors. Symbolism is built into the description of their character and strength, but the figures themselves should be understood to be literal.

In prophetic content, the timeline of Christ complements John's apocalyptic vision. So, when Jesus refers to signs and wonders in Matthew 24:24 as misleading tools of deception, we can go to His Revelation for further disclosure. As precursors to the day of the Lord, God has revealed that He will channel signs and wonders through six trumpets, 144,000 Jewish witnesses, including two of extraordinary abilities (Rev. 7:4–8, 11:3–12). But there will also be miracles of satanic origin in play, devised to erode all traces of humanity's faith in Jesus Christ. Luke 18:8 says, "When the Son of Man comes, will He find faith on the earth?" "Faith" in that verse means "the faith." When Jesus returns, will He find anyone who believes in Him? Apparently, He will because those who endure to the end will be saved, even if it's only a minority of the earth's population.

5. Look at Revelation 13:1–4. How does the world respond to this miraculous healing?

6. Who is the source of his power?

Verse 4 says, "And they worshiped the dragon, because he gave his authority to the beast; and they worshiped the beast, saying, 'Who is like the beast, and who is able to wage war with him?'" Before Christ's ministry began, Satan tried to derail Him with three temptations. On Satan's third attempt to entice defection— "Again, the devil took Him [Jesus] to a very high mountain and showed Him all the kingdoms of the world and their glory; and he said to Him, 'All these things I will give You, if You fall down and worship me.' Then Jesus said to him, 'Go, Satan! For it is written, "You shall worship the LORD your God, and serve Him only."'" Then the devil left Him; and behold, angels came and *began* to minister to Him" (Matthew 4:8–11).

Jesus refused Satan's temptations, but the Antichrist will not. The Antichrist is the man of lawlessness Paul wrote about in 2 Thessalonians 2:1–10. He will align himself with Satan and, as a result, be handed all the kingdoms of the world (1 John 5:19). Is this Satan incarnate? Why wouldn't he be? He is the antithesis of Christ, God incarnate. Additionally, he performs signs and wonders of supernatural origin by Satan's authority, just as Jesus performed literal signs and wonders by the authority of God (Acts 2:22). Yes, Satan was defeated at Calvary, but the kingdoms of this present world are not visibly relinquished to Christ until that seventh trumpet sounds (Heb. 2:8, Rev. 11:15). Even then, "He must reign until He has put all His enemies under His feet. The last enemy that will be abolished is death" (1 Corinthians 15:25–26). This is no doubt accomplished during Christ's literal one-thousand-year reign.

7. According to Revelation 13:5, how long is the reign of the Antichrist?

8. Revelation 13:12–14 also reveals a false prophet who promotes the Antichrist. What are his abilities?

Revelation 13 describes two beasts of evil origin. The first is the Antichrist, and the second is his protégé, the false prophet. Later, we look at these two counterfeits in more detail, but for now, note that they both perform signs and wonders designed to deceive the world. This warning is the prediction of a global tsunami that will threaten our lives and landscape. It is not to be marginalized, certainly not ignored. Would we prepare for a tsunami? Should we prepare ourselves for this forthcoming blitz of deception as well? You bet.

In the wake of such widespread deception, the Antichrist will reign for 42 months, which is a number similar in duration to the 1,260-day ministry of the two witnesses but not as precise. Jewish months vary in length from year to year because their calendar is lunar based—dependent upon moon cycles. But a day is 24 hours, a solar-based time frame. Therefore, these witnesses will preach for exactly 1,260 days. However, the 42-month tenure of the Antichrist is more ambiguous because moon schedules vary. Plus, Jesus said, "For the sake of the elect those days will be cut short" (Matthew 24:22). All of this together explains why "only the Father knows the exact day and hour" when Christ will return for His elect (Matt. 24:36).

9. Back to 2 Thessalonians 2:8. How does it end for the man of lawlessness?

When Jesus returns, the man of lawlessness meets his fate by the "appearance" of Christ's coming. Revelation 19:20–21 tells us that he and the false prophet will be thrown into the lake of fire. Satan—the deranged, defanged predator roaming about the earth with his foul and bitter breath—will be bound for 1,000 years during the reign of Christ. After that, he will be slain by the living, breathing, incredibly sweet Word of God (Rev. 20:1–2, 7–10). John wrote, "The Son of God appeared for this purpose, to destroy the works of the devil" (1 John 3:8). The end is in sight! The victory is secured and already declared!

Application

Jesus taught us to pray for His kingdom to come and His will be done on earth as it is in heaven (Matt. 6:10). Take a minute to pray as He taught us. Is that the desire of your heart?

YES   NO

Day Three Summary

Jesus warned us about the signs and wonders of false Christs and prophets designed to deceive even the elect. Then, He shared details regarding the abilities of the Antichrist and his false prophet through John's visions in Revelation. An awareness and understanding of the coming deception is to our advantage as the day of the Lord approaches.

Day Four: God's Christ

Jesus provided us with a timeline; He also sent visions to John and letters to a representation of churches in Asia—to prepare the saints for His return and the great tribulation (Rev. 1–3). In reality, any eschatological study should begin with Christ's timeline as a plumbline or spine of prophecy. When we do, the bones of the prophets and their prophecies in the Old Testament line up with New Testament apostolic teachings, Gospel accounts, and the book of Revelation. It is an amazing discovery! Now, if you prefer to stick to the theoretical, then that's your choice. But I encourage you to continue to study Christ's timeline and Revelation. Just in case Jesus is right.

1. **What directives have we covered so far in Matthew 24?**

   * See to it that no one _____ (v. 4).

   * See that you are not _____ (v. 6).

   * When you see the abomination of desolation, those in Judea should _____.

   * Pray that their flight not be _____.

2. **What additional directive is in Matthew 24:23?**

Matthew 24:23, Mark 13:21, and Luke 17:23 all record the same warning: "When they say the Christ has come—Do not believe them." Again, Jesus is not trying to scare us. He is preparing us. "Behold I have told you in advance" (Matthew 24:25). When we see the prophecies unfolding that were predicted in Scripture, our faith will be encouraged and strengthened rather than rattled. That's the point of Christ preparing us (John 13:19). Those caught unaware will be more vulnerable. We have been given ample notice, my friends, not to take the baited traps or believe the seductive lies. "Many," not a few, will be deceived (Matt. 24:11). "Many," not a few, will fall away (Matt. 24:10). You and I must determine not to be one of those "many."

3. How does Jesus return in Daniel 7:13, Revelation 1:7, and 1 Thessalonians 4:16–17?

In verse 28, Jesus said, "Wherever the corpse is, there the vultures will gather." Vultures feed from dead carcasses. Saints are not vultures. The elect of God have been brought into the family fold by the Good Shepherd, who returns for His sheep visibly in the clouds. He will *not* appear in a field, stadium, amphitheater, community center, or temple building as will the Antichrist. Jesus comes from above, from heaven like a bolt of lightning (Matt. 24:27)! Those unfamiliar with how Christ returns will be fodder for this vulture-feeding frenzy. Do not follow the crowd or let your curiosity get the best of you. Wait for Jesus to come back in the clouds as He promised.

Just imagine the impact of social media and news outlets during a time like the great tribulation. Information will be rampant, contradictory, and confusing. Deception will be saturating the airways through a multiplicity of influencers, interpreting the miraculous signs and wonders for their own purposes. Remember the warning of Christ—do not believe them.

4. In Matthew 24:27, Jesus said His coming would be like a flash of lightning. What did He mean? Let's look at a few verses from Revelation:

And behold, I am coming quickly. Blessed is he who heeds the words of the prophecy of this book. (Revelation 22:7)

Behold, I am coming quickly, and My reward *is* with Me, to render to every man according to what he has done. (Revelation 22:12)

He who testifies to these things says, "Yes, I am coming quickly." Amen. Come, Lord Jesus. (Revelation 22:20)

Behold, I am coming like a thief. Blessed is the one who stays awake and keeps his clothes, so that he will not walk about naked and men will not see his shame. (Revelation 16:15)

In those first three verses from Revelation, the Greek word for "quickly" is *tachu*, meaning "suddenly, quick, unexpectedly, or fast." *Tachu* does not mean that the coming of Jesus is imminent but that His return will be quick—like a flash of lightning or twinkling of an eye. For nonbelievers and those living in darkness, He will come like a thief in the night, while the saints watching in anticipation will recognize the signs of His return (1 Thess. 5:1–4). Yet neither demographic will be able to miss Jesus returning in the clouds!

5. What does Revelation 1:7 say about Christ's return?

6. Fill in the blanks from Revelation 19:11–16.

- He comes from _____ on a _____ horse.

- Armies in _____ come with Him following on _____ horses.

- From His mouth comes a _____.

- He treads the wine press of the fierce _____ of _____, the Almighty.

- On His robe and thigh is written, _____.

Think About It

How is it possible for every eye to see Jesus when He returns? First, with God, all things are possible (Luke 18:27). When heaven's luminaries fail to luminesce, the light of the world will break through the sky and dispense the darkness, which could explain why "every eye" sees Him. Jesus returns as the only heavenly light—visible. If the King of kings and Lord of lords has not descended in the clouds from heaven like lightning, on a brilliant white horse lighting up the sky with His mighty army on white horses, then Jesus has not yet returned. God said, "Light shall shine out of darkness" (2 Corinthians 4:6). Jesus is that light (John 8:12).

7. What does Acts 1:11 say about how Jesus returns?

The elect should be watching for Jesus Christ to descend from heaven. Just as He ascended into heaven, He will descend as the Bread of Life who comes from above (John 6:26–27, 35). Jesus will not return as a prophet who dazzles the world with wisdom, or great signs and wonders (Heb. 10:12–14). He has already done all of that.

8. Read 2 Thessalonians 2:1–4 again. What were the Thessalonians hearing?

9. What did Paul say would happen before the day of the Lord and Jesus returning?

Paul's teaching is very clear—the man of lawlessness will be revealed before Jesus returns and the day of the Lord begins. **Paul taught exactly what Jesus taught.** When the disciples asked Jesus, "What will be the sign of Your coming and the end of the age?" He pointed specifically to the abomination of desolation standing in the holy place (Matt. 24:15).

Next week, we go to Daniel for a brief study of the abomination of desolation. Remember, prior to that sign, we experience the beginning of birth pangs. After the abomination of desolation, the great tribulation begins and contractions escalate (Matt. 24:21). In Week Five, we venture into the book of Revelation, introduced this way: "I John, your brother and fellow partaker in the tribulation and kingdom and perseverance which are in Jesus, was on the island called Patmos **because of the word of God and the testimony of Jesus**" (Revelation 1:9). Your brother and fellow partaker. In the tribulation and kingdom. Because of the Word of God and the testimony of Jesus. Does that describe your journey with Jesus? It should, for "indeed, all who desire to live godly in Christ Jesus will be persecuted" (2 Timothy 3:12).

Application

Jesus said, "See to it that no one misleads you" (Matthew 24:4). Later, in verses 23–26, He warns us not to join those who congregate around false Christs. He also said, "For false Christs and false prophets will arise and will show great signs and wonders so as to mislead, if possible even the elect." That statement tells us that wolves in sheep's clothing will be baiting traps for God's elect. When tempted and pressured to "check them out," you and I must remember Christ's warning—do not go. Will you heed Christ's warning?

YES   NO

You may find the next two weeks of this study challenging, but I encourage you to stick with it! Too many within our church congregations will be blindsided by the abomination of desolation, yet both Jesus and Paul taught that this event precedes His return. The apostle John also mentioned the approaching Antichrist when he wrote, "Children, it is the last hour; and just as you heard that antichrist is coming; even now many antichrists have arisen; from this we know that it is the last hour" (1 John 2:18). Additionally, the Antichrist was revealed to Daniel in dreams and through visions to John on Patmos.

Coverage of this event is not warm and fuzzy material. I cannot apologize for that. Jesus shared what we need to know for our benefit, and it is supported by the whole writ of Scripture. A unique storm is on the horizon that will shake the existence of humanity and what we believe. I cannot apologize for that either. Since Scripture reveals the abomination of desolation as the final conflict for the saints before Christ returns, then it is God's design. And if it is His design, then we must commit to study it with open minds and hearts (Rom. 11:33–36) for our sakes, that of our families, and, most importantly, the glory of our coming Christ!

Day Four Summary

By studying and knowing Christ's timeline, we become beneficiaries of warnings designed to navigate us through the great tribulation tempest. Jesus Himself described it as a unique time—"such as not occurred since the beginning of the world." Daniel's and John's prophecies are validated by His timeline. The writings of Paul support the timeline of Christ as well.

Week Three Synopsis

The church of Jesus Christ is a union of Jews and Gentiles—God's elect,
who endure the great tribulation together.

Encourage each other as you see the day drawing near.
(Hebrews 10:25)

Week Three Worksheet

Matthew 24:15–28

Therefore when you see *the abomination of desolation* that was spoken of through Daniel the prophet, standing in the holy place [let the reader understand], then those who are in Judea must flee to the mountains. Whoever is on the housetop must not go down to get the things out that are in his house. Whoever is in the field must not turn back to get his cloak. But woe to those who are pregnant and to those who are nursing babies in those days! But pray that your flight will not be in the winter, or on a Sabbath.

For then there will be a *great tribulation*, such as has not occurred since the beginning of the world until now, nor ever will. Unless those days had been cut short, no life would have been saved; but for the sake of the elect those days will be cut short. Then if anyone says to you, "Behold, here is the Christ," or "There He is," do not believe him. For false Christs and false prophets will arise and will show great signs and wonders, so as to mislead, if possible, even the elect. Behold, I have told you in advance. So if they say to you, "Behold, He is in the wilderness," do not go out, or, "Behold, He is in the inner rooms," do not believe them.

For just as the lightning comes from the east and flashes even to the west, so will the coming of the Son of Man be. Wherever the corpse is, there the vultures will gather.

Observations

Therefore, when you see

-

Then, those in Judea must

-

For then, there will be a

-

Those days are cut short for the sake of

-

Do not believe the false

-

-

For just as the lightning comes from the east and flashes to the west, so will the

-

Vultures gather wherever

-

Antichrist/Israel Covenant		Abomination of Desolation		Jesus Returns
Dan. 9:27	3 1/2 years	great tribulation	3 1/2 years	1,000-year reign

Week Four

ABOMINATION OF DESOLATION

Day One: Ten Toes

This week, we begin to study the abomination of desolation, cited by Jesus as the sure sign of His coming. Paul referred to it too: "With regard to the coming of our LORD Jesus Christ ... Let no one in any way deceive you, for **it will not come unless the apostasy comes first**, and the man of lawlessness is revealed, the son of destruction" (2 Thessalonians 2:1–3). Paul is the apostle who wrote the Thessalonians about a rapture reunion in 1 Thessalonians 4:13–17. Same apostle. Same church congregation given the same order of events that are on Christ's timeline. What exactly is the abomination of desolation? We explore this event this week and next, visiting passages from the books of Daniel and Revelation. Matthew 24:15 says, "Let the reader understand." We are the readers. May God grant us an understanding of what Scripture elucidates and the spiritual fortitude to prepare.

1. **In Matthew 24:15, which prophet did Jesus refer to regarding the abomination of desolation?**

Numerous dreams and visions were recorded by Daniel regarding kingdoms and the abomination of desolation. First, we have the dream of King Nebuchadnezzar in chapter 2. That dream distressed the Babylonian king so much he threatened to kill all his advisers unless someone could: (1) recount the dream to him and (2) interpret its meaning. No one could comply with such a demand except for Daniel, a Hebrew captive in Babylon at the time (Isa. 39:7, Dan. 1:1–6). "Then the mystery was revealed to Daniel in a night vision and he blessed the God of heaven" (Daniel 2:19).

Daniel recounted the dream to Nebuchadnezzar just as the king had seen it. He saw a large statue with a head of gold, breast and arms of silver, thighs of bronze, and legs of iron. The feet on the statue were a mixture of iron and clay in its ten toes. A large stone "cut out without hands" struck the feet, collapsing the entire statue. "Then the iron, the clay, the bronze, the silver and the gold were crushed all at the same time, and became like chaff from the summer threshing floors; and the wind carried them away so that not a trace of them was found. But the stone that struck the statue became a great mountain and filled the whole earth" (Daniel 2:35).

The interpretation is found in Daniel 2:36–45:

This *was* the dream; now we will tell its interpretation before the king. You, O king, are the king of kings, to whom the God of heaven has given the kingdom, the power, the strength and the glory; and wherever the sons of men dwell, *or the* beasts of the field, or the birds of the sky, He has given *them* into your hand and has caused you to rule over them all. You are the head of gold. After you there will arise another kingdom inferior to you, then another third kingdom of bronze, which will rule over all the earth.

Then there will be a fourth kingdom as strong as iron; inasmuch as iron crushes and shatters all things, so, like iron that breaks in pieces, it will crush and break all these in pieces. In that you saw the feet and toes, partly of potter's clay and partly of iron, it will be a divided kingdom; but it will have in it the toughness of iron, inasmuch as you saw the iron mixed with common clay. And *as* the toes of the feet *were* partly of iron and partly of pottery, *so* some of the kingdom will be strong and part of it will be brittle. And in that you saw the iron mixed with common clay, they will combine with one another in the seed of men; but they will not adhere to one another, even as iron does not combine with pottery.

In the days of those kings the God of heaven will set up a kingdom which will never be destroyed, and *that* kingdom will not be left [passed on] for another people; it will crush and put an end to all these kingdoms, but it will itself endure forever. Inasmuch as you saw that a stone was cut out of the mountain without hands and that it crushed the iron, the bronze, the clay, the silver and the gold, the great God has made known to the king what will take place in the future; so the dream is true and its interpretation is trustworthy.

2. **How is the kingdom of ten toes described?**

3. **How is the kingdom of God described?**

4. On what day will God's kingdom "crush" all others (v. 44)?

Essentially, five dominions are depicted on the statue in King Nebuchadnezzar's dream: (1) a head of gold, (2) breast and arms of silver, (3) thighs of bronze, and (4) legs of iron extending into (5) the feet of iron and common clay.

Biblical and historical records reveal the first three kingdoms on Nebuchadnezzar's statue to be (1) the Babylonian Empire, the head of gold (Dan. 2:38); (2) the Medo-Persian Empire, breast and arms of silver (Dan. 8:20); and (3) the Grecian Empire, thighs of bronze (Dan. 8:21). The fourth kingdom of iron is believed to be the Roman Empire since it succeeded the Greeks. The feet of ten toes are an extension of the legs that will be re-established in the future as a fifth and final kingdom (vv. 44–45). Note that according to verse 44, it is "in the days of those kings" (ten toes) that the kingdom of God is set up, which transpires when Jesus returns (1 Cor. 15:23–24, Rev. 11:14).

5. Look again at Daniel 2:40. How is the fourth kingdom described?

Each kingdom or dominion prevailed over its predecessor through oppression, conquest, and enslavement. However, Rome was never conquered, only weakened by repeated invasions from Germanic tribes. Since it was not completely destroyed, Rome remains to reemerge.

What is the significance of the different materials in the feet, which are iron and clay? The ten toes will be an integrated alliance (they will combine with each other in the seed of men) who perhaps do not unite politically for geopolitical reasons (they will not adhere to each other, even as iron does not combine with pottery). An unknown number are stronger politically and militarily than others. (Some of the kingdom will be strong, and part of it will be brittle.) Though not a cohesive union, they will integrate with common interests for the purpose of achieving autocratic control.

Daniel 2:28 and 45 tell us that King Nebuchadnezzar's dream discloses what happens in the "latter days." All of the statute's kingdoms have emerged except for the fifth of ten toes. If that fourth kingdom of iron legs was indeed Rome, then the ten-toed kingdom could be a union of European leaders because ancient Rome ruled geographically where Europe exists today. While there are numerous interpretations and suggestions regarding the composition of this alliance, our purpose here is to become aware of the prophecy itself. Let's stay on course and avoid the weeds. We may find out soon enough!

Whether these ten toes are an extension of the Roman Empire or a different federation, we *will* see this dominion rise up in the future. How do we know?

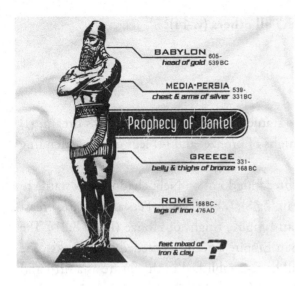

1- King Nebuchadnezzar was a pagan king. He would not be interested in fabricating a dream, predicting the demise of his own kingdom, or promoting the kingdom of God.

2- The other kingdoms on the statue emerged just as God revealed them.

3- Jesus Himself referenced this event in Matthew 24:15 as the notable sign of His coming.

4- Daniel declared that it would surface in the latter days. "There is a God in heaven who reveals mysteries, and He has made known to King Nebuchadnezzar what will take place in the latter days" (Daniel 2:45).

https://freebiblestudiesonline.wordpress.com/2012/03/04/image-of-daniel-2-chart/

In the days of King Nebuchadnezzar, the earth populated Northern Africa, Egypt, Asia, and Southern Europe. Today, the earth is inhabited globally. When this ten-toed empire does emerge, one question we might ask is, Will that final kingdom rule only over the Middle East region of biblical days, or will it rule over the entire world? Since the return of Jesus is a global event, my guess is that the tentacles of this final kingdom will infiltrate the entire world (Dan. 2:35). A ripple effect, so to speak, will pulsate throughout every continent on earth, originating in the Middle East as the primary area affected. The majority of Bible prophecies yet to be fulfilled relate to that geographic region specifically and the physical nation of Israel (Zech. 12:10–11).

God revealed this ten-toed kingdom over 2,600 years ago. It will be the last empire to rule "over the earth" before the kingdom of God becomes visibly established—the one "cut out of the mountain without hands" (Dan. 2:45). This kingdom has been initiated, designed, and continues to be built by God Himself. At the right time, God will stir up His enemies and choose the day of their demise (Deut. 28:7). Then, the victorious kingdom of His Son and saints will crush all other kingdoms—past, present, and future.

> And in the days of those kings the God of heaven will set up a kingdom which will never be destroyed, and that kingdom will not be left for another people; it will crush and put an end to all these kingdoms, but it will itself endure forever. (Daniel 2:44)

Application

This dream terrified King Nebuchadnezzar but not Daniel until he began to have dreams of his own. Daniel received more details regarding that fifth ten-toed dominion, which we will look at tomorrow. If these disclosures frighten you, then always stop and pray. Your heart and mind are moving in the direction of fleshly fear rather than spiritual faith in the Savior who says, "Do not fear, for I have redeemed you; I have called you by name; you are Mine! When you pass through the waters, I will be with you; And through the rivers, they will not overflow you. When you walk through the fire, you will not be scorched, nor will the flame burn you" (Isaiah 43:1–2). We follow and worship a faithful God! Don't ever forget that. Fear and doubt are not to be given a welcome mat into the lives of kingdom heirs.

First, let's be thankful for God's prophetic Word. Without it, we would know nothing of what to expect in the latter days. Secondly, the benefit of studying prophecy is that we are provided with the opportunity to prepare. When the fulfillment does transpire, our faith will be strengthened rather than weakened. Yet God doesn't reveal the minute details of how His prophecies play out. He gives us just what we need. Then, we are expected to trust Him with what we don't know and be faithful with what we do. Could anyone have predicted how the Messiah would be a Nazarene, born by a virgin in Bethlehem, and called out of Egypt with a ministry in Galilee? When we try to force the undisclosed details of God's plan, there is a huge risk of assuming erroneous conclusions. Interpreting wrongly. And the way we interpret Scripture consequently affects our application. The study of prophecy is a humbling, lifetime pursuit. Remain alert in the journey with a tender, receptive heart before God. The reward is in waiting, watching, and then witnessing His Word unfold exactly as predicted and precisely as intended (Num. 23:19). Are you willing?

YES   NO

Day One Summary

In King Nebuchadnezzar's dream, God revealed essentially five world kingdoms ruling over the earth prior to His coming kingdom. The first four emerged just as predicted, which verifies a pending fifth—a conflicted, divided confederation of ten leaders, iron and clay. This ten-toed kingdom will be more formidable than its predecessors but ultimately "crushed" by the kingdom of God, which endures *forever*!

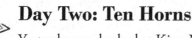 ## Day Two: Ten Horns

Yesterday, we looked at King Nebuchadnezzar's dream. He saw a large statue "of extraordinary splendor" depicting four world dominions, the fourth extending into a fifth. That fifth and final kingdom of ten toes rises up in the latter days as a divided, oppressive coalition, and "it will have the toughness of iron." What is the significance of that? Well, "iron crushes and shatters all things" (Daniel 2:40–41).

Now, let's look at a second dream in Daniel 7 regarding that fifth and final kingdom of ten kings. In Daniel's dream, he sees four beasts instead of four kingdoms, but they represent the same empires. The first three of Daniel's beasts resemble a lion (Babylon), a bear (Medo-Persia), and a leopard (Greece) (Dan. 7:1–6). We won't go into the details of those since it is Daniel's fourth beast that relates to this study and our understanding of the abomination of desolation. In verse 1, we read that this dream was given to Daniel in the first year of Belshazzar, king of Babylon.

This would have been after the reign of King Nebuchadnezzar (head of gold) but before Babylon fell to the Medes and Persians (chest and arms of silver).

> After this I [Daniel] kept looking in the night visions, and behold, a fourth beast, dreadful and terrifying and extremely strong; and it had large iron teeth. It devoured and crushed and trampled down the remainder with its feet; and it was different from all the beasts that were before it, and it had ten horns. While I was contemplating the horns, behold, another horn, a little one, came up among them, and three of the first horns were pulled out by the roots before it; and behold, this horn possessed eyes like the eyes of a man and a mouth uttering great boasts. (Daniel 7:7–8)

1. **How is Daniel's fourth beast like King Nebuchadnezzar's fourth kingdom in 2:40–41?**

2. **Describe the "little horn" and what he does.**

The fourth beast is described as "dreadful and terrifying" with iron teeth. It will emerge as a different and stronger dominion from all its predecessors. The ten horns on this beast represent the same union of ten toes on King Nebuchadnezzar's statue. Yet Daniel saw an extra detail. Three of those ten horns are defeated (militarily or politically) by a separate little horn. He has "the eyes of a man and a mouth uttering great boasts" (Daniel 7:8). This little horn is described with human characteristics because he is a man, not an ideology or symbolic representation. In cross-referencing Daniel's little horn with the beast in Revelation 13:18, we read, "Let him who has understanding calculate the number of the beast, for the number is that of a **man**; and his number is six hundred and sixty-six."

In the Bible, horns represent strength or power. For example, "Blessed *be* the Lord God of Israel, for He has visited us and accomplished redemption for His people, and has raised up a horn of salvation for us in the house of David His servant" (Luke 1:68–69). Let's revisit 2 Thessalonians 2:1–10 for another look at this man (little horn):

Now we request you, brethren, with regard to the coming of our Lord Jesus Christ and our gathering together to Him, that you not be quickly shaken from your composure or be disturbed either by a spirit or a message or a letter as if from us, to the effect that the day of the Lord has come. Let no one in any way deceive you, for *it will not come* unless the apostasy comes first, and the man of lawlessness is revealed, the son of destruction, who opposes and exalts himself above every so-called god or object of worship, so that he takes his seat in the temple of God, displaying himself as being God. Do you not remember that while I was still with you, I was telling you these things? And you know what restrains him now, so that in his time he will be revealed. For the mystery of lawlessness is already at work; only he who now restrains *will do so* until he is taken out of the way. Then that lawless one will be revealed whom the Lord will slay with the breath of His mouth and bring to an end by the appearance of His coming; *that is*, the one whose coming is in accord with the activity of Satan, with all power and signs and false wonders, and with all the deception of wickedness for those who perish, because they did not receive the love of the truth so as to be saved.

3. Who does the man of lawlessness claim to be?

4. What seat of authority does he take?

5. Who is he aligned with?

6. What abilities will he display?

7. When will he be revealed?

Previously, we looked at this passage regarding the apostasy or "falling away" because of the deceptive signs and wonders being accomplished. Now, our attention turns to this man of lawlessness or the "son of destruction" himself. He will display himself in the Jewish temple, taking a seat of authority as God Almighty. That is the sign Jesus points to as the sign of His coming— "When you see the abomination of desolation standing in the holy place" (Matthew 24:15).

Some think that Antiochus IV Epiphanes fulfilled Daniel's prophecy regarding this little horn. Antiochus IV was a Grecian king from the Seleucid Empire who attacked the second Jewish temple during his reign from 175 to 163 BC. He sacrificed a pig on the altar, persecuting or killing over eighty thousand Jews in three days and selling just as many into slavery (2 Macc. 5:11–14). However, that madman was not the little horn or man of lawlessness, fulfilling Daniel's prophecy. He served as a prototype instead. Jesus pointed to the abomination of desolation as a future sign. Neither was Antiochus IV slain by the breath of the coming Christ! Thus, we have not yet seen the man of lawlessness stand in the temple, seat himself as God, and perform miraculous signs and wonders with Satanic authority. Antiochus was merely a foreshadowing of this man to come.

Now, we can only speculate as to who or what the "restrainer" is. Only speculate. Some scholars propose the restrainer to be the Holy Spirit or church being removed from the earth when taken out of the way. Look closely. There is no mention of anyone being removed from the earth in that passage. The Scripture simply says that the restrainer is taken out of the way and no longer restrains the man of lawlessness, that's all. The pronoun utilized in reference to this restrainer is "he" rather than "she," as it would be if the church was the restrainer. "She" is the bride of Christ. It seems more conceivable that "he" refers to an archangel whose assignment is to restrain the man of lawlessness until "he" is removed by God's authority. Angels do participate in the restraining and releasing of evil principalities (Eph. 6:12, Rev. 9:14–15). If the Holy Spirit is being removed from the earth at this time, then God would be abandoning His elect during the great tribulation, which contradicts His promise to "never leave or forsake us" (Hebrews 13:5). Scripture reveals His elect are on earth during the great tribulation (Matt. 24:22; Rev. 7:9, 13–14; Dan. 7:21).

Paul did not mention the identity of the restrainer because (1) the Thessalonians already knew who it was or (2) the identity was irrelevant. Perhaps both. Paul was reinforcing previous teaching and reminding them that the apostasy and unveiling of the man of lawlessness would indeed precede Christ's return, which is what Jesus taught as well (Matt. 24:15).

This man of lawlessness or little horn has no power in and of himself to step onto the world stage until God removes His restrainer. Then, he temporarily acquires dominion. Do you remember how long his tenure lasts? Earlier in Revelation 13:5, we read, "There was given to him a mouth speaking arrogant words and blasphemies, and authority to act for forty-two months was given to him." The kingdom of God is the only kingdom that lasts forever. Forty-two months is less than a fraction of a nanosecond compared to the infinity of eternity.

Think About It

For the Antichrist to take a seat of authority in God's temple, a third Jewish temple must first be constructed. The first Jewish temple was destroyed by Babylon in 586 BC and the second by Rome in AD 70. Since 1987, plans have actually been underway to build a third, and the Temple Institute was established to promote the rebuilding. Implements have been crafted, and a priesthood is already trained. Animals for the sacrifices are being raised and prepared. The rebuilding of the third Jewish temple is underway! But a few large obstacles stand in the way. In the late seventh century, an Islamic Dome of the Rock shrine was erected over the original Temple site, which is where Orthodox Jews wanted to build. In addition, reinstating animal sacrifices is controversial and politically complicated (Reference: Encyclopedia Britannica; templeinstitute.org).

Application

"Then that lawless one will be revealed whom the LORD will slay with the breath of His mouth and bring to an end by the appearance of His coming" (2 Thessalonians 2:8). Though this evil figure is allowed to reign for forty-two months, Jesus returns to usher in His kingdom and reign forever. Don't ever forget that. Keep the Word of God at the forefront of your mind. When we allow ourselves to think along the lines of God's eternal plan, our perspective changes—and perspective is huge. "Seek first His Kingdom and His righteousness," and you won't be attracted to or deceived by the kingdom of the "lawless one" (Matthew 6:33). Are you willing?

YES   NO

Day Two Summary

In his dream, Daniel saw a beast with ten horns, the same as King Nebuchadnezzar's ten toes on the feet of a statue. Daniel also saw a separate "little horn" rising up to defeat three of those ten. In 2 Thessalonians 2:1–3, this little horn is described as the man of lawlessness or man of destruction. When he is no longer restrained, he will ascend to power and be revealed before the return of Jesus Christ and the day of the Lord. This is what we have so far—a confederation of ten horns or nations encounters a little horn or man of lawlessness (perhaps in war), and three will be defeated.

Day Three: Little Big Horn

Before proceeding with Daniel's dreams, let's consider a storm encountered by Christ's disciples recorded in Mark 4:35–40, and foreseen in Psalm 107:23-32 centuries beforehand. Romans 8:18 says, "For I consider that the sufferings of this present time are not worthy to be compared with the glory that is to be revealed to us." God doesn't waste our tribulations. He designs them to reveal His sufficiency.

After teaching all day from a boat offshore, Jesus summoned the disciples aboard, "Let us go over to the other side." He quickly secured a weathered cushion in the stern for reclining while the disciples released the rigging. Several were strong, seasoned seamen, able to handle the voyage with athletic dexterity. A trip to the other side should have been easily managed.

As the sun was setting, the air began to cool; a slight breeze beckoned the weary travelers to relax as they traveled. With Christ. They pushed the boat offshore. Distributing oars to one another, a discussion ensued over the parables Jesus had shared with the crowd regarding the kingdom of God. They might have had questions over the analysis. "When will the kingdom of God come? Is Jesus the king?" Jesus heard their conversation but did not engage, taking advantage of this rare opportunity to sleep.

Occupied by their debate and discussion, the disciples might have ignored the approaching cumulus clouds, cloaking the sapphire sky. One by one, the stars began to disappear. But when the moon suddenly vanished, a chilling darkness sounded an alarm. Streams of wind began to whistle in the upper atmosphere, causing the sails to sharply flap in attention. Swelling waves rocked their boat, pitching water over the sides in an attempt overtake it.

> For He spoke and raised up a stormy wind, which lifted up the waves of the sea. (Psalm 107:25)

Then, unexpectedly, a commanding squall dropped from beneath the clouds, challenging the disciples to keep their vessel stable. Blinding sheets of rain and spray lifted from the crest of rising waves, preventing visibility. They fought to steady the boat and stay afloat, shouting above the howling wind, "We're sinking! Can anyone see the shoreline? We're sinking!"

> They rose up to the heavens, they went down to the depths; their soul melted away in *their* misery. They reeled and staggered like a drunken man, and were at their wits' end. (Psalm 107:26-27)

Desperate and anxious, the disciples shook Jesus from His slumber, "Teacher, do you not care that we are perishing? Wow. Just think about that. The irony is stark. Jesus set aside His heavenly glory to become their Lamb sacrifice, yet His closest friends asked, "Do you not care that we are perishing?" Awakened, Jesus rebuked the wind and sea with "Hush, be still." The wind died down, and the storm abated. The Word of God had spoken. The storm had no recourse but to obey.

> Then they cried to the Lord in their trouble, and He brought them out of their distresses. (Psalm 107:28)

What an extraordinary experience for the disciples. But before they could celebrate, Jesus responded with, "Why are you afraid? How is it that you have no faith?" Ouch. A rebuke rather than a celebration. The wind had shackled them with fear and blinded their capacity for seeing (Heb. 11:1). Drenched and dripping, they glanced at one another. Someone asked, "Who then is this that even the wind and the sea obey Him?" Though they had traveled with Jesus in ministry, they had not yet seen who He was. And oddly, the storm was the revelator.

> He caused the storm to be still, so that the waves of the sea were hushed. Then they were glad because they were quiet, so He guided them to their desired haven. (Psalm 107:29-30)

John the Baptist knew who Jesus was. "Behold the Lamb of God who takes away the sin of the world!" (John 1:29). Do you know Him that way? The assurance is that if the blood of Jesus can cover the stain and pain of our sins and the Spirit can transform our hearts, then He will most certainly get us to the other side of any storm. Safely. Who is the King of God's kingdom? Jesus Christ—the Word of God—this is He! And this King is coming back to still all storms!

> I kept looking until thrones were set up and the Ancient of Days took His seat; His vesture was like white snow and the hair of His head like pure wool. His throne was ablaze with flames, its wheels were a burning fire. A river of fire was flowing and coming out from before Him; thousands upon thousands were attending Him, and myriads upon myriads were standing before Him; the court sat, and the books were opened. Then I kept looking because of the sound of the boastful words which the horn was speaking; I kept looking until the beast was slain, and its body was destroyed and given to the burning fire. (Daniel 7:9–11)

1. **Who takes His seat on the throne?**

2. **Who is given to the burning fire?**

The name "Ancient of Days" is seen in Daniel 7:9, 13, and 22 as a unique title referring to the Father member of the Trinity. In verses 9–10, He is seated on a wheeled throne ablaze with flames and a river of fire flowing from before Him. His mobile throne is capable of going anywhere and at any time judgment becomes necessary.

> I kept looking in the night visions and behold, with the clouds of heaven One like a Son of Man was coming and He came up to the Ancient of Days and was presented before Him. And to Him was given dominion, glory and a kingdom that all the peoples, nations and men of every language might serve Him. His dominion is an everlasting dominion which will not pass away; and His kingdom is one which will not be destroyed. (Daniel 7:13–14)

3. **How does the Son of Man come?**

4. **What is He given?**

The beast will not survive the blazing flames of God's throne or river of fire, but you and I will if Christ is within us—the hope of glory (Rom. 8:10, Col. 1:27). Without Christ, we too would perish in those flames. Instead, we have been positioned to reign alongside Him in His kingdom (2 Tim. 2:12, Dan. 7:27, Rev. 5:10). In verse 13, Jesus is presented before the Ancient of Days and given all the kingdoms of the world. Revelation 11:15 reveals this happening at the seventh and last trumpet: "The kingdom of the world has become *the kingdom* of our LORD and of His Christ; and He will reign forever and ever."

Daniel 7:13 is the first Scriptural mention of Christ coming in the clouds. It is the same reference John employs in Revelation 1:17 when he writes the churches of Jesus's returning. John wrote, "Behold, He is coming with the clouds, and every eye will see Him." The Scriptures never mention Jesus returning a third time to accomplish a private rescue. In the rapture passage itself, Jesus descends "with a shout, with the voice of the archangel, and with the trumpet of God" (1 Thessalonians 4:16). Jesus is announced and revealed in that passage. And when He is revealed, everyone sees Him!

As for me, Daniel, my spirit was distressed within me, and the visions in my mind kept alarming me. I approached one of those who were standing by and began asking him the exact meaning of all this so he told me and made known to me the interpretation of these things: "These great beasts, which are four in number, are four kings who will arise from the earth. But the saints of the Highest One will receive the kingdom and possess the kingdom forever, for all ages to come."

Then I desired to know the exact meaning of the fourth beast, which was different from all the others, exceedingly dreadful, with its teeth of iron and its claws of bronze, and which devoured, crushed and trampled down the remainder with its feet, and the meaning of the ten horns that were on its head and the other horn which came up, and before which three of them fell, namely, that horn which had eyes and a mouth uttering great boasts and which was larger in appearance than its associates. I kept looking, and that horn was waging war with the saints and overpowering them *until* the Ancient of Days came and judgment was passed in favor of the saints of the Highest One, and the time arrived when the saints took possession of the kingdom. Thus he said: "The fourth beast will be a fourth kingdom on the earth, which will be different from all the other kingdoms and will devour the whole earth and tread it down and crush it. As for the ten horns, out of this kingdom ten kings will arise; and another will arise after them, and he will be different from the previous ones and will subdue three kings. He will speak out against the Most High and wear down the saints of the Highest One, and he will intend to make alterations in times and in law; and they will be given into his hand for a time, times, and half a time.

"But the court will sit for judgment, and his dominion will be taken away, annihilated and destroyed forever. Then the sovereignty, the dominion and the greatness of all the kingdoms under the whole heaven will be given to the people of the saints of the Highest One; His kingdom will be an everlasting kingdom, and all the dominions will serve and obey Him." At this point the revelation ended. As for me, Daniel, my thoughts were greatly alarming me and my face grew pale, but I kept the matter to myself. (Daniel 7:15–28)

5. Describe the fourth kingdom.

6. Describe the additional horn.

7. How long is he in power?

8. What will be his judgment?

9. What promise can the saints anticipate and hope for?

Application

The little horn or Antichrist wages war against the saints and overpowers them for "a time, times, and half a time" until the Ancient of Days removes him. Tomorrow, we look at the origin of that time frame. Do not lose sight of how great our God is and the victory He has already accomplished through Jesus Christ. This same Redeemer is coming soon to establish His eternal kingdom on earth (Dan. 2:44, Rev. 11:15). Billy Graham once said, "The end will come with the return of Jesus Christ … That is why a Christian can be an optimist. That is why a Christian can smile in the midst of all that is happening. We know what the end will be: the triumph of the Lord Jesus Christ."

God disclosed that Jesus would visibly return—in the clouds—to reign. Beforehand, the Antichrist will take a seat of authority in the Jewish temple and rule for "a time, times, and half a time." This evil entity will manifest itself before the Son of God is revealed with His kingdom (Rom. 8:19–21). When you think about this approaching storm, remember Mark 4:35–40. My friends and family, we **will** make it to the other side! Jesus is in our boat and will not leave us, and He **will** stop the storm! Do you believe that?

YES   NO

If time permits, read the list of the trials that Paul endured in 2 Corinthians 11:22–28 and other saints in Hebrews 11. We must not be afraid of the fires that purge and prepare us for Jesus's coming. (Hab. 3:17-19) It may not be our plan, but it is definitely God's way of accomplishing eternal glory and the glories that follow us into eternity. Life after death. Fruitfulness (John 12:24). Beauty from ashes. Oil of gladness (Isa. 61:3). Favor. Joy in the morning (Ps. 30:5).

Application

How do you handle fear and doubt when your faith is weak? Pray for God to strengthen you and deal with these hindrances. He will! Then, believe what you pray for. When we pray in accordance with His will, God always answers (James 1:6, 1 John 5:14). Write a short prayer, petitioning the Ancient of Days, in the name of Jesus, for a fearless, enduring faith.

Day Three Summary

The disciples of Christ encountered a fierce storm traveling with Jesus, which He prevailed over. "Who is this that even the wind and the sea obey Him?" The great tribulation will be an intense turbulent storm for God's kingdom—a final fire of purging and preparing the elect for the glory of Christ and His kingdom. Daniel saw the Son of Man returning in the clouds and subduing the little horn who would be overpowering the saints. Jesus confirms Daniel's prophecy in His revelation to John and the churches in Revelation 1:7. No additional return is seen by Daniel, revealed by Jesus, or any other writer of Scripture.

Day Four: Saints of the Highest One

Wow, that's a lot to consider! May God bless you as you do. Daniel declared, "As for me, Daniel, my thoughts were greatly alarming me, and my face grew pale" (Daniel 7:28). Maybe you are reeling with the same uneasy feeling. When I first began to study these dreams as relevant to our future, my mind was reeling too. Listen, God has not left us in the dark regarding this forthcoming kingdom, revealing it to prepare us, not scare us. **"See to it that you are not frightened."**

Since God sets the hope of His coming kingdom before us, let's review:

Then the iron, the clay, the bronze, the silver and the gold were crushed all at the same time and became like chaff from the summer threshing floors; and the wind carried them away so that not a trace of them was found. But the stone that struck the statue became a great mountain and filled the whole earth. (Daniel 2:35)

In the days of those kings the God of heaven will set up a kingdom which will never be destroyed, and *that* kingdom will not be left for another people; it will crush and put an end to all these kingdoms, but it will itself endure forever. Inasmuch as you saw that a stone was cut out of the mountain without hands and that it crushed the iron, the bronze, the clay, the silver and the gold, the great God has made known to the king what will take place in the future; so the dream is true and its interpretation is trustworthy. (Daniel 2:44–45)

I kept looking in the night visions, and behold, with the clouds of heaven One like a Son of Man was coming, and He came up to the Ancient of Days and was presented before Him. And to Him was given dominion, glory and a kingdom, that all the peoples, nations and *men of every* language might serve Him. His dominion is an everlasting dominion which will not pass away; and His kingdom is one which will not be destroyed. (Daniel 7:13–14)

But the saints of the Highest One will receive the kingdom and possess the kingdom forever, for all ages to come. (Daniel 7:18)

I kept looking, and that horn was waging war with the saints and overpowering them until the Ancient of Days came and judgment was passed in favor of the saints of the Highest One, and the time arrived when the saints took possession of the kingdom. (Daniel 7:21–22)

He [the little horn] will speak out against the Most High and wear down the saints of the Highest One, and he will intend to make alterations in times and in law; and they will be given into his hand for a time, times, and half a time. But the court will sit *for judgment*, and his [little horn] dominion will be taken away, annihilated and destroyed forever. Then the sovereignty, the dominion and the greatness of *all* the kingdoms under the whole heaven will be given to the people of the saints of the Highest One; His kingdom *will be* an everlasting kingdom, and all the dominions will serve and obey Him. (Daniel 7:25–27)

1. **What does the Ancient of Days give the Son of Man?**

2. **What do the saints receive and possess forever?**

3. **When does this happen?**

4. **How long will God's kingdom last?**

Jesus and the "people of the saints of the Highest One" inherit the kingdom of God, in unity with the Godhead (John 17:21). This future acquisition is impossible for us to fully grasp. Impossible but promised. "Then the King will say to those on His right, 'Come, you who are blessed of My Father, inherit the kingdom prepared for you from the foundation of the world'" (Matthew 25:34). And in Romans 8:16–17, "The Spirit Himself testifies with our spirit that we are children of God, and if children, heirs also, heirs of God and fellow heirs with Christ, if indeed we suffer with *Him* so that we may also be glorified with *Him*." Glorified as heirs with Jesus Christ!

The final kingdom of ten toes or horns will tread down the earth, crushing it. A little horn among them speaks out against the Most High and wears down His saints for "a time, times and half a time" (Daniel 7:25). He will alter laws to benefit his own agenda, endowed with an authority (under the watchful, sovereign authority of God) that lasts for three and a half years. Jesus described this future period as the great tribulation (Matt. 24:21). How do we know that a time, times, and half a time equals three and a half years? The Hebrew word for "time" (*iddan*) could technically be any length. In this case, we know that *iddan* refers to a year because the same event in Revelation lasts forty-two months or three and a half years (Rev. 13:5). Therefore, replace the word "time" with "year," and you end up with year, years, and half a year (1 + 2 + 1/2 = 3 1/2).

The little horn or Antichrist rules for three and a half years, leaving three and a half more years unaccounted for, according to Daniel 9:24–27. That passage in Daniel reveals a seven-year time span for the remainder of God's prophecies to culminate. How did Daniel come by this disclosure? Well, after the Babylonians destroyed Solomon's temple and held Israel captive for seventy years, Daniel prayed for his people to be returned to Jerusalem. Jeremiah had predicted this seventy-year captivity because of their idolatries and sins (Jer. 25:11, 29:10). In conjunction, Isaiah prophesied that King Cyrus would rebuild Jerusalem (Isa. 44:28). In 539 BC when Babylon fell to the Medes and Persians under King Cyrus and their seventy years of captivity had been completed, Daniel knew the fulfillment of prophecy was at hand (Dan. 9:2). Read the answer that he received through Gabriel, an archangel, and note the distinction made between Messiah the "Prince" and the "prince" to come.

> Seventy weeks [490 years] have been decreed for your people and your holy city, to finish the transgression, to make an end of sin, to make atonement for iniquity, to bring in everlasting righteousness, to seal up vision and prophecy and to anoint the most holy place. So you are to know and discern that from the issuing of a decree to restore and rebuild Jerusalem until Messiah the Prince there will be seven weeks and sixty-two weeks [69 total weeks or 483 years]; it will be built again, with plaza and moat, even in times of distress. Then after the sixty-two weeks the Messiah will be cut off and have nothing, and the people of the prince who is to come will destroy the city and the sanctuary. And its end will come with a flood; even to the end there will be war; desolations are determined. And he will make a firm covenant with the many for one week [7 years], but in the middle of the week [after three and a half years] he will put a stop to sacrifice and grain offering; and on the wing of abominations will come one who makes desolate, even until a complete destruction, one that is decreed, is poured out on the one who makes desolate. (Daniel 9:24–27)

Daniel's 70 Weeks

5. **What will be accomplished in seventy weeks (490 years)?**

    a. To finish the _____

    b. To make an end of _____

    c. To make _____ for _____

    d. To bring in everlasting _____

    e. To seal up _____

    f. To anoint the _____

In seventy weeks (490 years), all of the above would be accomplished. Seventy weeks is the equivalent of 490 years (70 weeks x 7 years). After Israel's seventy-year Babylon captivity, the Persians under King Cyrus granted the Jews their freedom to rebuild Jerusalem. Successive Persian kings (Darius and Artaxerxes) maintained the edict of Cyrus and allowed that rebuilding to continue along with the reconstruction of Jerusalem's city walls in 445 B.C. So, from his decree to rebuild the city walls of Jerusalem to the Prince being "cut off" which is the Crucifixion of Christ, 483 years elapsed. If you divide 483 years by 7 years, the quotient is 69, leaving one more week of 7 years for the culmination of prophecy. This is why the tribulation period is thought to be 7 years in length. Note what happens at the beginning of that last 7-year week.

6. Who makes a firm covenant with the many for the final week?

7. What will happen in the middle of the week?

8. How long will the desolation last?

Messiah the Prince and His kingdom constitute the "rock cut out without hands" from the mountain of the Most High God. This rock will crush the feet of King Nebuchadnezzar's statue, collapsing all other kingdoms. Messiah the Prince is the Son of Man returning in the clouds for His people and saints, the one responsible for the redemption of His joint heirs (Rom. 8:17). He is the only one who could and did atone for our sin and the only one who can usher in everlasting righteousness. He will fulfill all remaining prophecies (Rev. 10:7). This is the Messiah who returns to anoint the holiest place in Jerusalem—Jesus Christ, the Word of God!

The prince of the people is the thief who "comes only to steal and kill and destroy," unlike the Prince who came that we may have life and have *it* abundantly (John 10:10). Did you notice that "the people of the prince" destroy the city and sanctuary? That prophecy was fulfilled in AD 70 when Herod's temple was destroyed just as Daniel's prophecy and Christ predicted (Matt. 24:2). In Week One, we read about it from the writings of Josephus. Just as the "people of the saints of the Highest One" (Dan. 7:27) constitute heaven's kingdom, the people of the prince are constituents of earthly kingdoms. The prince or man of lawlessness will covenant with the many for one week. In the middle of that seven-year week, he will break the treaty, stop the Jewish sacrifices, and desecrate their temple until the Ancient of Days decrees his destruction. That is the abomination of desolation, which initiates the great tribulation period.

69 Weeks (483 Years)			70ᵗʰ Week (7 Years)
7 Weeks	**62 Weeks**		**1 Week**
(49 Years) +	(434 Years)	Grace thru Christ	(7 years)
Decree	Messiah	*(Eph. 2:5-9)*	3 ½ + 3 ½
445BC *(Neh. 1-2)*	cut off	**Church empowered**	**One Body in Christ**
		Mt. 16:18; Acts 1:8	Eph. 2:14-15; 3:6; 4:4-6

The preceding chart illustrates Daniel's seventy weeks. Note the gap between the sixty-ninth and seventieth week. In this interim era, God's Gospel is preached until Christ returns. Prior to His Crucifixion and the Messiah being "cut off," keeping the laws of God was His prerequisite for kingdom membership—a covenant based upon works. "Now then, if you will indeed obey My voice and keep My covenant, then you shall be My own possession among all the peoples, for all the earth is Mine; and you shall be to Me a kingdom of priests and a holy nation" (Exodus 19:5–6). After Christ's redemptive work, the old covenant was replaced with a new covenant, one of forgiveness, championed by the sacrifice of Christ (Heb. 8:13). "For by grace you have been saved through faith; and that not of yourselves, *it is* the gift of God; not as a result of works, so that no one may boast" (Ephesians 2:8–9). What our works could not accomplish, Christ could, and did—on our behalf.

Daniel's seventy-week timeline in 9:24–27 has been titled "God's calendar for Israel." And it is. Israel was God's firstborn nation of people, appointed to conceive His firstborn Son, Jesus. His laws, prophecies, purposes, and plans have all been disclosed to the world through the history, patriarchs, and prophets of Israel. They were God's designated light in the world (Isa. 42:6). Daniel's calendar reveals final events on earth based upon the history of Israel because they were His chosen at the time. Yet His kingdom is comprised of all believers, not just Israel. He says in Hosea, "I will call those who were not My people, 'My people,' And her who was not beloved, 'beloved.' And it shall be that in the place where it was said to them, 'you are not My people,' There they shall be called sons of the living God" (Romans 9:25–26).

All believers are the Israel (chosen) of God (John 3:3, Gal. 6:16). He promised Abraham, "I will make you the father of a multitude of nations" (Genesis 17:5). Even before Christ came, Gentile believers were welcomed into the fold, considered "native" born, and included as heirs of the promised land (Ezek. 47:21–23, Eph. 3:6). Believers from all nations are the descendants of Abraham (Gal. 3:28–29). The prophetic promises made to Israel enlighten and affect us all. When Jesus returns, we will glorify God with one heart in one accord—together (Rom. 15:6, Ezek. 11:19, Jer. 32:39, Acts 4:32)! "For I know their works and their thoughts; the time is coming to gather all nations and tongues. And they shall come and see My glory" (Isaiah 66:18).

Application

Have you joined the people of the eternal Prince and kingdom of God? Or is your membership still with the people of the prince and temporary kingdoms of this world? How do your choices reflect the kingdom you live in? Is there room for better choices? What are your thoughts?

Day Four Summary

The people of the saints of the Highest One will inherit God's kingdom alongside the Messiah. Daniel 9:24–27 reveals a seventy-week calendar for all of God's prophecies to culminate regarding the people of the Prince versus the people of the prince. One week remains when the Antichrist enters into a seven-year peace treaty with the many but defaults halfway through. That is when the abomination of desolation occurs, and the great tribulation of three and a half years begins.

Week Four Synopsis

> Jesus returns to establish His kingdom in the days of the ten kings after the abomination of desolation and man of lawlessness is revealed.

Encourage each other as you see the day drawing near.
(Hebrews 10:25)

Week Five

REVELATION 12–13

Day One: Let's Talk

If I could, I would invite you to my back porch for coffee or tea so we could chat about what we've studied so far. We might even take a walk around the block together to share our thoughts. Listen, I am fully aware of how difficult it is to receive and process this information regarding the abomination of desolation. My journey with it began over twenty years ago, and initially, it felt like the storm the disciples encountered on the Sea of Galilee. Unexpected and uncomfortable to say the least. If Jesus had asked me, "Why are you afraid? Where is your faith?" I would have honestly replied, "Lord I believe. Help me in my unbelief" (Mark 4:40, 9:24).

Daniel's dreams of beasts waging war and overcoming the saints are difficult to disseminate, and we have not yet looked at John's visions in Revelation. That begins tomorrow, which is why we are having this discussion today. I don't want to overwhelm you with information, but the book of Revelation adds meat and muscle to the bones of this event. However, before we go there, I thought it would be advantageous to consider another record from the archives of Bible antiquity.

God's covenants are time-tested promises being fulfilled in the course of man's history—dependable certainties in contrast to the proposals and theories of men (2 Cor. 1:20). Let's look briefly at the Abrahamic covenant in Genesis 12:1–4:

> Now the Lord said to Abram, "Go forth from your country, and from your relatives and from your father's house, to the land which I will show you; and I will make you a great nation, and I will bless you, and make your name great; and so you shall be a blessing; and I will bless those who bless you, and the one who curses you I will curse. And in you all the families of the earth will be blessed." So Abram went forth as the Lord had spoken to him; and Lot went with him. Now Abram was seventy-five years old when he departed from Haran.

1. **In the passage above, underline or highlight the blessings that God promised Abram. How many families of the earth would be blessed?**

In Genesis 12:5–7, God also revealed to Abram that his descendants would possess Canaan and be blessed to bless: "You shall be a blessing." Then, Abram received another glimpse into the future—less thrilling but bookmarked inside the assurance of more covenant promises:

> *God* said to Abram, "Know for certain that your descendants will be strangers in a land that is not theirs, where they will be enslaved and oppressed four hundred years. But I will also judge the nation whom they will serve, and afterward they will come out with many possessions." (Genesis 15:13–14)

2. What was the unappealing disclosure?

3. Yet the outcome would be?

God disclosed the descendants of Abraham would endure four hundred years of enslavement—information that must have been puzzling. It doesn't make sense to promise national prolificity and then insert four generations of captivity into the narrative. Why would God include a "furnace of affliction" instead of simply proceeding with their establishment in the promised land? I think most would agree this addendum qualifies as a complicated twist in the narrative. And difficult to comprehend. But God's ways are vastly different from ours. He has eternal purposes in mind, built into the design of every trial that we encounter.

> "For My thoughts are not your thoughts, nor are your ways My ways," declares the Lord. (Isaiah 55:8)

What was the promised outcome? "I will also judge the nation whom they will serve, and afterward they will come out with many possessions" (Genesis 15:14). Four hundred and thirty years elapsed, four hundred of those spent in Egyptian slavery before God delivered Israel and enacted judgment against their captors (Exod. 12:40–41). He destroyed Egypt's agriculture and livestock, even killing the firstborn of everyone who refused to apply the Passover blood to their doorposts (Exod. 7–12). When the Pharaoh pursued Israel, God drowned the entire Egyptian army (Exod. 14:28). Six hundred thousand Hebrew men and their families left Egypt with "many possessions," just as God had promised (Exod. 12:37).

Rejection, persecution, and loss—these are unwanted crucibles of fire—fierce flames that God implements for purposes of refinement. Just as precious metals are smelted in forging fires to achieve purification, refinement is also necessary for the apples of God's eye—His kingdom. (Ps. 17:8; Zech. 2:8, 13:9) The furnace process transforms saints from dust to glory and glory to glory. Out of one fire and into another. From hopeless situations to positions of spiritual fortitude. In the process, the quantitative fat of our faith is measured. We may have a substantial amount of fat or discover that our faith lacks substance. Whatever the realization is, trust the process and designer to be faithful in attaining its purpose. Fires of affliction compel us to seek God and His ways. And when we seek Him, we will find and know Him (Jer. 29:13, Matt. 7:7).

It is reasonable to assume that God's elect should be prepared prior to inhabiting His kingdom as joint heirs with Jesus Christ. This enterprise is of heavenly origin, not earthly origin, whose constituents are called out of the world. Do we automatically know how to operate in the realm of Christ's righteousness? No. Thus, we must trust the training process God has in place. He is faithful. Contemplating the great tribulation might be daunting but no more so than this challenge— "If anyone wishes to come after Me, he must deny himself, and take up his cross and follow Me. For whoever wishes to save his life will lose it; but whoever loses his life for My sake will find it" (Matthew 16:24–25). Did the predicted four hundred years of enslavement frighten Abram? Apparently not. That complicated twist incorporated into Israel's future wasn't a deal breaker for Abraham, Isaac, Jacob, or their families. Even though God is a consuming fire, a smelter and a purifier, He is a God who prospers and blesses. He brought Israel out of the iron furnace and into the Promised Land as a people for His own possession (Deut. 4:20, 6:23). God has blessed His elect with every heavenly spiritual blessing in Christ (Eph. 1:3). His abundant love is being perfected in us daily (1 John 4:12). Just as Abraham and his descendants had the promise of Canaan for an inheritance, we have the return of Christ and the eternal kingdom of God set before us.

4. What did God say to Abram in Genesis 15:1?

The covenant God made with Abram and his descendants was a certainty. Though Israel was to endure a furnace of affliction, He promised to be their shield and their reward would be very great (Heb. 11:6, 24–27). Affliction is uncomfortable—unwanted—yet God has promised to be with us and rewards us beyond expectation, beyond what we can imagine (Phil. 4:6–7). When Jesus returns, His family of faith will see His covenant assurances fulfilled. The kingdom of God will be visually established. We will be reunited with deceased loved ones. Sin and evil will be removed. Peace will replace the suffering, pain and chaos. Our bodies will be made whole. The earth will be filled with the glory of God. These are just a few of the blessings we can and should anticipate!

Jesus wrote this to the Laodicean church, "I advise you to buy from Me gold refined by fire so that you may become rich, and white garments so that you may clothe yourself, and *that* the shame of your nakedness will not be revealed; and eye salve to anoint your eyes so that you may see. Those whom I love, I reprove and discipline; therefore be zealous and repent" (Revelation

3:18–19). Only by the heat of an intense fire can inferior metals and impurities be removed from gold which is the most priceless metal of all.

5. What does 1 Peter 1:3–9 say about the importance of testing?

John's visions in Revelation are for the church of Jesus Christ (Rev. 1:4, 2–3, 22:16). In them, Jesus disclosed the difficulties of the great tribulation but that He and His bond servants would overcome. As a finale, Jesus revealed His glorious return, His millennial reign and the recreation of heaven and earth. Revelation opens with Christ standing in the midst of seven golden candlesticks or churches (a candlestick was a tabernacle furnishing), sending letters to each one in preparation. The visions close with "I, Jesus, have sent My angel to testify to you these things **for the churches**. I am the root and the descendant of David, the bright and morning star" (Revelation 22:16). The great tribulation is revealed by the world's Messiah to His church, Jew and Gentile. To the faithful saints in Philadelphia, Jesus promised,

> Because you have kept the word of My perseverance, **I also will keep you** from the hour of testing, that *hour* which is about to come upon the whole world, to test those who dwell on the earth. (Revelation 3:10)

The Greek word for "keep," *tereo*, is the same word utilized by Christ when He prayed that the Father not take us out of the world but "keep" or "guard" us in it (John 17:14–15). Marvin Vincent and Greek scholar (1834–1922), says that the preposition *from* in Revelation 3:10 is better translated as *in*. Jesus promised to guard His faithful *in* the hour of testing or great tribulation. W. E. Vine, another Greek scholar, defines *tereo* as "watched over," referring to the keeping power of God the Father and Son being exercised over His redeemed. *Tereo* should not be interpreted as God removing us from the great tribulation but as God watching over and guarding us while in it.

Application

In Week One, Day Two, you were asked if it would make a difference in your commitment to Christ to discover that you will be hated, betrayed, or even killed for following Jesus. In countries like North Korea, Afghanistan, Somalia, Libya, Pakistan, Eritrea, Yemen, Iran, Nigeria, China, and India, persecution is widespread and commonplace. The cost of following Jesus Christ and His Word of truth is known and considered upfront. David Curry, president and CEO of Open Doors USA, recently stated, "You might think that [list of countries] is all about oppression. ... But the [list] is really all about resilience" (Reference: Open Doors – top 10 countries of Christian oppression).

When we follow Jesus, suffering will be entailed—period. Participation in the sufferings of Christ should be expected and embraced (1 Pet. 4:12–13). The disciples and apostles made sacrifices to follow Jesus. Are we willing to do the same? And why do we hesitate to believe God would ask His church and kingdom to endure the tribulation period prior to His return? "Why are we afraid? How is it that we have no faith?" (Mark 4:40).

6. What does 2 Corinthians 4:17–18 say?

Application

God's mystery of Christ and His church, shrouded in the Old Testament, was disclosed to the apostles and writers of the New Testament. The descendants of Abraham are not exclusively Jewish; they are Gentile too—a congregation. All believers have Abraham as their father and Jesus as their Savior, who broke down the dividing wall between them (Eph. 2:14, Gal. 3:7). Once united, can the elect of Christ be divided (1 Cor. 1:13)?

> There is neither Jew nor Greek, there is neither slave nor free man, there is neither male nor female; for you are all one in Christ Jesus. And if you belong to Christ, then you are Abraham's descendants, heirs according to promise. (Galatians 3:28–29)

How would you have reacted to God's revelation of a forthcoming four-hundred-year captivity?

What are your thoughts regarding His disclosure of a three-and-a-half-year great tribulation?

Jesus, Daniel, Paul, and John describe this time as an intense period of persecution and falling away. Jesus sent letters to prepare His church for this time of testing, saying, "Blessed is he who reads and those who hear the words of the prophecy, and heed the things which are written in it; for the time is near" (Revelation 1:3). We heed John's visions in Revelation by accepting the content and responding with preparation and readiness.

Just like the false prophets in the Old Testament, there are those today who minimize the warnings. Preach the opposite and render the saints ill prepared (Jer. 23:16–40). "'Behold, I am against those who have prophesied false dreams,' declares the LORD, 'and related them and led My people astray by their falsehoods and reckless boasting; yet I did not send them or command them, nor do they furnish this people the slightest benefit,' declares the LORD" (Jeremiah 23:32). Embrace the value of present trials, permitted and designed to prepare us for those of tomorrow. God is sovereign over all of it. If you are of Gentile origin, examine your willingness to **endure to the end** with the nation of Israel in preparation for the kingdom of God. Are you willing?

YES   NO

Why or why not?

Day One Summary

After enduring four hundred years of affliction, God delivered Israel to be His priesthood, steward His laws, and exalt His Son—the world's Redeemer. If we are asked to endure the great tribulation, it will be to prepare us to receive this Savior and reign with Him as heirs of an eternal kingdom and priesthood (Rev. 20:6). Be willing to suffer with Christ and for Christ—and trust His plan. "For you have been called for this purpose, since Christ also suffered for you, leaving you an example for you to follow in His steps" (1 Peter 2:21).

Day Two: A Great Sign

Consider what we cannot see, such as viruses, bacteria, distant planets, and galaxies. What about people of other nations and neighborhoods? These are invisible to the naked eye without leaving our yards or utilizing satellites and microscopes, yet they do exist, right? Is Satan any different? We cannot see him, but it should be obvious that there are driving forces behind the evil behavior in our world. Should we refuse to acknowledge the source of these forces just because they are invisible (Eph. 6:12)?

The day is approaching when the invisible will become a visible reality. Jesus Christ will be revealed along with His saints and kingdom. Before that, however, the Antichrist will first become visible and enthrone himself in Jerusalem. Today, we look at a chapter that provides insight into the history of past, present, and future events, explaining what is happening in our world and why. Revelation 12 is a synopsis of four significant players. For your benefit, mark the words "woman" and "she" with a yellow highlighter and the words "dragon" and "he" in red. This helps with observations.

The Woman

A great sign appeared in heaven: a woman clothed with the sun, and the moon under her feet, and on her head a crown of twelve stars; and she was with child; and she cried out, being in labor and in pain to give birth.

The Red Dragon

Then another sign appeared in heaven: and behold, a great red dragon having seven heads and ten horns, and on his heads were seven diadems. And his tail swept away a third of the stars of heaven and threw them to the earth. And the dragon stood before the woman who was about to give birth, so that when she gave birth he might devour her child.

The Male Child

And she gave birth to a son, a male child, who is to rule all the nations with a rod of iron; and her child was caught up to God and to His throne. Then the woman fled into the wilderness where she had a place prepared by God, so that there she would be nourished for one thousand two hundred and sixty days.

The Angel

And there was war in heaven, Michael and his angels waging war with the dragon. And the dragon and his angels waged war, and they were not strong enough, and there was no longer a place found for them in heaven. And the great dragon was thrown down, the serpent of old who is called the devil and Satan, who deceives the whole world; he was thrown down to the earth, and his angels were thrown down with him. Then I heard a loud voice in heaven, saying, "Now the salvation, and the power, and the kingdom of our God and the authority of His Christ have come, for the accuser of our brethren has been thrown down, he who accuses them before our God day and night. And they overcame him because of the blood of the Lamb and because of the word of their testimony, and they did not love their life even when faced with death.

"*For this reason*, rejoice, O heavens and you who dwell in them. Woe to the earth and the sea, because the devil has come down to you, having great wrath, knowing that he has only a short time." And when the dragon saw that he was thrown down to the earth, he persecuted the woman who gave birth to the male child. But the two wings of the great eagle were given to the woman, so that she could fly into the wilderness to her place, where she was nourished for a time and times and half a time, from the presence of the serpent. And the serpent poured water like a river out of his mouth after the woman, so that he might cause her to be swept away with the flood. But the earth helped the woman, and the earth opened its mouth and drank up the river which the dragon poured out of his mouth. So the dragon was enraged with the woman, and went off to make war with the rest of her children, who keep the commandments of God and hold to the testimony of Jesus.

1. How is the woman depicted?

2. Describe her labor before giving birth to the child?

First, a great sign appears in heaven—the woman, Israel. She is clothed with the sun (light), ruling above the moon (over darkness). She has a crown of twelve stars, which are the twelve tribes or sons of Jacob. Before she birthed Christ, labor pains were experienced through King Herod's decree. "When Herod saw that he had been tricked by the magi, he became very enraged, and sent and slew all the male children who were in Bethlehem and all its vicinity, from two years old and under, according to the time which he had determined from the magi. Then what had been spoken through Jeremiah the prophet was fulfilled: 'A voice was heard in Ramah, weeping and great mourning, Rachel weeping for her children; and she refused to be comforted, because they were no more'" (Matthew 2:16–18).

3. Describe the great red dragon.

Then, another sign appeared in heaven—a great red dragon having ten horns and seven heads with seven crowns. The dragon is identified as the devil, Satan. In Daniel's dream, he saw these ten horns on a fourth beast, described as "dreadful, terrifying and extremely strong with iron teeth—different from all the beasts that were before it" (Daniel 7:7). King Nebuchadnezzar saw the same ten horns as a kingdom of ten toes on the feet of a great statue. They will be the final beast to rule as a kingdom on earth. In the end when the kingdom of God is set up, the entire statue of earthly kingdoms will be crushed by a "stone, cut out without hands" (Dan. 2:34–35, 44). Details regarding the seven heads of the beast will be studied tomorrow.

4. How did the dragon attempt to destroy the child?

This vision in Revelation 12 provides us with background and insight into a conflict that began in heaven long ago. When the dragon was thrown down to earth, one-third of heaven's hosts were ejected along with him. We can assume that this battle was both significant and disruptive. The Bible mentions three archangels: Michael, Gabriel, and Lucifer. Perhaps each archangel commands one-third of the angels, so when Satan fell, the legions under his authority did too. Fiery and venomous, they swarmed the earth like mad hornets encircling a collapsed nest, later to engage Judea as their primary target. In verse 6, those who flee into the wilderness will be protected for 1,260 days, which, according to verse 14, is a "time, times, and half a time." This is the Antichrist's allotted tenure for reigning (Dan. 7:25). Because God provides a place of protection for those in Judea who flee, Satan and his demons or fallen angels go after the rest of her children identified as those who "keep the commandments of God and hold to the testimony of Jesus Christ." This demographic appears to include believers worldwide who are not being protected in the wilderness of Judea.

5. How does this coincide with Christ's instructions following the abomination of desolation in Matthew 24:16–20?

We are at war, my friend, and on a much grander scale than we care to think about. This battle involves angelic beings hidden from sight until their influence visibly solidifies under the reign of the Antichrist. Then they will exhibit a formidable authority that no one can stop but Jesus Christ alone. The great red dragon is the same shifty, slithering serpent of old, permitted by God to pour out his wrath against the earth during the great tribulation period, in particular, the elect of God. Make no mistake. The time of tribulation is not God's wrath unfolding because the elect are still on the earth. It is Satan's "great wrath" coming against humanity and persecuting His elect. According to Revelation 11:15–18, God's wrath follows the seventh trumpet (Rev. 11:15–18).

In Genesis 3, we are introduced to Satan, the crafty "beast" who deceived Eve and essentially destroyed humanity (John 8:44). Speaking directly into his dark, beady eyes, God vowed, "I will put enmity between you [Satan] and the woman [Israel] and between your seed [the Antichrist] and her seed [the Christ]. He [the Christ] shall bruise you [Satan] on the head, and you [Satan] shall bruise Him [the Christ] on the heel" (Genesis 3:15). This oath was God's Adamic covenant and promise of a Messiah to come, after which He trekked through history to accomplish. No one could conceive and author such a script, fulfilling its prophecies and covenants, except for the Creator and sustainer of heaven and earth Himself. No one but God.

Satan enticed Herod to kill Bethlehem's infants in an attempt to thwart the fulfillment of God's Adamic covenant. He tried again through the Crucifixion of Christ, enticing Judas as his accomplice (Luke 22:3). Paul wrote that the rulers of that age did not understand what they were doing, for "if they had understood it they would not have crucified the LORD of glory" (1 Corinthians 2:8). They did not foresee the miracle of Christ's resurrection. His heel was bruised (crushed) at the cross. The serpent's head was bruised (crushed) as well. Death was overcome, and our sin debt was absolved—the realization and revelation occurring in the day of the Lord (Heb. 2:8).

Do you believe that Satan is your enemy—your worst enemy? He is not a flesh-and-blood opponent but an invisible entity (Eph. 6:12). If you are a member of God's elect, then you are engaged in a battle that began in heaven and will culminate on earth. Perhaps it doesn't seem fair for God to expel these demonic angels from His turf onto ours, but if it is God's plan, then there is a divine reason enacting a perfect purpose (Rom. 8:28). "'For I know the plans that I have for you,' declares the LORD, 'plans for welfare and not for calamity to give you a future and a hope'" (Jeremiah 29:11). We must trust His plan for us. Because the Lord of glory was crucified and resurrected from the dead, all things have been put in subjection under His feet. Consequently, our feet too. We have been blessed with every spiritual blessing in the heavenly places in Christ (Eph. 1:3, 18–23). Every. Spiritual. Blessing.

6. In Revelation 12:5, who is to rule all the nations with a rod of iron?

7. Where is He now?

8. Why does verse 12 say, "Woe to the earth"?

9. In verse 11, how do we overcome this enemy?

God is presently establishing an eternal kingdom of glory fighters and holy priests who have been redeemed from Satan's kingdom by the blood of His Son's sacrifice (Heb. 2:10). "For He rescued us from the domain [authority] of darkness, and transferred us to the kingdom of His beloved Son" (Colossians 1:13). The great red dragon has been defeated, defanged, and Christ's victory over him declared when He overcame the grave (Heb. 2:14). Yet this toothless predator continues to wander the earth—accusing, maiming, and devouring prey—until Jesus Christ returns. When we find ourselves engaged in this battle, we are walking through a fight, already fought and won by the Child who was caught up in heaven until the time of His return (1 Pet. 5:8–9).

Application

We overcome by the blood of the Lamb (sacrifice of Christ), the word of our testimony (confession of faith), with a willingness to face persecution head-on even unto death (martyrdom) (Rev. 12:11). Does that describe you? Why or why not?

Think About It

Your head may be spinning with all that you have studied thus far. But I pray that you realize the following:

- A great tribulation is on the horizon. The Word of God has recorded and revealed it.

- We have an active adversary whose wrath will be unleashed against God's elect and intensify during that tribulation period.

- We prepare by being aware of God's prophecies and covenant promises. It is to our advantage that we separate from sin and endure the smaller tribulations of today. Hebrews 12:1–2 says, "Let us also lay aside every encumbrance and the sin which so easily entangles us, and let us run with endurance the race that is set before us, fixing our eyes on Jesus, the author and perfecter of faith, who for the joy set before Him endured the cross, despising the shame, and has sat down at the right hand of the throne of God." We must lay aside the hefty weights of sin if we want to endure the race set before us (Heb. 3:13). Read the Word of God often. Pray unceasingly. Identify the sins in your life and believe His Word over the lies of Satan, who has been ejected from heaven. We too must deny him access to our lives, minds and hearts. Throw him out! And finally, fix your eyes on Jesus. He has provided the example of running and winning this race against Satan. He is running it again with us—we are not alone!

Day Two Summary

Revelation 12 is a synoptic view of what is happening in our world and why. There is a spiritual battle taking place and battleground on earth where God's elect have been positioned for war. Israel is regarded as a "great sign" because she is the "firstborn" of God's elect. Thrown out of heaven, Satan fights against her with a vengeful vendetta, but the saints will overcome. Satan cannot possibly win. His defeat was declared through the Adamic covenant and proclaimed by the Resurrection of Jesus Christ.

Day Three: Beast from the Sea

Why would God reveal the distant future so long ago? Why not wait until we get closer? King Nebuchadnezzar reigned over Babylon from 605 to 562 BC, so the dreams in Daniel were disclosed hundreds of years prior to the birth of Christ and thousands before His return. Why would God do that? Because the first four kingdoms of Nebuchadnezzar's statue emerged exactly as predicted. Therefore, we can know assuredly that the fifth and final kingdom will too.

This final kingdom of ten toes will surface like a submerged barnacled submarine concealed in cold, murky waters. No one will be able to stop its course—except for the Christ who has already declared Satan's fate. "The court will sit for judgment and his [Satan's] dominion will be taken away, annihilated and destroyed forever" (Daniel 7:26).

In the dreams of both Nebuchadnezzar and Daniel, God's kingdom crushes and removes that of the Antichrist. All earthly kingdoms are brief in tenure; the kingdom of God lasts forever. Satan's attack against God's elect will cease, and whatever losses we might suffer, God has promised to restore with greater gains. In Christ, we can only win. Only win. Do not fear any temporary losses or separation from worldly possessions. A future restoration is on the books!

"Therefore all who devour you will be devoured; and all your adversaries, every one of them, will go into captivity; and those who plunder you will be for plunder, and all who prey upon you I will give for prey. For **I will restore you** to health and **I will heal you** of your wounds,' declares the LORD" (Jeremiah 30:16–17). Zechariah 9:12 says, "Return to the stronghold, O prisoners who have the hope; this very day I am declaring that I will restore double to you." Rest assured, just as Israel left Egypt with many possessions, we as heirs of God and joint heirs with Jesus Christ, will too (Rom. 8:17).

In Revelation 19, John saw Jesus returning and in chapter 20, Satan was bound (Rev. 20:2–3, 7). The saints are resurrected to reign alongside Him for 1,000 years when Jesus returns (Rev. 20:4). It is during this millennial period that they begin to enjoy their restoration and freedoms. Whatever losses we have suffered will be reinstated and increased exponentially. Do you remember the story of Job? He lost everything—his friends, his children, and his health. Even Job's wife, his covenant companion, turned against him.

1. **Read Job 42:10–13. What does the first part of verse 12 say?**

2. What does Isaiah 32:16–18 say about this future era?

Jesus will return to bring in God's righteousness and justice, reigning until He has put all enemies under His feet (Isa. 42:1–4, 1 Cor. 15:25). "The last enemy that will be abolished is death" (1 Corinthians 15:26). The glory of the Lord will fill the earth because Jesus Christ is reigning. "For a child will be born to us, a son will be given to us; and the government will rest on His shoulders; and His name will be called Wonderful Counselor, Mighty God, Eternal Father, Prince of Peace" (Isaiah 9:6). Jesus inherits the throne of David and his kingdom forever (Luke 1:32–33). The nations will travel to Jerusalem to learn from Him (Isa. 2:2–3) as they did in the days of King Solomon (Matt. 12:42).

In the interim, we might suffer losses and experience storms like the disciples did in their travels with Jesus. We are never promised otherwise. For his faith, John suffered exile on the Isle of Patmos in AD 95, where he received the apocalyptic visions of Revelation (Rev. 1:9). What was the purpose of those visions? To prepare God's saints or "bond servants" for "the things that must shortly take place" (Revelation 1:1). Let's look at Revelation 13 for additional insight into the event Jesus designated as the unmistakable sign of His coming—the abomination of desolation. Paul reiterated this sign on Christ's timeline in 2 Thessalonians 2:1–4. Paul taught what Jesus taught.

Nebuchadnezzar (a pagan king) and Daniel (Hebrew captive) were the first to receive the disclosure of this event. John (a disciple) was the last (Rev. 1:1). God has revealed the abomination of desolation as a dreadful event preceding the return of the Son of Man, Jesus Christ (Dan. 7:13, Rev. 1:7). Yet, how many of us are aware and familiar?

> And the dragon stood on the sand of the seashore. Then I saw a beast coming up out of the sea, having ten horns and seven heads, and on his horns were ten diadems, and on his heads were blasphemous names. And the beast which I saw was like a leopard, and his feet were like those of a bear, and his mouth like the mouth of a lion and the dragon gave him his power and his throne and great authority. I saw one of his heads as if it had been slain, and his fatal wound was healed and the whole earth was amazed and followed after the beast; they worshiped the dragon because he gave his authority to the beast; and they worshiped the beast, saying, "Who is like the beast, and who is able to wage war with him?" (Revelation 13:1–4)

3. What is standing on the sand of the seashore?

4. How many horns did the beast have?

5. How many heads?

6. Compare the origin of this beast to those in Daniel 7:2–3?

The beasts in Daniel 7:2–3 and Revelation 13:1 rise up from the sea. Revelation 17:15 interprets **seas** as **nations**. These ten-horned beasts will emerge from the sea of Gentile nations. Daniel's beasts are similar in appearance to those of John's—a leopard, a bear, and a lion—which typifies their strength and character. All these kings have the same source of authority—the dragon. Both Daniel and John saw ten horns with diadems (crowns), referring to kings or leaders of nations. Essentially, God has revealed a ten-member coalition as a tyrannical beast under Satan's authority (the dragon) that will emerge in the future. John also saw the origin of the Antichrist. In addition to the ten horns, he saw seven heads with blasphemous names, empowered by the same dragon. One of those seven heads will be slain in battle but revives, mimicking the Resurrection of Jesus. We touched on this "healing" in our discussion of signs and wonders in Week Three, Day Three. Since these heads have blasphemous names, it seems plausible that they represent leaders of nations with apostate religions. The one whose "fatal wound was healed" proves to be the Antichrist.

7. How does this healing affect the whole earth?

8. What is the perception of the beast's strength?

Note: This being healed from a "fatal wound" may or may not be an authentic resurrection. We can't be certain. If it is, then God has authorized it to accomplish a "deluding influence," in order to judge against the ungodly (2 Thess. 2:8–12). No one rises from the dead without God being the instigator. Interpreting this as a legitimate miracle comes the wording "I saw one of his heads **as if it had been slain**." Similar wording is utilized by John in Revelation 5:6 when referring to the Resurrection of Christ. "And I saw between the throne and the elders a Lamb standing **as if slain**." The Greek word for "slain" in both places is *sphazo*, meaning "slaughtered."

Remember that the ten toes in Nebuchadnezzar's dream are synonymous with the ten horns in Daniel's dream—a coalition of ten leaders. Daniel saw three of these ten "pulled out by the roots" by a separate little horn (Dan. 7:8). In John's vision, this little horn comes from a group of seven heads fueled by the same power source—the dragon. The little horn is the one who is slain and yet revives, astonishing the world. Subsequently, the earth will worship this little horn, saying, "Who is like the beast, and who is able to wage war with him?" (Revelation 13:4). The tribulation period is undoubtedly characterized by wars and their effects, described as the beginning of birth pangs by Jesus. The first four scroll seals and their apocalyptic horsemen disclose the same characterizations. These conflicts provide the setting for the little horn to die by "the sword" in battle (Rev. 13:14) and then miraculously recover.

> There was given to him a mouth speaking arrogant words and blasphemies, and authority to act for forty-two months was given to him. And he opened his mouth in blasphemies against God, to blaspheme His name and His tabernacle, that is, those who dwell in heaven. It was also given to him to make war with the saints and to overcome them, and authority over every tribe and people and tongue and nation was given to him. All who dwell on the earth will worship him, everyone whose name has not been written from the foundation of the world in the book of life of the Lamb who has been slain. If anyone has an ear, let him hear. If anyone is destined for captivity, to captivity he goes; if anyone kills with the sword, with the sword he must be killed. Here is the perseverance and the faith of the saints. (Revelation 13:5–10)

9. **How long is the beast given authority to act?**

10. **Who does he blaspheme?**

11. **Who does the beast overcome?**

12. **How far does his authority extend?**

13. **Who will worship this beast?**

The beast is given authority to tread down and overcome the saints from every nation. Verse 10 declares, "Here is the perseverance and the faith of the saints." "Every tribe, people, tongue, and nation" refers to people of **all nations** who have placed their faith in Jesus Christ. Here, again, we should realize that (1) the saints of God are on earth during the great tribulation and that (2) they are not just from the nation of Israel. The Scriptures disclose Satan being permitted for forty-two months (three and a half years) to dispense his wrath and fury against the family of faith, knowing he only has a short time remaining (Rev. 12:7–12). Remember—God revealed this to Daniel as well. "He will speak out against the Most High and **wear down the saints** of the Highest One, and he will intend to make alterations in times and in law; and they will be given into his hand for a time, times, and half a time" (Daniel 7:25).

Allow me to reiterate that the great tribulation is **not** when God's wrath is poured out since the Scriptures reveal the saints to be enduring. "Here is the perseverance and the faith of the saints." Satan's wrath is being unleashed—not God's wrath (Rev. 12:12).

Application

One of the seven heads appears "as if slain" in battle, but then his "fatal wound" is healed (Rev. 13:3). As a result of this miracle, Satan will have accomplished the most important item on his bucket list—to be worshipped as God. Let's not forget Christ's two commands found in Matthew 24:4–6: (1) "See to it that no one misleads you," and (2) "See that you are not frightened." What would be the significance of those directives? False messiahs and prophets will be prolific. The Antichrist will be enthroned over the Middle East, perhaps the world. Nations will be dealing with municipal chaos and political turmoil, wars resulting in shortages, famine, and loss of life. The kingdom of God will suffer widespread persecution, with many falling away from the faith. Lawlessness will govern in a world spinning out of control. These are not inconsequential difficulties!

Jesus never taught that His redeemed would be removed from these great tribulation challenges, except for those in Judea who flee and are protected. Instead, He provided preparatory directives for our protection and endurance. Then He promised "the one who endures to the end, he will be saved" (Matthew 24:13). We can and must trust the same God who released us from the penalty of our sins to lead us through every temptation and tribulation (Heb. 2:16–18). Jesus is the Way, the Truth, and the Life. Instead of allowing fear to throttle our faith, let's allow Jesus to show us how to navigate threatening storms (Ps. 91, Mark 4:35–41). The Holy Spirit resides within us for this very purpose (Deut. 31:6). Are you willing to rise to this challenge and let the Holy Spirit lead you?

YES   NO

Day Three Summary

John's beast rising from the sea is the same ten toes on the feet of Nebuchadnezzar's statue and the same ten-horned beast in Daniel's dreams. This confederation of ten leaders will come from Gentile nations. Three of the ten fall to a member of a separate group of seven heads. Described as a "little horn," he secures the attention of the whole world and will be worshipped as God after a miraculous healing from a fatal wound in battle.

Day Four: Beast from the Earth

After the beginning of birth pangs, Jesus highlighted the abomination of desolation as a sure sign of His coming. Antichrist(s), wars, famine, death, and earthquakes are merely the beginning of birth pangs. Hard contractions begin with martyrdom and the abomination of desolation, peaking in the day of the Lord (Isa. 13:6). Last week, on Day Four, we read in Daniel 9:27:

> And **he** will make a firm covenant with the many for one week, but in the middle of the week **he** will put a stop to sacrifice and grain offering; and on the wing of abominations will come **one who makes desolate**, even until a complete destruction, one that is decreed, is poured out on the **one who makes desolate**.

Who is this Scripture talking about? Daniel described him as the little horn who becomes larger than his associates (Dan. 7:20). Paul designated him to be the man of lawlessness or son of destruction. John saw him as one of seven heads who is slain by the sword but healed, a miracle that captivates the world. The Antichrist will mimic the Christ and Holy Spirit, deceive the world and if possible, the elect which explains why this period is distinct from all others (Mt. 24:24). "For then there will be a great tribulation, such as has not occurred since the beginning of the world until now, nor ever will" (Matthew 24:21). Such deception will be overwhelming, especially for the unprepared.

By way of review, yesterday we read in Revelation 13:1–10 that the beast of ten horns and seven heads will rise up from the sea of nations. Daniel saw that as well (Dan. 7:2–3). It is a confederation of ten Gentile nations, three of them falling to the little horn from a separate group of seven heads. Blasphemous names were written on the heads, indicating these seven might be an alliance of seven false religions or factions, possibly even seven nations with apostate leadership. The little horn or renegade head declares war on the kingdom of God. More details are disclosed regarding this little horn in Revelation 13:12–18:

> Then I saw another beast coming up out of the earth; and **he** had two horns like a lamb and **he** spoke as a dragon. **He** exercises all the authority of the first beast in his presence. And **he** makes the earth and those who dwell in it to worship the first beast, whose fatal wound was healed. **He** performs great signs, so that **he** even makes fire come down out of heaven to the earth in the presence of men. And **he** deceives those who dwell on the earth because of the signs which it was given **him**

to perform in the presence of the beast, telling those who dwell on the earth to make an image to the beast who had the wound of the sword and has come to life. And it was given to **him** to give breath to the image of the beast, so that the image of the beast would even speak and cause as many as do not worship the image of the beast to be killed. And **he** causes all, the small and the great, and the rich and the poor, and the free men and the slaves, to be given a mark on their right hand or on their forehead, and **he** provides that no one will be able to buy or to sell, except the one who has the mark, either the name of the beast or the number of his name. Here is wisdom Let him who has understanding calculate the number of the beast, for the number is that of a **man**; and **his** number is six hundred and sixty-six.

1. **Where does this beast come from?**

2. **What does this second beast look like?**

3. **How does he speak?**

4. **Who is the earth forced to worship?**

5. **How does he deceive the earth?**

6. **What is the image able to do?**

Revelation 19:20 identifies this second beast who rises from the earth to be the "false prophet." His origin is not from the sea of nations but the earth of man's beginnings—the Middle East, where God's final prophecies unfold. He will be a "lamb-like" religious figure, promoting the little horn (Antichrist) while performing signs to enhance the deception and corroborate his platform. The false prophet engineers the construction of an image in order to mandate worship of the Antichrist. This could be a digital hologram or virtual-reality projection. John would not have been aware of twenty-first-century technology capable of relaying electronic images globally. Today, imageries are routinely transmitted through televisions, theaters, computers, tablets, watches, and phones. Cloning or even artificial intelligence could be the tools implemented to produce this image.

7. What mark does he require all men to take?

8. Where is the mark placed?

9. What happens to those who do not worship the image?

This mark that identifies the Antichrist is a mockery of the Holy Spirit who preserves and seals the saints of God for redemption and eternal life (Eph. 1:13–14). First, Satan mimics the Resurrection of Christ when the Antichrist survives a fatal wound, then he imitates the eternal sanctuary of the Spirit by marking those who choose worldly prosperity and safety under his reign, albeit temporary.

Application

The mark of the beast scares the pants off most Christians living in America. It's sad, really. Gospel messages void of the cross of Christ have insulated and weakened the American church. Congregants are consequently, so terrified of the mark of the beast that the pre-tribulation rapture theory is lauded and applauded over clear Biblical teaching. It is time, if not past time, for the church of Jesus Christ in America to unashamedly shake her shaker of salt—challenge herself to adhere to the disciplines of the faith and her calling—prepare for the great tribulation rather than ignore it—embrace the fallout of persecution and suffering—most importantly—trust God with her future. The crux of Christianity is His challenge, accepted by faith: "If anyone wishes to come after Me, he must 1) deny himself, and 2) take up his cross and 3) follow Me. For whoever wishes to save his life will lose it; but whoever loses his life for My sake will find it" (Matthew 16:24–25). Jesus delineated the truth of what it means to follow Him. The truth.

Any gospel presentation void of the cross of Christ is a compromised, false gospel, lacking the power to save anyone (1 Cor. 1:17–18). Removing the cross from our theology has opened the door for a wide range of erroneous and inaccurate interpretations of the Scriptures. Ask yourself—Am I willing to be persecuted for my faith in Christ? To allow the Holy Spirit to lead me out of sin? If so, you will be counted worthy of the kingdom of God (2 Thess. 1:5). If so, you have undoubtedly counted all things as loss in order to gain Christ (Phil. 3:8, Ps. 31:20). If so, then you have recognized the hopelessness of your sinful self, embraced the Christ of the cross and the cross of the Christ as God's way and provision for salvation. Does that describe you?

10. Look at Ezekiel 9:4. How are the men who are marked by God being described?

> In what context does a Christian live, move, act, think, decide? It must be the context of God's kingdom. We either live in that kingdom or we live in the world. (Elisabeth Elliot from *Keep a Quiet Heart*)

Our attitude toward sin reveals our heart toward God. "Hate evil, you who love the Lord, Who preserves the souls of His godly ones" (Psalm 97:10). No one is perfect or without fleshly struggles, but our pursuits do reflect our faith or lack thereof. God's kingdom is one of righteousness, not unrighteousness spurred on by evil passions. The Israelites marked the doorposts of their homes with the sacrificial blood of the Lamb (Exod. 12). They identified themselves as God's chosen people—set apart, holy, and marked for redemption. If the Holy Spirit resides within us, then we too have been set apart, holy, and marked for redemption. We will not be able to agree with sin (John 16:8, Titus 2:11–12). We will not be able to habitually participate in sinful behavior without experiencing conviction and regret (1 John 1:5–10, 3:9–10). 2 Timothy 2:19 says, "The firm foundation of God stands, having this seal, 'The LORD knows those who are His,' and, 'Everyone who names the name of the LORD is to abstain from wickedness.'" Do you groan over sin?

YES   NO

11. According to Revelation 14:9–11, what future awaits those who take the mark of the beast?

Those who identify with the Antichrist and take his mark will think they are safe when, in reality, they are marked for eternal destruction. It is a clear choice set before humanity in the latter days. That mark will be a decision to align oneself with the satanic, anti-Semitic, anti-Christian manifesto of the Antichrist who rejects Jesus Christ, His saints, and God's firstborn nation, Israel.

In addition, the Antichrist will enlist a protégé—his bootlicking, bad-to-the-bone, false prophet. Out of the abysmal fungal community of deceived prophets, one will arise preeminently and be appointed to stand beside the Antichrist and mandate his worship. This protégé prophet has deceived himself into thinking he has hitched his insignificant, rickety wagon to an infallible star. Yet they both as a dynamic duo have already been sentenced to a predetermined, eternal destruction (Matt. 16:26).

12. What does Revelation 19:20 say about the outcome for the beast and false prophet?

Application

If you knew that Satan would be granted a throne of authority over the earth (the Middle East, in particular), what would you do to prepare? Well, now you do know. Satan (the dragon) abhors the kingdom of God. He loathes the cornerstone and each precious stone built upon the cornerstone, as well as the binding mortar of the Holy Spirit. Think about that the next time he entices you to sin against your Creator and Savior. Be faithful, my friend (Ps. 31:23, Rev. 2:10). Be holy (Rom. 12:1, 1 Cor. 3:16–17). Live by faith as a holy people of God, preparing not only for the glorious return of Jesus Christ but for the great tribulation beforehand.

Taking the mark of the beast (Antichrist) is a conscious decision to reject God's Son. "By this you know the Spirit of God: every spirit that confesses that Jesus Christ has come in the flesh is from God; and every spirit that does not confess Jesus is not from God; this is the *spirit* of the antichrist, of which you have heard that it is coming, and now it is already in the world" (1 John 4:2–3). In the great tribulation, those living in the Middle East and perhaps globally will be required to choose between Christ and the Antichrist. In a very real sense, we are making that decision today. We are either for Jesus Christ or against Him—now, at this very hour. There is no in-between, invisible gray area for Christians to inhabit. Matthew 12:30 says, "He who is not with Me is against Me; and he who does not gather with Me scatters." Neither is Christianity a spectator sport. Christianity is living by faith in the redemptive power of Jesus—living free from sin. "I have been crucified with Christ; and it is no longer I who live, but Christ lives in me; and the life which I now live in the flesh I live by faith in the Son of God, who loved me and gave Himself up for me" (Galatians 2:20).

Whose mark do you currently bear? How do you see yourself faring without the ability to make financial transactions, obtain medicine, or purchase meals from a favorite restaurant? That is a baseline question to consider. Be honest first. Then, be willing to pick up your cross and follow Christ without qualifying that He provide you with material prosperity and a tribulation escape pod. We overcome Satan by (1) the blood of the Lamb, (2) our confession of faith in Jesus Christ, and (3) a willingness to endure even unto death (Rev. 12:11).

If you struggle with anxiety regarding the mark of the beast, then pray for God to strengthen you. That's what He does! The Holy Spirit strengthens, enlightens, empowers, and comforts. Just ask. This entire study revolves around awareness and preparedness for this final battle between the saints and Satanic forces (Dan. 7:21–26). Just as with any strength training exercise, start where you are. Free and forgiven, without condemnation. Evaluate the ground you are standing on. Is it a dependable, solid rock (the Word of God) that can withstand tribulation storms, or are you standing on the shifting sands of uncertainty and false gospels (Matt. 7:24–27)? Prepare yourself by praying and yielding to the work of the Holy Spirit. The Son of God came to save us;

the ministry of the His Spirit is to anoint and prepare us to reign alongside Christ in the kingdom of God (2 Tim. 2:11–12). As an overcomer. A holy priest. And an heir of God.

> These things I have spoken to you, so that in Me you may have peace. In the world
> you have tribulation, but take courage; I have overcome the world. (John 16:33)

We have completed our study of the abomination of desolation. You qualify as a warrior of the faith if you made it to this point because these have been difficult lessons to process. Please hear me when I say—God would never disclose information to scare us—only to prepare us. If you feel frightened, then ask yourself why. A spirit of fear is not the Spirit of God (2 Tim. 1:7). It would never be God's intention to frighten those He has redeemed and delivered from the power of Satan, sin, and fear. Confront your anxiety by reminding Satan of his future demise and destination. Then, turn to Jesus as your shelter of refuge. "You are my hiding place; You preserve me from trouble; You surround me with songs [shouts] of deliverance. *Selah*" (Psalm 32:7).

Day Four Summary

A false prophet will support and promote the little horn (Antichrist). He authorizes the building of an image that will demand inhabitants in the Middle East (perhaps the world) to take his mark. Noncompliance will result in either execution or exile. But God is our source of strength. We can face the great tribulation as an overcomer with the blood of Jesus coursing freely through our lives, facing fear, rejection, persecution, and anything else we encounter when we pick up our cross and follow the Lamb of God.

Week Five Synopsis

> The Antichrist reigns for three and a half years prior to Jesus
> returning and visibly establishing His kingdom on earth.

Encourage each other as you see the day drawing near.
(Hebrews 10:25)

Week Six

MATTHEW 24:29–31

Day One: Heavens Are Shaken

We have covered quite a bit of material in the past five weeks. You were asked to postpone the use of outside resources until after Week Five because honestly, Bible scholars vary so profusely in their interpretations of prophecy, it gets confusing. But don't let that discourage you. Please don't. The Bible is for everyone. The Holy Spirit is capable of disclosing "what is to come" to all of Christ's body (John 16:13), and it would never contradict the overall counsel of Scripture—since all Scripture is inspired by God (2 Tim. 3:16). Remember that. Even in the day of Jesus, Jewish scholars differed in their doctrinal views, many even rejecting Him as their Messiah (Luke 11:53–54, Mark 3:6). Remember that too.

1. **What does 2 Peter 1:20–21 say about our interpretations?**

The Holy Spirit has revealed God's plan through Scripture, and the veracity of its constitution will never change because of our differing opinions. Study His Word. His plan will unfold exactly as He declared and determined (Isa. 55:11). We may find the abomination of desolation and great tribulation to be unsettling, but rest assured—God's plan has been and always will be for us, never against us (Rom. 8:31–33). This week, we finish the timeline of Christ and next week, we finish our study. You have been amazing! I mean flat-out amazing. It takes discipline, raw stamina, and a strong, healthy heart to do a prophetic study packed with Scripture for your analysis. Yet you have done it! My prayer is that these last two weeks will bring it all together and that you will be able to agree with God's plan, unafraid to travel with the one who commands the wind and seas (Mark 4:35–41).

Please begin with the Week Six Worksheet on Matthew 24:29–31 at the end of this week's lesson and fill in the blanks on the right side. There's a brief review exercise on the back side of that worksheet. See how you do!

2. **Describe the "shaking" of the heavens.**

We take for granted the dependability of the sun, moon, and stars, don't we? These luminaries were placed in the heavens on the fourth day of creation to support life on earth. Yet light actually appeared on the first day—before the luminaries (Gen. 1:4–5, 14–19). That light was God! (1 John 1:5) Evidently, when the heavens are shaken and darkened, the light of God's presence returns (Ps. 44:3). Hebrews 1:10–12 says, "You, LORD, in the beginning laid the foundation of the earth, and the heavens are the works of Your hands; they will perish, but You remain; and they all will become old like a garment, and like a mantle You will roll them up; like a garment they will also be changed. But You are the same, and Your years will not come to an end."

In Week Two, Day Three, we discussed the heavens being "shaken" as the sign Old Testament prophets predicted would predicate the day of the Lord. This sign is also unveiled by the sixth scroll seal in Revelation 6:12–17. The seals reveal the contents of the scroll: (1) Antichrist(s), (2) war, (3) famine, (4) death, and (5) martyrdom. Jesus defined these as birth pangs that increase in intensity prior to the heavens being shaken, disclosed by seal (6). The significance of these seals duplicating the signs on Christ's timeline cannot be overstated. Jesus is revealing an overview or characterization of the tribulation period in both places (see appendix "The Sixth Seal"). The sixth seal discloses the wrath of the Lamb (God), which according to Revelation 11:15–18, happens after the seventh and last trumpet.

3. Look at the elements of the sixth seal in Revelation 6:12–14 and fill in the blanks:

- A great _____

- _____became black as sackcloth

- _____became like blood

- _____of the sky fell to the earth

- The _____was split apart like a scroll when it was rolled up.

- Every _____and _____were moved out of their places.

The sixth seal depicts a great earthquake and cataclysmic failure of the earth's luminaries. The sun is blackened; the moon turns red. Stars fall from heaven as the sky splits apart which is difficult to comprehend. There might be scientific explanations that we could consider, such as a solar or lunar eclipse, perhaps even the atmospheric effects of a nuclear blast or volcanic eruption. But stars falling to earth and the sky splitting apart defy all human logic. Whether this luminary failure is a natural or supernatural phenomenon or a combination of both, Jesus designated it as the sign of the Son of Man and the end of the age. The day of the Lord will then begin (Ps. 94:1–2)! Old Testament prophets predicted this shaking of the heavens, and Jesus positioned it on His timeline as the climactic sign of His return.

4. In Revelation 6:12–17, how does the earth respond?

What an astounding turn of events. God's two-sided celestial coin is irreversibly flipped. When the abomination of desolation occurs, those in Judea are to flee from Satan's wrath; God protects and provides for them there (Matt. 24:15–16, Rev. 12:14). But there is no place for the unrighteous to hide from the wrath of the Lamb! No protection. No provisions. No place of refuge. Revelation 6:16–17 says, "Hide us from the presence of Him who sits on the throne, and from the wrath of the Lamb; for the great day of their wrath has come, and who is able to stand?"

> Wail, for the day of the LORD is near! It will come as destruction from the Almighty. Therefore all hands will fall limp, and every man's heart will melt. They will be terrified, pains and anguish will take hold of *them*; they will writhe like a woman in labor, they will look at one another in astonishment, their faces aflame. Behold, the day of the LORD is coming, cruel, with fury and burning anger, to make the land a desolation; and He will exterminate its sinners from it. For the stars of heaven and their constellations will not flash forth their light; the sun will be dark when it rises and the moon will not shed its light. Thus I will punish the world for its evil and the wicked for their iniquity; I will also put an end to the arrogance of the proud and abase the haughtiness of the ruthless. (Isaiah 13:6–11)

5. What does God's wrath accomplish?

> Sun *and* moon stood in their places; they went away at the light of Your arrows, at the radiance of Your gleaming spear. In indignation You marched through the earth; In anger You trampled the nations. You went forth for the salvation of Your people, for the salvation of Your anointed. You struck the head of the house of the evil to lay him open from thigh to neck. *Selah.* (Habakkuk 3:11–13)

6. Who is saved in the day of the Lord?

"The LORD keeps all who love Him, but all the wicked He will destroy" (Psalm 145:20). Other Old Testament prophets such as Isaiah (Isa. 2:2–4, 13:6–13); Jeremiah (Jer. 46:10); Ezekiel (Ezek. 30:3); Amos (Amos 5:18), Obadiah (Obad. 1:15); Zechariah (Zech. 14:1–4); and Zephaniah (Zeph. 1:7–8) describe this day as the appointed time for God's judgment against all enemies of righteousness. Since Jesus Christ sacrificed Himself as the pardon and release from our sins, in Him we become righteous—saved, sanctified, and sealed for eternity (Heb. 10:14, Eph. 4:30). The elect who are marked by the blood of the Lamb will be rescued from God's wrath (1 Thess. 1:9). "You went forth for the salvation of Your people, for the salvation of Your anointed" (Habakkuk 3:13).

And the timing according to Jesus? **Immediately after the great tribulation**, "the sun will be darkened, and the moon will not give its light, and the stars will fall from the sky, and the powers of the heavens will be shaken. And then the sign of the Son of Man will appear in the sky." Here, Jesus returns as the light of the world (John 8:12)! The luminaries are no longer necessary to support life on earth because the omnipotent, omniscient, omnipresent light arrives (Rev. 21:23)! You and I are lights too (Matt. 5:14–16; Phil. 2:15). When Jesus comes back and His saints are resurrected and caught up to join Him in the air, He and we will light up the sky together! Can you imagine? Then, "we will be like Him, because we will see Him just as He is" (1 John 3:2). Brilliant, pure, and without defect because He is brilliant, pure, and without defect. We will shine like stars in harmony with the Son of God. I don't know about you, but that humbles me beyond adequate words. Peter wrote,

> Blessed be the God and Father of our Lord Jesus Christ, who according to His great mercy has caused us to be born again to a living hope through the resurrection of Jesus Christ from the dead, to *obtain* an inheritance *which is* imperishable and undefiled and will not fade away, reserved in heaven for you, who are protected by the power of God through faith for **a salvation ready to be revealed in the last time**. In this you greatly rejoice, even though now for a little while, if necessary, you have been distressed by various trials, that the proof of your faith, *being* more precious than gold which is perishable, even though tested by fire, may be found to result in praise and glory and honor **at the revelation of Jesus Christ**. (1 Peter 1:3–7)

Application

Your imperishable inheritance is reserved in heaven for you—if you have been born again by the blood and the Spirit of the Lord Jesus Christ (John 3:5–6). You are protected by the power of God through faith for salvation, ready to be revealed when Jesus is revealed. Today, we walk by faith, and our faith is being refined. The redeemed are being made ready (Rev. 19:7). When Christ returns in glory, we will be glorified as well, and the time of testing and refinement will be finished (Rom. 8:17–19, James 1:2–4). There will be praise, glory, and honor for the Christ who comes to "be glorified in His saints" (2 Thessalonians 1:10). We have been born again to this very hope of a glorious future with Him. Do not give up on the faithfulness of God. He will not give up on you!

Day One Summary

Immediately following the great tribulation, the heavens are shaken. This is the second of two unmistakable signs preceding Christ's return, the first being the abomination of desolation. This second sign or shaking of the heavens is also disclosed by the sixth scroll seal. It initiates the wrath of the Lamb from which no man escapes except for the redeemed, just like in the days of Noah.

Day Two: Jesus Returns

Let's reflect briefly on the opening verses of Matthew 24. God in the flesh—our eternal, sovereign Savior—walked out of the Jewish temple for the last time, knowing His final hour was at hand. No doubt, the mind of Jesus was on God's altar of sacrifice and the agony ahead of Him (Isa. 53:7–8). But the topic of conversation for the disciples was the infamous Jewish temple, their nation's reminder of God's selection and presence (Deut. 14:2). We often gravitate to temporary things for comfort and strength—beauty, wealth, health, and success—cheering ourselves on with material possessions when those of eternity should be our anchor and assurance. It is almost a certainty that the last thing on the mind of Jesus as He walked out of the temple that day was its ornate structure and historical representation. His foreknowledge of the imminent battle ahead would have been pressing in against Him with enormous weight.

Transitioning from Herod's temple to God's eternal work and building, Jesus diverted the disciple's attention to the future. He began by predicting the destruction of their treasured temple. Not a single stone would remain upon another (Matt. 24:2). How could He possibly know that? Jesus. Is. God. This divine disclosure solicited questions from the disciples, just as He intended:

> As He was sitting on the Mount of Olives, the disciples came to Him privately, saying, "Tell us, when will these things happen, and what *will be* the sign of Your coming, and of the end of the age?" (Matthew 24:3)

In His answer, Jesus revealed a timeline of signs that will signal His coming. What were the saints to do with it? Toss it aside for theological, theoretical timelines? No. He meant for us to adhere to His timeline so that we're not caught off guard in the latter days. Not only the nation of Israel but the entire church of Jesus Christ to whom the book of Revelation was addressed (Rev. 22:16). The destruction of the temple in AD 70 happened just as Jesus predicted. Not one stone remained upon another. The rest of His prophetic signs will transpire just as Jesus predicted too.

With precision and clarity, Jesus answered, "What will be the sign of Your coming?" First, the initial birth pangs. Next, the abomination of desolation recorded by the prophet Daniel, initiating three and a half years of great tribulation. Lastly, "But immediately after the tribulation of those days the sun will be darkened, and the moon will not give its light, and the stars will fall from the sky, and the powers of the heavens will be shaken. And then the sign of the Son of Man will appear in the sky, and then all the tribes of the earth will mourn, and they will see the Son of Man coming on the clouds of the sky with power and great glory" (Matthew 24:29–30).

After the great tribulation and **after** the heavens are shaken, **then** the "sign of the Son of Man will appear in the sky." That is the final sign of His coming. "They will see the Son of Man coming on the clouds of the sky with power and great glory." Jesus again resourced Daniel who said, "I kept looking in the night visions, and **behold, with the clouds of heaven One like a Son of Man was coming**, and He came up to the Ancient of Days and was presented before Him" (Daniel 7:13). We should note that the same reference is utilized by Jesus in the opening of His revelation to the churches, "**Behold, He is coming with the clouds**, and every eye will see Him, even those who pierced Him; and all the tribes of the earth will mourn over Him. So it is to be. Amen" (Revelation 1:7). Jesus is seen standing in the midst of seven golden candlesticks (the churches) when He quotes Old Testament prophets (Daniel and Zechariah) to His New Testament church (Zech. 12:10–14).

1. Review Hebrews 9:28 and write it out:

The Scriptures reveal only two comings of Christ—first for the sinner and then for His saints, those who "eagerly await Him." This Second Coming is the focus of the book of Revelation, written to prepare and encourage His church:

> And I saw heaven opened, and behold, a white horse, and He who sat on it *is* called Faithful and True, and in righteousness He judges and wages war. His eyes *are* a flame of fire, and on His head *are* many diadems; and He has a name written *on Him* which no one knows except Himself. *He is* clothed with a robe dipped in blood, and His name is called The Word of God. And the armies which are in heaven, clothed in fine linen, white *and* clean, were following Him on white horses. From His mouth comes a sharp sword, so that with it He may strike down the nations, and He will rule them with a rod of iron; and He treads the wine press of the fierce wrath of God, the Almighty. And on His robe and on His thigh He has a name written, "KING OF KINGS, AND LORD OF LORDS." (Revelation 19:11–16)

To the Thessalonians, Paul wrote,

> But we do not want you to be uninformed, brethren, about those who are asleep, so that you will not grieve as do the rest who have no hope. For if we believe that

Jesus died and rose again, even so God will bring with Him those who have fallen asleep in Jesus. For this we say to you by the word of the LORD, that we who are alive and remain until the coming of the LORD, will not precede those who have fallen asleep. For the LORD Himself will descend from heaven with a shout, with the voice of *the* archangel and with the trumpet of God, and the dead in Christ will rise first. Then we who are alive and remain will be caught up together with them in the clouds to meet the LORD in the air, and so we shall always be with the LORD. (1 Thessalonians 4:13–17)

2. **Compare the above passages from Revelation 19 and 1 Thessalonians 4. Do you think these are different events? Why or why not?**

The visions in Revelation were sent by God to Jesus through an angel to John for the purpose of preparing the bond servants (church) of Jesus Christ (Rev. 1:1). We have already established that in this study. Revelation 19 is a vision of Jesus coming to deal with unrighteousness, the Antichrist, false prophet, and Babylon. Judging against them, He will tread the winepress of the fierce wrath of God (Rev. 19:15). Did you catch that? The wrath of God commences when Jesus returns after the seventh and last trumpet (Rev. 11:15–18). Also disclosed by the sixth scroll seal (Rev. 6:12–17).

In 1 Thessalonians 4:13–17, Paul affirms the resurrection and reunion of the saints rather than Christ's judgment and wrath. The saints in Thessalonica needed that confirmation. Both passages provide insight into the return of Christ but with a different emphasis. Revelation 19 highlights the day of the Lord, His glory, and His wrath. First Thessalonians 4 highlights the gathering and reunion of the elect. There are many aspects involved in the return of Christ scattered throughout Scripture; no single passage presents them all in one place.

Paul wrote about the return of Christ in numerous other places as well. Such as:

So that you are not lacking in any gift, awaiting eagerly **the revelation of our LORD Jesus Christ**, who shall also confirm you to the end, blameless in the day of our LORD Jesus Christ. (1 Corinthians 1:7–8)

For as in Adam all die, so also in Christ all shall be made alive. But each in his own order: Christ the first fruits, after that those who are Christ's at His coming, then comes the end, when He hands over the kingdom to the God and Father, when He has abolished all rule and all authority and power. (1 Corinthians 15:22–24)

For I am confident of this very thing, that He who began a good work in you will perfect it **until the day of Christ Jesus**. (Philippians 1:6)

And this I pray, that your love may abound still more and more in real knowledge and all discernment, so that you may approve the things that are excellent, in order to be sincere and blameless **until the day of Christ**; having been filled with the fruit of righteousness which comes through Jesus Christ, to the glory and praise of God. (Philippians 1:9–11)

When Christ, who is our life, **is revealed**, then you also will be revealed with Him **in glory**. (Colossians 3:4)

For after all it is only just for God to repay with affliction those who afflict you, and to give relief to you who are afflicted and to us as well **when the LORD Jesus will be revealed from heaven with His mighty angels in flaming fire**, dealing out retribution to those who do not know God and to those who do not obey the Gospel of our LORD Jesus. (2 Thessalonians 1:6–8)

In addition to Matthew 24:30 and Revelation 1:7, 19:11–16, Jesus said,

For the Son of Man is going to come **in the glory of His Father** with His angels, and will then repay every man according to his deeds. (Matthew 16:27)

But when the Son of Man **comes in His glory**, and all the angels with Him, then He will sit on His glorious throne. (Matthew 25:31)

For whoever is ashamed of Me and My words in this adulterous and sinful generation, the Son of Man will also be ashamed of him when **He comes in the glory of His Father** with the holy angels. (Mark 8:38)

3. Do the teachings of Paul and Christ reflect a glorious return of Jesus or a silent, private return?

The Scriptures you just read are not exhaustive but an accurate sampling of what Christ and His apostles taught throughout the New Testament. They are a representation of the whole. The return of Jesus Christ initiates the day of the Lord, which entails a reunion and revelation of His kingdom saints and the execution of His wrath against sin by His angels. A third return as a precursor before the day of the Lord is never mentioned in Scripture. Never. Paul wrote the Corinthians that we now eagerly await "the revelation of our Lord Jesus Christ" (1 Corinthians 1:7). He wrote a letter to Titus telling him that **we are now waiting for** the blessed hope, which is **the appearance of His glory**:

For the grace of God has appeared, bringing salvation to all men, instructing us to deny ungodliness and worldly desires and to live sensibly, righteously and godly in the present age, looking for the blessed hope and the appearing of the glory of our great God and Savior, Christ Jesus, who gave Himself for us to redeem us from every lawless deed, and to purify for Himself a people for His own possession, zealous for good deeds. (Titus 2:11–14)

4. How does Titus 2:11–14 say we should be living as we wait?

Application

God has extended grace through Christ and temporarily stayed His righteous wrath against sin. Have you ever wondered why the Old Testament is so different from the New Testament? The Old Testament reveals the righteousness of God in conflict with sin and the sinner. The New Testament reveals God's grace, releasing sinners from their sins. Both testaments conclude with the day of the Lord and the revelation of God's kingdom. Today is the day of salvation! When Jesus returns, the day of the Lord begins. The opportunity to receive God's grace and forgiveness will then be over (John 11:25–26, 2 Cor. 6:2).

How are we to live prior to the day of the Lord? "Live sensibly, righteously and godly in the present age, looking for the blessed hope and the appearing of the glory of our great God and Savior, Christ Jesus" (Titus 2:12–13). Psalm 98:8–9 says, "Let the rivers clap their hands, let the mountains sing together for joy before the Lord, for He is coming to judge the earth; He will judge the world with righteousness and the peoples with equity."

Whose gospel and creed do you live by? That of the living Word of God, who separates us from sin and calls us to live as holy lights, or the false, seductive gospel, promoting promises of finding our identity by reveling and remaining in sin? Romans 8:13–14 says, "For if you are living according to the flesh, you must die; but if by the Spirit you are putting to death the deeds of the body, you will live. For all who are being led by the Spirit of God, these are sons of God." When Jesus returns for His kingdom saints, it will be those who have separated from sin unto righteousness—those who identify with Christ and are identified by His Spirit.

"Become sober minded as you ought, and stop sinning" (1 Corinthians 15:34). God has never approved of sin because sinful behaviors destroy us; they do not enhance our lives and certainly cannot free us. A freedom to sin is not a freedom from sin (Rom. 6:1–7). "It was for freedom that Christ set us free; therefore keep standing firm and do not be subject again to a yoke of slavery" (Galatians 5:1). If we choose to remain in sin, we are choosing to remain in bondage rather than freedom. It is impossible to find our identity through sinful, licentious living. We can only find identity and purpose by connecting

> "Too many think lightly of sin and therefore think lightly of the Savior" (Spurgeon)

to the source of life, love, and liberty—Jesus Christ—all the way home as pilgrims enduring this present difficult journey toward heaven (Heb. 11:13). Does that describe you? Are you committed to following your Redeemer all the way home?

YES   NO

The night is almost gone, and the day is near. Therefore let us lay aside the deeds
of darkness and put on the armor of light. (Romans 13:12)

Day Two Summary

Jesus will return in power and glory for the saints to establish His kingdom and remove all unrighteousness. That is what the Scriptures teach regarding the Second Coming of Christ—the only testimony provided by both Old and New Testament writers, from Daniel's dreams to John's visions, and—the only way Jesus depicts it Himself. A stealthy coming of Christ prior to the great tribulation to remove the saints is not revealed in Scripture. As we wait in anticipation of Christ's return and the revelation of His glory, saints and kingdom, let us live sensibly, righteously, and godly every day—all the way home. He is coming back for all who eagerly await Him (Heb. 9:28)!

Day Three: All the Tribes Will Mourn

Today's topic is the restoration of Israel and the return of God's favor to a nation that mismanaged His laws and rejected His Son. Do they deserve His mercy? Does anyone? Yet God promised, "I will restore you [Israel] to health and I will heal you of your wounds, declares the LORD" (Jeremiah 30:17).

At the end of Christ's timeline, we see, "Immediately after the tribulation of those days the sun will be darkened, and the moon will not give its light, and the stars will fall from the sky, and the powers of the heavens will be shaken. And then the sign of the Son of Man will appear in the sky, and then all the tribes of the earth will mourn and they will see the Son of Man coming on the clouds of the sky with power and great glory" (Matthew 24:29–30).

Earlier, in verse 15, Jesus referenced Daniel for the abomination of desolation. Here, at the end of His timeline, Jesus recounts prophecies from Daniel, Isaiah, Ezekiel, Joel, Amos, and Zephaniah regarding the day of the Lord and Israel's renaissance. The Old Testament is not irrelevant as some insist. In fact, its contents are not only necessary but essential to understanding the New Testament, especially the timeline of Christ and His revelatory visions. When Jesus reaches back into ancient texts and connects them to future events, it should be obvious that the Old Testament forecasts the New Testament and the New fulfills the Old. Hand in glove, they declare God's story and glory.

1. What does 2 Timothy 3:16 say?

The "tribes of the earth" is a reference to the nation of Israel. Think back to Revelation 12:1 (Week Five, Day Two). "And a great sign appeared in heaven—a woman clothed with the sun, and the moon under her feet, and on her head a crown of twelve stars." These twelve stars are the twelve tribes of Israel. There is a distinction made in Scripture between the "physical" nation of Israel (Abraham's descendants by birth) and the "spiritual" Israel of God (Abraham's descendants by rebirth) (Rom. 9:8, Col. 3:11). The physical nation of Israel is comprised of twelve tribes, stemming from the twelve sons of Jacob, Isaac's son and Abraham's grandson.

In Week Four, Day Four, we discussed Daniel 9:24–27 and Israel's prophetic calendar. Seventy weeks were decreed for the physical nation of Israel. Sixty-nine of those seventy weeks (483 years) transpired from the edict of Artaxerxes to rebuild Jerusalem to the coming of Messiah the Prince. Therefore, one week of seven years remains for prophecy to culminate in regard to this nation. At the onset of those seven years, the prince or Antichrist will sign a peace treaty with "the many" for seven years, but he breaks it halfway through. That is when the abomination of desolation occurs, initiating three and a half years of great tribulation.

Every Scriptural prophecy regarding the nation of Israel and their (our) Messiah has been literally fulfilled in granular detail. The future events Jesus alludes to with His timeline and in His Revelation to the churches will be literally fulfilled as well. Yes, there is symbolic representation built into the descriptions of proceedings and their actors, but if we categorize the events themselves as allegorical, we will get lost in the thicket of a mystical forest—without a working compass. Don't underestimate God's ability to literally accomplish these future events. His signs and wonders executed in Egypt were literal. If not, why did Pharaoh release over a million Hebrew slaves (Exod. 12:37)? If the parting and closing of the Red Sea was not a literal event, how did the entire Egyptian army of six hundred chariots drown (Exod. 14:5–9, 28; Heb. 11:29)? The birth, crucifixion, and resurrection of Christ were authentic, literal events. When He comes again, the final prophecies contained in Daniel's seventieth week will be fulfilled literally as well, just as Scripture predicts—not symbolically, parabolically, or allegorically. Literally.

69 Weeks (483 Years)				70th Week (7 Years)
7 Weeks	**62 Weeks**			**1 Week**
(49 Years) +	(434 Years)		Grace thru Christ	(7 years)
Decree		Messiah	*(Eph. 2:5-9)*	3 ½ + 3 ½
445BC *(Neh. 1-2)*		cut off	**Church empowered**	**One Body in Christ**
			Mt. 16:18; Acts 1:8	Eph. 2:14-15; 3:6; 4:4-6

Afterward the sons of Israel will return and seek the LORD their God and David their king; and they will come trembling to the LORD and to His goodness in the last days. (Hosea 3:5)

2. Who returns to seek the Lord in the last days?

I will pour out on the house of David and on the inhabitants of Jerusalem, the Spirit of grace and of supplication, so that they will look on Me whom they have pierced; and they will mourn for Him, as one mourns for an only son, and they will weep bitterly over Him like the bitter weeping over a firstborn. (Zechariah 12:10)

3. Who will mourn for the one they pierced?

God's nation, chosen to birth and proclaim Jesus Christ, relinquished Him to Roman authorities for crucifixion. They pierced His hands and feet with nails, His head with a crown of thorns, and His side with a centurion's spear. Betrayed. Rejected. Crucified. Yet the house of David can and will be forgiven when they acknowledge His sacrifice, just as they were healed in the wilderness after looking to the bronze serpent on the pole (Num. 21:8–9, John 3:14–15). "He made Him who knew no sin *to be* sin on our behalf, so that we might become the righteousness of God in Him" (2 Corinthians 5:21). Will the entire nation be saved? Scripture indicates it to be a remnant (Rom. 9:27, Isa. 10:20–22).

4. When does Romans 11:25–27 say God returns to Israel?

We discussed this "fullness of the Gentiles" in Week Three, Day Two. After the Gospel has reached all nations, it will be time for God's firstborn nation to be awakened (Matt 24:14). Their disconnected, dry bones will come back to life (Ezek. 37:1–6, Jer. 31:33–34, Zech. 12:10). "For this is the covenant that I will make with the house of Israel after those days, says the LORD: I will put my laws into their minds, and I will write them on their hearts. and I will be their God, and they shall be My people" (Hebrews 8:10).

In deference to those who insist on removing Gentile believers or the church of Jesus Christ from the earth in a pre-tribulation rapture, this explains why. God's focus switches to Israel. The seventy-week calendar disclosed to Daniel for his "people and the holy city" is primarily Jewish theater. The main arena for Old Testament prophecies to unfold is in Jerusalem and the Middle

East. In the Jewish temple, the Antichrist commits the abomination of desolation. The protagonist (Jesus) is from the lineage of David—Jewish. The antagonist (Satan) will set his sights first on eradicating Israel before making "war with the rest of her children, who keep the commandments of God and hold to the testimony of Jesus" (Revelation 12:17).

If God's focus returns to Israel in Daniel's seventieth week, the time of "Jacob's trouble," what about the rest of the world (Jer. 30:7)? Are Gentile believers still on the planet, or are they removed when the "fullness of the Gentiles" comes in? Maybe, but that's a tentative maybe. We don't see that proposal taught anywhere in Scripture. The removal of the church prior to the return of Jesus Christ is a theological theory, hypothetical, dependent upon Scriptures being extracted and then amalgamated for its construction.

This cutting and pasting of Scripture to support a "pre-tribulation rapture" is compelling until you examine both context and content of the passages. For instance, consider the context of "only the Father knows the day of the hour," used frequently to support Christ's imminent return. Jesus made that statement in a sermon where He revealed signs we should expect to see prior to His coming—His glorious coming. Yes, only the Father knows the precise timing, but Jesus knows the signs we should watch for and shared them with us. His return in the "twinkling of an eye" is also utilized to say Christ's coming is imminent. That phrase comes from 1 Corinthians 15:50–53, where Paul explained to the church that Jesus would return in the twinkling of an eye at the last trumpet when the righteous are resurrected. Paul is the same apostle who told the Thessalonians that the righteous resurrection would precede the rapture. The Bible reveals the timing of the righteous resurrection to be on the last day (John 6:39–40, 44, 54). When the heavens are no longer (Job 14:12).

Then, 2 Thessalonians 2:6–8 is referenced to say the church and Holy Spirit are the restrainers being removed from earth when he who restrains "is taken out of the way (2 Thessalonians 2:1–9). We covered this in Week Four, Day Two. The restrainer is not identified nor the rapture mentioned by Paul in that passage. Paul's emphasis is on the Antichrist being revealed **before Jesus returns**. The restrainer could be the archangel Michael—we just don't know. Paul clarifies that the "lawless one" or Antichrist will take his seat in the temple of God and claim to be God, which is the sign Jesus said to watch for—the abomination of desolation. In 2 Thessalonians, Paul is speaking to the same congregation he wrote regarding the rapture. (1 Thess. 4:13–17).

Are the visions in Revelation primarily for the nation of Israel or is it for the entire church of Jesus Christ? Revelation opens with Jesus standing in the middle of seven churches, sending letters to prepare each one. Then Revelation concludes with "I Jesus, have sent My angel to testify to you these things for the churches" (Revelation 22:16). When a book opens and closes by identifying its recipients to be the churches, then the entire book is for His church—both Jew and Gentile.

> After these things I looked, and behold, a great multitude which no one could count, from every nation and *all* tribes and peoples and tongues, standing before the throne and before the Lamb, clothed in white robes, and palm branches *were* in their hands; … These are the ones who come out of the great tribulation, and they have washed their robes and made them white in the blood of the Lamb. (Revelation 7:9, 14)

5. Who comes out of the great tribulation?

Revelation 12 reveals four main players involved in the earth's history (Week Five, Day Two). The first and "great sign" is the woman—Israel. She is God's firstborn nation, chosen to be a light to the Gentile nations and bring the Lamb sacrifice into the world. God's Word to Israel is His Word of promise to everyone who partakes of this sacrifice. In addition to God's kingdom being established on earth when Jesus returns, unrighteousness will be removed. Satan loses his temporary throne, and Jesus acquires His eternal throne in the city of God, Jerusalem. The glory of the LORD will fill the earth (Num. 14:21)! In that final week of Daniel's seventy-week calendar, the nation of Israel is definitely in the spotlight—center stage. But that does not preclude the presence of Christ's church being among the "bond servants" waiting for Him to return and reveal His kingdom.

Apart from Daniels's seventy-week calendar in the Old Testament, the only other eschatological timeline we have was provided by Jesus in the New Testament. Two timelines. One from the prophet Daniel. The other from the prophet Jesus. And don't forget this: In Revelation 1:7, Jesus referenced Daniel 7:13. In the book of Revelation, which is sent to the churches, Daniel is again quoted regarding His return. What would that mean? Simply put, Jesus validates Daniel's dreams as applicable to His church. In Revelation 1:7, He also says "Every eye will see Him" and quotes from Zechariah 12:10–14 when He says, "Even those who pierced Him; and all the tribes of the earth will mourn over Him." Every eye will see Him is not a private rapture rescue; it is a full-blown revelation and "all the tribes of the earth will mourn Him." This is situated on Christ's timeline after the great tribulation. Look at it again.

6. Review Matthew 24:30–31, Daniel 7:13, and Revelation 1:7. Do these passages depict the same event? Why?

On Day One this week, we looked at Scriptures connecting the day of the Lord to the shaking of the heavens. "For the stars of heaven and their constellations will not flash forth their light; the sun will be dark when it rises and the moon will not shed its light" (Isaiah 13:10). Yesterday, on Day Two, we looked at the Son of Man returning in glory as an event absolutely no one can miss (Rev. 1:7). Our Creator and judge will suddenly illuminate the darkness like lightning streaking across a midnight sky and rescue His elect. Grace and forgiveness will have been presented to all nations including the nation of Israel. Those "willing to turn from their transgressions" will recognize Jesus as the Messiah, and all the tribes of the earth will mourn. "You will arise *and* have compassion on Zion; for it is time to be gracious to her, for the appointed time has come" (Psalm 102:13). Then, "the Son of Man comes on the clouds of the sky with power and great glory." These prophetic events, foretold by prophets in the Old Testament, are accounted for on Christ's timeline and detailed in His revelation in the New Testament.

Just Like the Days of Noah was not written to discredit any anointed saints of God or dishonor their ministry in kingdom service. Nor was it written to exacerbate division within the church body over our differing views. We should be able to disagree in areas of eschatology without angry discord, especially in the gray areas of theoretical uncertainty. Our love for God and one another must remain a pinnacle priority lest we disparage the household of God and our calling as ambassadors for Christ. We have been commissioned to share the Gospel of salvation and win souls, not arguments.

As long as the church has boots on the ground, she is to be Christ's light of righteousness and love. Jesus was full of grace and truth (John 1:14). Truth entails a commitment to the kingdom of God, to His ways, and to His will (Matt. 6:33). Be ready for the return of Jesus and familiar with the great tribulation, not caught off guard by either one. First Thessalonians 4:13–17 has been designated as the pre-tribulation church escape passport and mode of transport. But that is not a certainty. It is a theological supposition. Invest your heart and mind in the clear revelations of Scripture rather than the proposals. I said this earlier in this study and will say it again: God can do whatever He wants. I am not opposed to a sudden transfer from Earth to heaven for any reason. But while we remain on this planet, the church of Jesus Christ should invest in what is clear rather than what is not.

Many of the pastors I listen to are of dispensational persuasion. I cherish them and am blessed by their teaching and outreach. My prayer is that our differences can complement one another, and the Spirit unite us through His wielding process of iron sharpening iron (Prov. 27:17). Perhaps the greatest challenge the American church faces today is her reluctance to embrace and endure adversity for the sake of God's kingdom. Without a doubt, her timidity has contributed to the popularity of a preferred escape plan. Will Gentiles eagerly receive the mantle of God's priesthood and blessings from heavenly places yet refuse to identify with Christ's sufferings (Eph. 1:3–6)? Where is her willingness to say, "Our God is able to deliver us but if He does not, let it be known O king that we are not going to serve your gods or worship the golden image that you have set up" (Daniel 3:17–18)?

Israel was chosen and set apart from the other nations, just as all of God's redeemed have been separated from the world. The true Israel of God is His house, "in whose house we are" (Gal. 6:16, Heb. 3:6). Those redeemed by the blood have been emerging as a lineage of saints from the beginning of creation: Adam, Abel, Seth, Enoch, Methuselah, Lamech, Noah, and other "sons of glory" who lived prior to Abraham and Christ (Heb. 2:10, 3:3–6). This assembly of saints did not begin at Pentecost. God's family began with Adam, and His invitation to join will remain open until Jesus returns. God's congregation is the mystery of Christ and His body—His church, His elect and redeemed (Eph. 3:4–10, 1 Cor. 12:12–14). Gentiles have joined the nation of Israel as heirs of the same promises (Exod. 12:48–49, Lev. 24:22, Num. 15:14–16, Ezek. 47:21–23). God's congregation of saints and His brethren have collectively emerged through the same Father and through the same sacrifice as constituents of the same kingdom (Heb. 2:11). One family. One return of Jesus Christ. One resurrection of the righteous. One rapture for those who endure to the end. One reunion and gathering of the saints as One eternal bride (Isa. 54:5–8, Eph. 5:22–27).

7. According to Hebrews 12:26–29, what will and won't be shaken?

God's kingdom cannot be shaken. In the day of the Lord, Christ will reveal and present the kingdom of His redeemed to His Father (Rom. 8:19, 1 Cor. 15:22–24). The Antichrist will have tenured temporarily on a throne in Jerusalem as the prince of this world before being removed by the sovereign Prince. "Then the sovereignty, the dominion, and the greatness of all the kingdoms under the whole heaven will be given to the people of the saints of the Highest One; His kingdom will be an everlasting kingdom, and all the dominions will serve and obey Him" (Daniel 7:27).

Why would the church even want to leave before the return of Jesus Christ—before the revelation and finale of God's glory? Events to unfold in Daniel's seventieth week will be the buzz of conversation for the entirety of eternity. Can we even imagine? Consider the trumpet signals taking place, reminiscent of the signs and wonders displayed in Egypt. The Gospel of salvation will be heralded to God's firstborn nation through 144,000 Jewish witnesses, including two who are supernaturally protected for 1,260 days (Rev. 11:3–4, Matt. 24:14). We will witness the fulfillment of prophecy being broadcast globally by media reporting unprecedented events taking place in the Middle East. Our Jewish brethren will be drawn by the Holy Spirit to the very Messiah they cut off and crucified (Dan. 9:26, Isa. 53:8). It doesn't get any sweeter than this, my friends, to hear the Gospel of Jesus Christ proclaimed as it encircles the earth from the city of David, Jerusalem!

Men of Israel, listen to these words:

Jesus the Nazarene, a man attested to you by God with miracles and wonders and signs which God performed through Him in your midst, just as you yourselves know––this *Man*, delivered over by the predetermined plan and foreknowledge of God, you nailed to a cross by the hands of godless men and put *Him* to death. But God raised Him up again, putting an end to the agony of death, since it was impossible for Him to be held in its power. (Acts 2:22–24)

Therefore let all the house of Israel know for certain that God has made Him both Lord and Christ—this Jesus whom you crucified. Now when they heard *this*, they were pierced to the heart, and said to Peter and the rest of the apostles, "Brethren, what shall we do?" Peter *said* to them, "Repent, and each of you be baptized in the name of Jesus Christ for the forgiveness of your sins; and you will receive the gift of the Holy Spirit. For the promise is for you and your children and for all who are far off, as many as the LORD our God will call to Himself." (Acts 2:36–39)

Application

The final week on Israel's calendar sits on our horizon. Sin and demonic activity are rapidly escalating, bolstered by the world's increasing appetite and acceptance of depravity. Laws are being rewritten and enforced to protect sins unthinkable just a decade ago yet applauded and lauded today as worthy, healthy pursuits. And if we refuse to fall in line like stringed puppets, then we are the ones considered senseless.

Consider again the storm encountered by the disciples in Mark 4:35–41. Think of it in terms of today's swelling turbulence. Gross immorality. Human rights overriding the laws of heaven. The gender confusion insanity. Escalating criminal violence. Rogue autocratic governments establishing formidable alliances. Global displacement of refugees. This tornadic activity is destroying humanity and planet Earth. How do we respond? We should secure our footing on the clear truth of God's Word and fix our hope on Jesus Christ! Soon, our Heavenly Father will initiate the day of the Lord, still the storm, and remove the pervasive evil that is demanding humanity's undivided allegiance. Soon.

We have a place of refuge, the secret place of Christ's presence (Psa. 31:20). Even though Jesus was asleep in the boat with His disciples, they were in His presence. They could have rested with Him, but they panicked instead and asked, "Do you not care that we are perishing?" He replied, "How is it that you have no faith?" Jesus was in their boat. He was with them. It might not have felt like He was, but He was. Rest in the shelter of His presence. Trust His faithfulness. Allow Jesus Christ to reveal His sovereignty over the turbulence because He is taking us to the other side of the storm (Isa. 43:2). "The LORD will rescue me from every evil deed, and will bring me safely to His heavenly kingdom; to Him be the glory forever and ever. Amen" (2 Timothy 4:18). Can you trust and rest in the presence of Christ?

YES   NO

Jesus did not disqualify the disciples for their weak faith. He did not allow the storm to overtake them. He stilled the storm and stayed in the boat. Jesus might rebuke us when our faith is weak, but He will not abandon us. (Psa. 11:4). With a willingness to trust the Navigator, we can always earnestly pray, "I believe, LORD. Help me in my unbelief" (Mark 9:23–24).

Day Three Summary

When the heavens are shaken, the sign of the Son of Man will appear, and the day of the Lord begins. God's promise to return and restore Israel will be fulfilled. Those who mourn and call on His name will be saved. The church will remain on earth to see Jesus return in glory. The

Scriptures do not teach otherwise. This will be an extraordinary testimony of God's faithfulness before the world—a display of power and majesty we will recount and rehearse for all eternity!

Day Four: Gathers and Separates

A woman in labor has only one thing on her mind—delivery. As the birth approaches, she is unable to think about neighborhood teas, book clubs, recipes, politics, or anything else but bringing that baby out of the womb. It is a unique and miraculous experience, all-consuming and painfully dramatic. Contractions intensify and become more frequent as the baby descends into the birth canal. Finally, the groaning mother makes one final ginormous push, bringing her baby into the world. The labor is then done, and a new life for the family begins. Was there a shout from heaven or a trumpet blast accompanying the delivery? No, but there is a family gathering to celebrate. The family of God will be gathered as well with a hallelujah chorus! (Rom. 8:22–23) For those who have suffered tragedy in childbirth or been unable to conceive, you are not alone, and you are greatly loved by the one who sees your plight. He has not abandoned or forgotten you, and He never will. Trust the one who sees: El Roi (Gen. 16:13). Trust the one who has promised to restore your losses (Joel 2:25, Zech. 9:12).

Finishing Christ's timeline today, we read, "And He will send forth His angels with a great trumpet and they will gather together His elect from the four winds, from one end of the sky to the other" (Matthew 24:31).

1. **What are His angels tasked with?**

2. **How are these angels sent?**

Immediately following the great tribulation, the heavens will be shaken, and the sign of the Son of Man appears. Christ returns to gather His elect with a great trumpet. He gathers and reunites. He also separates. Trumpets relating to the return of Christ are mentioned in the following Scriptures:

➢ In the rapture passage (Complete Jewish Bible): "For the LORD Himself will come down from heaven with a rousing cry, with a call from one of the ruling angels, and with God's shofar; those who died united with the Messiah will be the first to rise; then we who are left still alive will be caught up with them in the clouds to meet the LORD in the air; and thus we will always be with the LORD" (1 Thessalonians 4:16–17).

➢ At the last trumpet: "Behold, I tell you a mystery; we will not all sleep, but we will all be changed, in a moment, in the twinkling of an eye, at the last trumpet; for the trumpet will sound, and the dead will be raised imperishable, and we will be changed" (1 Corinthians 15:51–52).

➢ In a series of seven: "And I saw the seven angels who stand before God, and seven trumpets were given to them" (Revelation 8:2). "Then the seventh angel sounded; and there were loud voices in heaven, saying, 'The kingdom of the world has become the kingdom of our LORD and of His Christ; and He will reign forever and ever'" (Revelation 11:15).

Bible scholars disagree over the purpose of those seven trumpets in Revelation and whether or not the seventh is Paul's "last" trumpet in 1 Corinthians 15:52. Sequentially, the seventh is "the last," following a series of six. It is also unique from the other trumpets in designation. This last trumpet announces the kingdom of Christ. According to Revelation 11:18, the wrath of God ensues, which supports the seventh trumpet as Paul's last—the one announcing Christ when He returns to first resurrect and gather His elect.

When we allow God's Word to speak freely without censorship, the Scriptures flow like tributaries into a larger mainstream. But when we disconnect or block them in an attempt to force human interpretation, then the intended target does not receive or collect water properly. God's prophetic plan has been revealed and placed on a timeline by the Lord Jesus Christ, the Son of God. It would benefit His church to study His timeline comprehensively and allow the tributaries of prophetic Scripture to flow and pool as intended. Then, the vast sea of conflicting and confusing interpretations would dry up and disappear.

3. In Hebrews 1:1–2, who is God's spokesman in these last days?

4. Who is the source of the timeline in Matthew 24 and John's visions in Revelation?

At the end of the book of Revelation, we read, "I, Jesus, have sent My angel to testify to you these things for the churches. I am the root and the descendant of David, the bright morning star" (Revelation 22:16). Jewish Jesus provided visions through John to benefit all His bond servants—the church of the firstborn, enrolled in heaven as the house and kingdom of God (Heb. 10:21, 12:23). Through John's visions, **Jesus prepares** His household of faith by unveiling latter-day events. With His timeline, **Jesus designates** when those future events will take place.

In Matthew 24:31, Jesus said He would be announced with a great trumpet. If you track the Jewish feasts as prophetic of Christ's first and second comings, then the great trumpet refers to the shofar of Yom Kippur. Perusing the Jewish feasts is like visiting God's Believe It or Not Museum of

Fine Arts. It is a fascinating, faith-building tour of an orchestrated plan way beyond the capability of human design. As mentioned previously, the four Jewish spring feasts enacted after Israel's deliverance from Egypt were fulfilled in the first coming of Christ and during their appointed celebrations (see appendix "Seven Jewish Feasts"). Jesus was crucified on Passover as the sinless Unleavened Bread of God. Three days later, He was resurrected during the Feast of First Fruits (1 Cor. 15:20). Fifty days after Passover, during the Feast of Pentecost, the Holy Spirit descended to baptize and sanctify the kingdom of God (Acts 2). Such fulfillment doesn't happen by chance. It just doesn't. Only God could write a nation's history to establish prophetic festivals and then fulfill them centuries later by His Son. Only God could do that. Only God would do that!

The fourth spring feast, Pentecost, commemorates God gathering Israel to receive His laws at Mount Sinai. That encounter is the first Scriptural mention of "the trumpet of God."

5. What does Exodus 19:16–17 say about the purpose and origin of that shofar?

The three Jewish fall feasts will be fulfilled in the Second Coming of Christ. The Feast of Trumpets or Rosh Hashanah is the first of the fall feasts, celebrated months after Pentecost. Rosh Hashanah is observed in preparation for the second fall feast and holiest day of the year: the Day of Atonement or Yom Kippur. Thirdly, there's the Feast of Tabernacles or Ingathering which will be fulfilled after Jesus returns, gathers His saints and begins His one-thousand-year reign (Rev. 20:4). Understanding the purpose of the Feast of Trumpets clarifies the first six trumpets in Revelation to be viable opportunities for repentance—in preparation for the Day of Atonement. Those trumpets are mere trailers of the bowls of wrath that ensue after Jesus returns, similar to the trumpets but more comprehensive in their destruction.

Just as the plagues in Egypt were opportunities for repentance, the trumpet warnings will be as well. God's wrath upon Egypt came in the last plague: the plague of death. In Revelation 11:15–18, God's wrath follows the seventh and last trumpet. Thus, the trumpets are judgment warnings prior to God's wrath. By the sixth and before the seventh trumpet, repentance will have ceased. Revelation 9:21 says, "And they did not repent of their murders nor of their sorceries nor of their immoralities nor of their thefts."

Yom Kippur is the most solemn of all the Jewish feasts—Judgment Day. It follows the Feast of Trumpets. The name, Yom Kippur, actually means "day of covering" in honor of the high priest who entered the Holy of Holies to sprinkle sacrificial blood over the mercy seat on the Ark of the Covenant. When the seventh and great trumpet blows to announce the Christ, and the elect are gathered, it will be a day of covering for the redeemed because the blood of the Lamb covers God's eternal mercy seat (Rom. 3:25, Heb. 9:5–11). Hallelujah! Let the 1,000-year reign begin—fulfilling the last fall feast—the feast of Tabernacles.

In Matthew 24:31, Jesus again pulls from the Old Testament.

> In that day the LORD will start *His* threshing from the flowing stream of the Euphrates to the brook of Egypt, and you will be gathered up one by one, O sons of Israel. It will come about also in that day that a great trumpet will be blown, and those who were perishing in the land of Assyria and who were scattered in the land of Egypt will come and worship the LORD in the holy mountain at Jerusalem. (Isaiah 27:12–13)

> And He will lift up a standard for the nations and assemble the banished ones of Israel, and will gather the dispersed of Judah from the four corners of the earth. (Isaiah 11:12)

What does the New Testament say? In the parable of the wheat and tares, found in Matthew 13:24–30, angels gather God's elect and separate the righteous from the unrighteous. In that parable, Jesus said, "Allow both to grow together until the harvest; and in the time of the harvest I will say to the reapers, 'First gather up the tares and bind them in bundles to burn them up; but gather the wheat into my barn'" (Matthew 13:30). Read the interpretation of that parable:

> Then He left the crowds and went into the house. And His disciples came to Him and said, "Explain to us the parable of the tares of the field." And He said, "The one who sows the good seed is the Son of Man, and the field is the world; and *as for* the good seed, these are the sons of the kingdom; and the tares are the sons of the evil *one*; and the enemy who sowed them is the devil, and the harvest is the end of the age; and the reapers are angels. So just as the tares are gathered up and burned with fire, so shall it be at the end of the age. The Son of Man will send forth His angels, and they will gather out of His kingdom all stumbling blocks, and those who commit lawlessness, and will throw them into the furnace of fire; in that place there will be weeping and gnashing of teeth. Then the righteous will shine forth as the sun in the kingdom of their Father. He who has ears, let him hear." (Matthew 13:36–43)

6. **When does this gathering take place?**

7. **Where are the tares being gathered from?**

8. Who shines forth in the kingdom of their Father?

Jesus first gathers and attends to His elect. Remember Hebrews 9:28? "So Christ also, having been offered once to bear the sins of many, will appear a second time for salvation without *reference to* sin, to those who eagerly await Him." God's saints are resurrected and reunited, and all the stumbling blocks are removed. Currently, our churches have been infiltrated with the distractions of superficial chaff, but when this wild grass is removed, "the righteous will shine forth as the sun in the kingdom of their Father" (Matthew 13:43). "How great is Your goodness, which You have stored up for those who fear You, which You have wrought for those who take refuge in You before the sons of men!" (Psalm 31:19). Now, look at the parable of the net:

> Again, the kingdom of heaven is like a dragnet cast into the sea, and gathering *fish* of every kind; and when it was filled, they drew it up on the beach; and they sat down and gathered the good *fish* into containers, but the bad they threw away. So it will be at the end of the age; the angels will come forth and take out the wicked from among the righteous, and will throw them into the furnace of fire; in that place there will be weeping and gnashing of teeth. (Matthew 13:47–50)

9. The kingdom of heaven attracts what kind of fish?

10. Who comes to separate the wicked from the righteous?

In your Bible, look up Matthew 25:31–46.

11. Who is gathered before Christ when He returns?

12. Who is separated?

13. What does He say to His sheep?

14. What is the fate of the goats?

After Jesus returns and the great trumpet sounds, his angels will accompany Him to gather and separate the righteous from the unrighteous. Judgment does, in fact, begin with the house of God (1 Pet. 4:17). The concept of judgment makes us cringe if we prefer the trendy view of God being passionate about our fleshly passions. The truth is that the majority of Scripture must be redacted to construct a god without a throne—one with no interest or intention of preserving life and truth, one who considers worldly pleasures as more significant than attaining "the resurrection of the dead" (Phil. 3:10). In the parable of the wheat and tares, Satan is the source of the tares so God uproots and removes them at the proper time. Only the wheat will be gathered to dwell with Him forever—only those redeemed by the blood of the Lamb and set apart by the Holy Spirit (Ps. 101:6–7).

Application

"Therefore, prepare your minds for action, keep sober *in spirit*, fix your hope completely on the grace to be brought to you at the revelation of Jesus Christ. As obedient children, do not be conformed to the former lusts *which were yours* in your ignorance, but like the Holy One who called you, be holy yourselves also in all *your* behavior; because it is written, 'You shall be holy, for I am holy'" (1 Peter 1:13–16). God is passionate for us, not our fleshly passions. Are your passions set upon Jesus Christ?

YES   NO

The Second Coming of Christ initiates the day of the Lord and His righteous judgment. We currently live in an era of grace. The day of the Lord is an era of judgment against evil, all enemies of righteousness, and Satan's entourage. David wrote, "He is coming to judge the earth. He will judge the world in righteousness, and the peoples in His faithfulness" (Psalm 96:13). When that great and last trumpet blows, His judgment begins with His own house. The kingdom of God is built upon Jesus Christ—the perfect, sinless Son of God whose shed blood purchased every single brick in His building (Heb. 3:6). His redeemed will be revealed when He returns (Rom. 8:19, 1 Cor. 1:7–8). The wheat are gathered and presented to the Father as His kingdom (1 Cor. 15:24). The chaff is removed. Are you ready? Next week, we talk more about this readiness—our last week together.

Day Four Summary

At God's last trumpet, Jesus will return in astonishing glory. When this great trumpet sounds, judgment begins with the house of God, and all tares are removed. Only the saints will tabernacle with Christ in the kingdom of God together and forever with Him.

Week Six Synopsis

> Scripture presents one return of Jesus Christ, one day of the Lord, one resurrection of the righteous, and one gathering of the elect.

Encourage each other as you see the day drawing near.
(Hebrews 10:25)

WEEK SIX WORKSHEET

Matthew 24:29–31

But immediately after the tribulation of those days the sun will be darkened, and the moon will not give its light, and the stars will fall from the sky, and the powers of the heavens will be shaken.

And then the sign of the Son of Man will appear in the sky, and then all the tribes of the earth shall mourn, and they will see the Son of Man coming on the clouds of the sky with great power and great glory. And He will send forth His angels with a great trumpet, and they will gather together His elect from the four winds, from one end of the sky to the other.	Observations
	
	Immediately after …
	
	The tribulation of those days
	
	• The sun will be
	
	• The moon will not
	
	• The stars will fall from
	
	• The powers of the heavens will be
	
	And then …
	
	• The sign of the Son of Man
	
	  will _____.
	
	• All the tribes of the earth shall mourn.
	
	• They will see the Son of Man coming on the clouds of the sky with power and great glory.
	
	• He will send forth His angels with a great trumpet, and they will
	
	  _____.

Antichrist/Israel Covenant		Abomination of Desolation		Jesus Returns
Dan. 9:27	3 1/2 years	great tribulation	3 1/2 years	1,000-year reign

Review

Draw a line to match the following:

Matthew 24:1–14   Abomination of desolation

Matthew 24:15–28   Heavens are shaken.

Matthew 24:29–31   Beginning of birth pangs

Week Seven

MATTHEW 24:32–41 AND 24:42–51

Day One: Fig Tree Parable

Blessings to you! You have been faithful to endure. Keep going! This week, we will finish our study, *Just Like the Days of Noah*. You have five full days of study, so please adjust your schedule accordingly. Take your time. These are not difficult lessons, and you will gain so much more if you do them separately with time to think and pray in between.

Two Week Seven Worksheets are provided for you at the end of this week. Look at the first worksheet on Matthew 24:32–41 and observe the text, highlighting notable truths in the passage while filling in the blanks on the right side. Then, answer the following questions:

1. **How does a fig tree signal that summer is near?**

2. **When is Jesus coming?**

3. **How close is His coming at that point?**

4. **Which generation will see the coming of the Lord?**

5. **Who alone knows the day and hour?**

When the leaves of a fig tree begin to bud, summer is near. When birth pangs escalate, we know a baby is coming, yet the precise timing remains unknown. The analogy is clear. When the events that Jesus said to watch for transpire, **then His return is imminent**, yet only the Father knows the exact day and hour.

Jesus provided us with a timeline of specific events that will signal His return. Afterward, He said, "Now, learn the parable from the fig tree: when its branch has already become tender and puts forth its leaves, you know that summer is near; so you too, when you see all these things, **recognize that He is near, right at the door**" (Matthew 24:32–33). What are those things?

- ✓ Beginning of birth pangs
- ✓ Abomination of desolation
- ✓ Great tribulation (initiated by the abomination of desolation)
- ✓ Heavens are shaken

Israel waited for the first coming of Christ with a fervent hope that it would be soon. Should we not anticipate His Second Coming in the same way? Watching for the signs? Waiting in a state of readiness with a willingness to endure? He comes as a thief only to those who live in darkness, not to those who know the signs and are prepared (1 Thess. 5:1–6). "Only the Father knows the day and hour" does not mean we are clueless regarding the time of His coming. Jesus Himself highlighted two Old Testament prophecies that must first be fulfilled: (1) the abomination of desolation and (2) the cataclysmic failure of heaven's luminaries. These two signs should be ingrained into our thinking processes—taught, understood, and acknowledged when they appear on the radar. Matthew 16:2–3 says, "When it is evening, you say, 'It will be fair weather, for the sky is red.' And in the morning, 'There will be a storm today, for the sky is red and threatening.' Do you know how to discern the appearance of the sky but cannot discern the signs of the times?" We have been given specific signs of Jesus returning. An awareness of those signs will strengthen our faith as we see them unfold, which is why they were revealed.

6. What did Jesus say in John 13:19?

Look at 1 Thessalonians 5:1–6 again. This paragraph immediately follows the rapture passage in 1 Thessalonians 4:13–17. Peter also taught that the day of the lord would come like a thief in the night (2 Pet. 3:10). And Paul connects that day to the return of Jesus in 2 Thessalonians 2:1–2.

7. To whom does Jesus come like a thief in the night?

8. What messages are they listening to?

9. How should we live before Jesus returns?

In 1 Thessalonians 5:1, Paul said it was unnecessary to reiterate his teaching on the "times and epochs" regarding the day of the Lord. They had already been taught. Referring to those in darkness, he said, "While they are saying, 'Peace and safety!' then destruction will come upon them suddenly like birth pangs upon a woman with child, and they shall not escape" (1 Thessalonians 5:3). Preachers who preach messages of "peace and safety" in a day of looming destruction are lulling their listeners to sleep with appealing lullabies. True prophets warn of the pending disaster, providing listeners with an opportunity to repent before God's corrective measures become necessary (Ps. 94:12). Evidence for this is found throughout the Old Testament (Jer. 6:11–14, Micah 3:5). False prophets refused to sound the alarm and warn God's people. Instead, they affirmed His blessings despite Israel's national waywardness, thwarting repentance and essentially solidifying their doom. To the church in Sardis, Jesus warned, "If you do not wake up, I will come like a thief, and you will not know at what hour I will come to you" (Revelation 3:3). Sardis was asleep, and their garments were soiled. They were in danger of being caught off guard by Christ's return.

> They have misled My people by saying, "Peace!" when there is no peace. And when anyone builds a wall, behold, they plaster it over with whitewash … Thus I will spend My wrath on the wall and on those who have plastered it over with whitewash; and I will say to you, "The wall is gone and its plasterers are gone, *along with* the prophets of Israel who prophesy to Jerusalem, and who see visions of peace for her when there is no peace," declares the LORD God. (Ezekiel 13:10, 15–16)

Ignorance is bliss until we find ourselves standing before the Judge of heaven and earth, and we all will in the day of the Lord—judgment day. At that moment, it doesn't matter what has been preached or what our preferences are. Neither ignorance nor false teaching will perpetuate a solace of peace for us in God's courtroom, only sobriety and preparedness (Eccl. 12:13). First Thessalonians 5:6 says, "Let us not sleep as others do, but let us be alert and sober." Know the signs. Be ready. Not because His coming is imminent but because it is certain.

The following passage, authored by Luke, is often used to say we do not know the signs of His coming, yet we do. Let's look at it together:

The first account I composed, Theophilus, about all that Jesus began to do and teach, until the day when He was taken up *to heaven*, after He had by the Holy Spirit given orders to the apostles whom He had chosen. To these He also presented Himself alive after His suffering, by many convincing proofs, appearing to them over *a period of* forty days and speaking of the things concerning the kingdom of God. Gathering them together, He commanded them not to leave Jerusalem, but to wait for what the Father had promised, "Which," *He said*, "you heard of from Me; for John baptized with water, but you will be baptized with the Holy Spirit not many days from now."

So when they had come together, they were asking Him, saying, "LORD, is it at this time You are restoring the kingdom to Israel?" He said to them, "It is not for you to know times or epochs which the Father has fixed by His own authority; but you will receive power when the Holy Spirit has come upon you; and you shall be My witnesses both in Jerusalem, and in all Judea and Samaria, and even to the remotest part of the earth." And after He had said these things, He was lifted up while they were looking on, and a cloud received Him out of their sight. And as they were gazing intently into the sky while He was going, behold, two men in white clothing stood beside them. They also said, "Men of Galilee, why do you stand looking into the sky? This Jesus, who has been taken up from you into heaven, will come in just the same way as you have watched Him go into heaven." (Acts 1:1–11)

10. What promise did Jesus recount to His disciples?

11. What subject were the disciples more interested in?

After forty days of teaching on the subject of His kingdom, Jesus transitioned to a different topic— the baptism and promise of the Holy Spirit. Yet the disciples remained fixated on the kingdom and attempted a correlated question, "Is it at this time You are restoring the kingdom to Israel?" Jesus replied, "It is not for you to know times or epochs which the Father has fixed by His own authority but you will receive power when the Holy Spirit has come upon you and you shall be My witnesses both in Jerusalem, and in all Judea and Samaria and even to the remotest part of the earth." The disciples were attempting to pinpoint the timing of Christ's return and Kingdom by asking if that would happen when the Spirit descended. They already had His timeline. The signs of His coming had been given. At this juncture, they were to wait for the Father's promise of the Holy Spirit. "But you will receive power when the Holy Spirit has come upon you; and you shall be My witnesses both in Jerusalem, and in all Judea and Samaria, and even to the remotest part of the earth." In effect, the next event on God's calendar was not His return or the revelation of His kingdom. It was the baptism of the Holy Spirit. Proclaiming the Gospel to all nations was a necessary prequel to the day of the Lord and they needed His anointing.

God is omniscient (all-knowing)—a Trinity comprised of the Father, Son, and Holy Spirit. According to Scripture, God the Father has a position of authority and knowledge unique to the Son and the Holy Spirit. For instance, in John 5:19, He said, "The Son can do nothing of Himself, unless *it is* something He sees the Father doing; for whatever the Father does, these things the Son also does in like manner." In 1 Corinthians 15:24, Jesus submits the kingdom to His Father after He puts all enemies under His feet. And the book of Revelation opens with:

> The Revelation of Jesus Christ, which God gave Him to show to His bond-servants, the things which must soon take place; and He sent and communicated *it* by His angel to His bond-servant John, who testified to the word of God and to the testimony of Jesus Christ, *even* to all that he saw. (Revelation 1:1–2)

12. Who supplied Jesus with the revelation for His bond-servants?

Understanding that God the Father is the revelator and ultimate sovereign, explains the phrase, "only the Father knows the day and hour" and Jesus telling His disciples, "It is not for you to know times or epochs which the Father has fixed by His own authority." Jesus isn't privy to the precise timing of His return but does know the signs, which is why He said, "When you see all of these things, recognize that He is near, right at the door" (Matthew 24:33).

Application

It is to our advantage to know the signs of Christ's coming. The sons of Issachar were men who "understood the times," knowing what to do (1 Chron. 12:32). As "sons and daughters of the light," we too should be alert to the times, knowing what to do and how to respond. Then the day will not "overtake" us like a thief as it will those living in ignorance and darkness.

In 1 Thessalonians 5:8, Paul wrote, "Since we are of the day, let us be sober, having put on the breastplate of faith and love, and as a helmet, the hope of salvation." Sobriety is an exercise of self-control over relentless, wandering hearts and selfish, wayward flesh. The breastplate of faith and love protects our hearts. The helmet of the hope of salvation protects our minds. "Let us be sober" means to be aware of our sinful desires that are in conflict with the righteousness of God. Our sins do not define us; they only destroy us. Paul elaborated on this armor in Ephesians 6:10–11, "Be strong in the LORD and in the strength of His might. Put on the full armor of God, so that you will be able to stand firm against the schemes of the devil." Know the signs of the times. Exercise faith and live in the light of God's truth, separating from the deceptive, destructive deeds of darkness (1 John 1:5–7). Take up the full armor of God. Everyday.

Romans 13:11–14 says, "Do this, knowing the time, that it is already the hour for you to awaken from sleep; for now salvation is nearer to us than when we believed. The night is almost gone, and the day is near. Therefore let us lay aside the deeds of darkness and put on the armor of light. Let us behave properly as in the day, not in carousing and drunkenness, not in sexual promiscuity and sensuality, not in strife and jealousy. But put on the LORD Jesus Christ, and make no provision for the flesh in regard to *its* lusts." David wrote, "Depart from evil and do good, so you will abide forever" (Psalm 37:27). Putting on the LORD Jesus Christ and our armor of light means separating from the deeds of darkness in preparation for His return. Are you willing?

YES   NO

Day One Summary

Jesus gave us a timeline of signs. Then He said, "When you see all these things, I am near, right at the door. Heaven and earth will pass away, but My words shall not pass away." We can believe the Word of God and the timeline of Jesus to be both accurate and dependable. While only God the Father knows the day and hour, God the Son knows the signs of His return and shared them for our benefit.

Day Two: Just Like the Days of Noah

The title of this Bible study is *Just Like the Days of Noah* because Jesus compares the day of His coming to the days of Noah. And Lot (Luke 17:28). God judged against the world in Noah's day and destroyed all but one family (1 Pet. 3:20, Gen. 6:17). In the days of Lot, He destroyed two cities "reducing *them* to ashes, having made them an example to those who would live ungodly *lives* thereafter" (2 Peter 2:6). What solicited such harsh judgments? Let's find out. You might want to review your Week Seven Worksheet on Matthew 24:32–41. Then, answer the following:

1. **How did Jesus describe the days of Noah?**

   - The people were

   - They did not

Jesus described normal activities continuing until Noah entered the ark and "the flood came" (Matt. 24:38–39; Luke 17:27). Evidently, a sense of normalcy, though perhaps limited, will continue until Jesus returns as well. Isn't that the point of the comparison? It is when Jesus returns that ordinary activities completely cease and God's extraordinary acts of renewal commence (Acts 3:19–21, Isa. 66:22, 2 Pet. 3:13).

2. According to Matthew 24:39, what was lacking prior to the flood?

Noah did all that God commanded (Gen. 6:22, 7:5). Can you and I say the same? He was a preacher of righteousness who, along with seven others, survived God's decision to "blot out from the face of the land every living thing" (Genesis 7:4). They were the only ones to escape God's wrath (2 Pet. 2:5). The world had lost a right "understanding" and refused to acknowledge their Creator as sovereign—the one who rightfully judges His creation and will (Acts 17:31). They rejected God and Noah, God's messenger. Disregarded both. Ignored them entirely, choosing instead to live depraved lifestyles and worship lifeless idols (Eph. 5:3–5). They did not believe God would destroy the earth or that their behavior solicited His judgment (Gen. 6:6). Therefore, the earth declined God's ark of protection only to be swept away by the flood. David wrote, "The LORD sat as King at the flood; yes the LORD sits as King forever" (Psalm 29:10). Many today reject God's existence as our Creator and righteous judge, and refuse to believe His ark of provision (Jesus Christ) is the only way of salvation.

3. What does Proverbs 9:10 say about understanding?

A right understanding begins with accepting God as He revealed, "I am who I am" (Exodus 3:14). We respect, reverence, and fear God for who He is rather than who we want Him to be. We cannot redefine God and His attributes. To do so is to fashion gods with our own hands, false gods, lifeless idols designed to gratify sinful, fleshly lusts (Isa. 2:8, Psa. 115:1–8). Idols cannot hear or answer us because they are not alive. They did not create us. We created them.

> Listen to the word of the LORD, O sons of Israel, for the LORD has a case against the inhabitants of the land, because there is no faithfulness or kindness or knowledge of God in the land. There is swearing, deception, murder, stealing and adultery. They employ violence, so that bloodshed follows bloodshed. Therefore the land mourns, and everyone who lives in it languishes along with the beasts of the field and the birds of the sky, and also the fish of the sea disappear. (Hosea 4:1–3)

4. **What was missing in Hosea's day?**

My people [Israel] are destroyed for lack of knowledge. Because you have rejected knowledge, I also will reject you from being My priest. Since you have forgotten the law of your God, I also will forget your children. (Hosea 4:6)

5. **Whose laws are forgotten when we reject God?**

6. **Consequently, who will God forget?**

Hosea was a contemporary of Isaiah. Both prophets warned Israel of pending disaster unless the people returned to God. "They have stopped giving heed to the LORD" (Hosea 4:10). God did not create us to destroy us. We bring destruction upon ourselves and our children when we reject Him. If we expel God from our homes, lives, institutions, and churches, then we will quickly lose sight of His righteousness. His laws clarify the difference between righteous and unrighteous pursuits. How can we follow Christ without regard for His righteous ways? How can we expect to reign with Him in the kingdom of God if we refuse to embrace His righteousness? We can't. And we won't. Psalm 119:73 says, "Your hands made me and fashioned me; give me understanding, that I may learn Your commandments."

God's righteousness protects the blessings of life, such as peace, prosperity, joy, and freedom (Isa. 32:17). His Word promotes equality, love, and reconciliation. Is there anything wrong with these blessings? No. But they are lost when we reject God and His kingdom laws. And how do we lose such understanding? False teachers. False prophets and pastors propagating error. It is our willingness to believe their lies and unify around popular, godless pursuits that erodes peace, incentivizes crime, and promotes violence. Genesis 6:5 reveals that the wickedness of humanity was great in the days of Noah, and their hearts were consumed by evil. This perilous state was the by-product of making erroneous choices and losing sight of God as their Creator and judge over His creation.

Romans 1:24–32 states that when we exchange the truth of God for a lie and worship the creature rather than the Creator, God gives us over to our degrading passions and depraved minds. "Their women exchanged the natural function for that which is unnatural and in the same way also the men abandoned the natural function of the woman and burned in their desire toward one another, men with men committing indecent acts and receiving in their own persons the due penalty of their error" (Romans 1:26–27). Sounds familiar? How long will God permit the unhealthy sexual activity we see escalating today? Or the rising violence? What about human trafficking? Child and spousal abuse, abortion, infanticide, greed, deceit, and an insatiable lust for wealth? All these are the by-products of egotistical self-worship and narcissistic gratification—outliers of sinful flesh. Listen, choices have consequences, and our world is choosing to ignore the reality of where such blatant sins are taking us. A right understanding of God and His righteousness is so far gone today, that His corrective response could be the only solution of remedy. Isaiah 26:9 says, "When the earth experiences Your judgments, the inhabitants of the world learn righteousness."

We can pray for a sweeping revival, but God may have already summoned His angelic army, prepared and assigned to the day of the Lord (Matt. 16:27). God maintains and reigns from a throne of righteousness as a Trinity cohesively supporting what is right and comprehensively judging against what is not. This union of the Father, Son, and Holy Spirit can see what we promote and are participating in. Together, they will faithfully exact a justice through judgments that will correct the world's waywardness exactly as Scripture reveals.

> These are *the records of* the generations of Noah. Noah was a righteous man, blameless in his time; Noah walked with God. Noah became the father of three sons: Shem, Ham, and Japheth. Now the earth was corrupt in the sight of God, and the earth was filled with violence. God looked on the earth, and behold, it was corrupt; for all flesh had corrupted their way upon the earth. Then God said to Noah, "The end of all flesh has come before Me; for the earth is filled with violence because of them; and behold, I am about to destroy them with the earth. (Genesis 6:9–13)

Corruption and violence are the insatiable thieves of righteousness and peace.

7. How was Noah distinguished as different?

8. Describe the earth's inhabitants at that time?

9. What is said about "all flesh"?

We are left to speculate about Noah's "behind the scenes" family dynamics. Not in regard to Noah and his sons but their wives and the extended families of their wives. Did they struggle with leaving parents and siblings behind? Were they ridiculed for associating with a heretic family who warned of a cataclysmic flood? And what did the world think of Noah preaching that the ark was God's only way of salvation? Difficult choices had to be made, but all three women decided to take refuge in the ark with their husbands – Noah's sons. Now, let's compare Lot's family:

> Then the *two* men [angels] said to Lot, "Whom else have you here? A son-in-law, and your sons, and your daughters, and whomever you have in the city, bring *them* out of the place; for we are about to destroy this place, because their outcry has become so great before the Lord that the Lord has sent us to destroy it." Lot went out and spoke to his sons-in-law, who were to marry his daughters, and said, "Up, get out of this place, for the Lord will destroy the city." But he appeared to his sons-in-law to be jesting. When morning dawned, the angels urged Lot, saying, "Up, take your wife and your two daughters who are here, or you will be swept away in the punishment of the city." (Genesis 19:12–15)

10. How did the sons-in-law respond?

11. Who left the city with Lot?

The sons or sons-in-law didn't go, and Lot's wife disobeyed God's command as they left. Even Lot hesitated when the angels told him to leave (Gen. 19:15–16). We don't see the same resilience displayed in Lot's family as the Scripture reveals regarding Noah's. When it came time to make the difficult choices, their faith faltered and fractured. Even when Lot was directed to flee to the mountains, he pleaded for a city residence instead. Perhaps his love for the conveniences and material wealth of trade is why he never left Sodom, even though he was "oppressed by the sensual conduct of unprincipled men" and "felt his righteous soul tormented day after day with their lawless deeds" (2 Peter 2:7–8). The difference also may have been that Noah, a preacher of righteousness, was more vocal about his faith. Lot was more reserved; therefore, his family was less committed (2 Pet. 2:5). A silent faith is often a compromised faith, lacking conviction and therefore largely ineffective. It is a hidden light that benefits no one else, including those we love the most (Matt. 5:14–16).

We cannot control the choices of others but we can determine ours. Lot's faith was weak. He loved the bustle of a city more than a mountain sunrise, even though he was surrounded by sin, oppressive enough for the Lord to say, "The outcry of Sodom and Gomorrah is indeed great, and their sin is exceedingly grave" (Genesis 18:20). Whether we live in the mountains, suburbs, or city, all of God's elect are called to "come out of her My people!" (Jer. 51:45; 2 Cor. 6:17; Rev. 18:4). Be willing to separate from worldly sinful pursuits, share the light of truth, and reach those seeking salvation. "For you were formerly darkness, but now you are Light in the Lord; walk as children of Light" (Ephesians 5:8).

Make no mistake, love characterizes our Creator and the good news of His Gospel. Because God is love, He provided the way of salvation. God's love embodies Christians through the Holy

Spirit and should exude from our lives (John 13:35, Gal. 5:22–23). Jesus taught that justice, mercy, and faithfulness are the weightier provisions of the law (Matt. 23:23). Mercy and grace must be at the forefront of our thinking and relationships (Heb. 5:1–2) but never to the point of compromising the Gospel of Jesus Christ or being compromised ourselves. That is a bridge too far and a lifetime of waste that you and I will give an account for (John 12:48, Matt. 16:27). Be intentional regarding the kingdom of God and sharing the love of Jesus. Come out from under the cultural mandates of this world. Be a light!

Years ago, I encountered a man standing on the courtroom steps of my city with a microphone, preaching a somber, chilling message. His audience included people such as myself arriving and leaving the justice building for traffic violations. I approached and suggested he should include God's grace in his message, to which he promptly announced over a loudspeaker, "Now, what we have here, ladies and gentlemen, is a 'bona fide Jezebel.'" I was not given the opportunity for rebuttal, so I ambled away slowly, somewhat wounded. I was also saddened by his presentation being so completely void of compassion. Folks, we have a Gospel of grace and good news to deliver (Heb. 4:2)! Judgment is certainly an element, but apart from God's love and forgiveness, there is no Gospel of good news.

Application

The world is pursuing what pleases the eyes rather than what is right in the sight of God (Jude 21:25). And many within church gatherings are only listening to what tickles the ears (2 Tim. 4:3). We are exchanging truth for lies to gratify lusts of the flesh (Rom. 1:25). "For all that is in the world, the lust of the flesh and the lust of the eyes and the boastful pride of life, is not from the Father, but is from the world" (1 John 2:16). When you see the world rejecting God and living by fleshly desires, seduced by sin—open the Word of God. Read the truth provided by the Holy Spirit out loud! You will find the strength that you need for holy living as His light on this dark planet (2 Tim. 3:16, James 1:22–24, Phil. 2:15). And make no mistake, that is our calling (2 Tim. 1:9). We are to set ourselves apart for Christ as He has set Himself apart for us. The Scriptures are absolutely *filled* with helpful exhortations in assistance, such as the following:

> Therefore if you have been raised up with Christ, keep seeking the things above, where Christ is, seated at the right hand of God. Set your mind on the things above, not on the things that are on earth. For you have died and your life is hidden with Christ in God. When Christ, who is our life, is revealed, then you also will be revealed with Him in glory. Therefore consider the members of your earthly body as dead to immorality, impurity, passion, evil desire, and greed, which amounts to idolatry. For it is because of these things that the wrath of God will come upon the sons of disobedience, and in them you also once walked, when you were living in them. But now you also, put them all aside: anger, wrath, malice, slander, *and* abusive speech from your mouth. (Colossians 3:1–8)

12. How would setting your mind on "things above" affect your lifestyle?

Think About It

Prior to Christ's return, the earth will experience a push for global unity to attain peace, prosperity, and security worldwide. Treaties will be signed. Solutions will be applauded. Compromises will be made. This scenario played out after the flood at the Tower of Babel in the plain of Shinar, the birthplace and cradle of Babylon. Though Noah, Ham, Shem, and Japheth had seen God's wrath firsthand, their descendants had not. Later generations needed their patriarchal parents to be steadfast, godly testaments of righteousness. Instead, God's Genesis 3:15 covenant and edict to fill and subdue the earth was forsaken. Forgotten. Knowledge and understanding were lost, so the Lord acted and judged against their united defiance. He descended from heaven and confused the language of the "whole earth." He separated the descendants of Noah because they had opted out of establishing God's kingdom to build their own (Gen. 11:4–8). When Jesus returns, He will again descend from heaven to judge against the world kingdoms and separate the godly from the ungodly. At that point, those who lack understanding will acquire it, but it will be too late. Just like the days of Noah. And Lot.

> The fear of the Lord is the beginning of wisdom; **a good understanding** have all those who do *His commandments*; His praise endures forever. (Psalm 111:10)

Day Two Summary

If you haven't already, you might want to read the prologue to this study regarding the days of Noah. Our world has lost a right understanding of God. Consequently, we are currently sliding into an abyss of bizarre, violent, and depraved behavior. We have disconnected from the source and sustainer of life itself, Jesus Christ, who embodied the Word of God and now sits at the right hand of the Father, prepared to judge His creation. As we demand ownership of our own bodies, killing and abusing our offspring, living as if there is no accountability for these actions or carnal affections, we are, in effect, soliciting God to intervene. If our day is not just like the days of Noah— it is far worse.

Day Three: Taken or Left

Jesus compared the time of His return to the days of Noah, relating normal activities continuing until the flood came. Not for Noah's family, however, who spent years constructing an ark larger than the length of a football field. When Noah wasn't cutting trees and assembling timbers, he searched for an audience willing to listen (2 Pet. 2:5). Noah's life was not "normal." Regardless of how odd he appeared to peers and family, Genesis 6:8–9 says, "Noah found favor in the eyes of the Lord—Noah was a righteous man, blameless [perfect, having integrity] in his time; Noah walked with God." Walking with God means to journey in His direction, which explains the downfall of Noah's generation. Instead of walking with God, they walked away from Him. "Teach me Your way, O LORD; **I will walk in Your truth**; unite my heart to fear Your name" (Psalm 86:11).

We can safely assume Noah was never voted most likely to succeed, yet he was successful in the eyes of God, the only eyes that matter. He walked with God rather than hand in hand with his generation, singing, "We are the world" or "I did it my way." When we do it our way or devise schematics for walking with the world and God simultaneously, hoping for acceptance or persuasive inroads, we are not walking with God (1 John 2:15–17). And if we are not walking with God, then we are walking away from Him. "You adulteresses, do you not know that friendship with the world is hostility toward God? Therefore whoever wishes to be a friend of the world makes himself an enemy of God" (James 4:4). God's elect will never fit into an atheistic, immoral, greedy, narcissistic culture operating against heaven's righteousness. Why would we even want to? Do you fit in? I hope not.

YES   NO

In the decades required for Noah to build that ark, ample opportunity would have been extended to his generation for repentance, but they did not repent. They refused to believe a flood of judgment was coming or that the ark was God's sole provision for salvation. Listen, if the world makes you feel insignificant, foolish, and close-minded, remember Noah. Do you think he was esteemed for his faithfulness to obey the Word of God or to preach the truth? Not by the world, he wasn't. Hebrews 11:7 says, "By faith Noah, being warned *by God* about things not yet seen, in reverence prepared an ark for the salvation of his household, by which he condemned the world, and became an heir of the righteousness which is according to faith." Because he walked with God, Noah built the ark. As a result, his family was saved and he became an heir of God—saved by faith.

1. According to Matthew 24:39, when did the people of Noah's day finally understand?

When that single door on the ark closed, the time to repent had expired. Any opportunity to choose life over death at that moment no longer existed. In Matthew 24:40–41, Jesus depicts a similar scenario, and only those in God's ark (Jesus Christ) will be saved.

2. In Matthew 24:40–41, what happens?

The coming of the Son of Man will be just like the days of Noah. People were left standing outside of the ark when God's judgement came, just as people will remain on the ground when Jesus returns. This segment of Scripture has become controversial because if Jesus is referring to the saints being caught up as Paul taught in 1 Thessalonians 4:17, then His timeline contradicts the dispensational pre-tribulation rapture theory. Let's consider

Taken *paralambano*: "to receive near, associate with, take with, accept"

Left *aphiemi*: "to send away, forsake, a separation"

the context. Jesus compares the days of His return to the days of Noah. And Lot (Luke 17:26–31). The righteous were saved immediately before God's wrath, not years or months prior. The unrighteous were left for judgment. Look at the Greek word meanings above for "taken" and "left."

3. What are your thoughts?

Should we ignore clear revelation in preference for the theoretical? Matthew Henry, a prominent theologian from the 1800s, interprets verses 40–41 as the rapture of the saints. It wasn't until after the mid-1800s that the view of a pre-tribulation rapture gained momentum, and Bible commentators began to interpret it differently (see appendix "Rapture"). Some dispensationalists interpret those verses as the unrighteous being taken for judgment while the righteous are left. They employ the parable of wheat and tares in Matthew 13:24–30, speaking of the wicked being removed before the righteous. Yet in that parable, Jesus reveals the timing to be the consummation of the age which may refer to the wicked being extracted before God's recreation of heaven and earth (Matt. 13:40–43).

On their last night together, Jesus promised His disciples, "If I go and prepare a place for you, I will come again and receive you to Myself, that where I am, *there* you may be also" (John 14:3). The Greek word Jesus used for "receive" in John 14:3 is the same word He used in Matthew 24:40–41, translated as "taken" [*paralambano*], which means "to receive near, associate with, take with, accept." When Jesus utilized the same word to say, "I will come again and receive [*paralambano*] you to Myself," as He did when He said, "One will be taken [*paralambano*] and one will be left," shouldn't we interpret verses 40–41 as Jesus speaking of the rapture and gathering His elect?

Let's look again at the rapture reference in 1 Thessalonians 4:13–18:

But we do not want you to be uninformed, brethren, about those who are asleep, so that you may not grieve as do the rest who have no hope. For if we believe that Jesus died and rose again, even so God will bring with Him those who have fallen asleep in Jesus. For this we say to you by the word of the LORD, that we who are alive and remain until the coming of the LORD, will not precede those who have fallen asleep. For the LORD Himself will descend from heaven with a shout, with the voice of the archangel and with the trumpet of God, and the dead in Christ shall rise first. Then we who are alive and remain shall be caught up together with them in the clouds to meet the LORD in the air, and so we shall always be with the LORD. Therefore comfort one another with these words.

> caught up *harpazo*: "seized"

4. **Complete the order of events in 1 Thessalonians 4:13–18.**

- The Lord descends from heaven with _____

- God brings with Him those who have _____

- _____ shall rise first.

- Then we who are alive and _____ shall be _____

  _____

In 1 Thessalonians 4:13–18, Jesus is announced with a shout and a trumpet as He descends from heaven. Again, this does not describe a silent, private return. The righteous are resurrected first. Graves release bodies from around the world! Then, those who are "alive and remain [after the great tribulation] will be caught up with them in the clouds to meet the LORD in the air." Can we even begin to fathom this revelation of Jesus and His saints (Col. 3:4)? We've covered it already; but just to reiterate, when Jesus comes again, He replaces our worn-out, debilitated body suits with those of righteous perfection and immortal quality (1 Cor. 15:50–54, Phil. 3:20–21). That's worth repeating, rehearsing, and remembering, especially for those of us who suffer from diseases and afflictions. Jesus returns for His saints to resurrect, rapture, reunite, and restore them as originally designed—in His image (1 John 3:2, Gen. 1:27).

5. **What does Philippians 3:20–21 say?**

6. According to Acts 3:19–21, when does Jesus return?

7. Look at Genesis 19:12–16, the record of Sodom and Gomorrah's destruction. Why did the angels come for Lot and his family?

8. How were they rescued (v. 16)?

Lot and his family were rescued right before the destruction of Sodom and Gomorrah. Angels "seized" their hands. The elect will be caught up or seized prior to God's wrath. Jesus is coming

> seized *chazaq*: "to fasten upon, seize"

back for His elect! Those who have died before us will be the first to meet Him in the air. Then, the saints who remain alive will be raptured. This gathering is something we will celebrate and enjoy for all eternity!

Just think of it. No more diseases, handicaps, or pain. No more struggles with the flesh! Jesus took all of that to the cross on our behalf and declared, "It is finished." Yet we continue to deal with ailments and sinful inclinations because sin remains caustic in our world and flesh. When Jesus returns, this dramatically changes which is why we can live by faith in the promises of what is to come and why we are taught to fix our hope on the saving grace yet to be revealed (1 Pet. 1:13). "And everyone who has this hope *fixed* on Him purifies himself, just as He is pure" (1 John 3:3).

Dispensationalists who do interpret verses 40–41 as a rescue, contend it is only the Jewish elect that are being saved. In fact, they also believe Christ's timeline in Matthew 24 applies to the Jews only. For either to be reliable interpretations, the Bible should elucidate two rapture rescues of the saints, therefore two returns of Christ and two righteous resurrections – one for the Jews and another for the rest of Christendom. But it doesn't. Additionally, they claim Matthew was Jewish, writing to a Jewish audience at the time, so Christ's teaching is selectively Jewish. Yet every other New Testament book of Scripture was written by Jewish authors except for Luke's gospel and his book of Acts. Are we to segregate God's audience by the ethnic origin of a book's author? Or delineate what teaching applies to whom based upon the nationality of the congregation receiving God's truth?

The church of Jesus Christ is both Jew and Gentile. We are saved, sealed, and sanctified forever as His glorious kingdom of priests who have overcome the world, sin, and Satan by the blood of the same Lamb of God (Rev. 12:11). We overcome together because Jesus overcame for all of us. We have a Redeemer who will return to resurrect and rapture His saints prior to His reign, restoration, and renewal of heaven and earth. This is what Scripture declares—One God—One Kingdom. One return. One resurrection of the righteous. One rapture rescue. One gathering for the millennial reign of Christ. What will it be like to stand with Jesus Christ as He presents His kingdom to the Father that you and I belong to? I can't wait to find out!

Yet those who have rejected God's Redeemer will themselves be rejected, excluded from the peaceful reign of Jesus Christ and unable to experience restoration or renewal (Matt. 10:32). What will that be like? I can't fathom the regret or heartache.

Paul wrote this to Timothy:

> It is a trustworthy statement: For if we died with Him, we will also live with Him; If we endure, we will also reign with Him; If we deny Him, He also will deny us; If we are faithless, He remains faithful, for He cannot deny Himself. (2 Timothy 2:11–13)

Application

The rapture of Christ's church is a divisive topic—almost as divisive as politics. Please be respectful of the miscellany of diverse opinions. It is much too easy to fall into the trap of dogmatically debating and offending one another. Instead, savor the Savior and blessing of His revelatory and promissory Word. Jesus has come and is coming again to fulfill every prophetic detail as written, which may differ from our interpretations. Listen patiently to the insights of others, maintaining His command to love one another (John 13:34). We all have more to learn and gain from one another—we all do. Anyone who assumes the position of "knowing it all," is not operating according to the design of God's body of saints. Jesus is the Head. We are each a member of His body, individuals of the whole with complementary giftings (Eph. 4:1–13). This study was not written to cause division or enflame debates regarding the rapture of the saints. The appointment was to excavate and examine Matthew 24, the timeline of Jesus Christ. His timeline will challenge everyone's thinking and certainly has mine! If there is room for enlarging our minds, let God's Word be the catalyst under the direction of the Holy Spirit. Not a book or apocalyptic novel. Not a preacher. Or personal preference. Trust what the Scriptures reveal. Trust the living and written Word of God.

Day Three Summary

Jesus said that when He returns, some will be taken, and others will be left. Is He speaking of the church rapture? Consider the context and Greek words being utilized. Cross-reference other Scriptures such as John 14:3, where Jesus promised to receive us (*paralambano*) when He comes again, as He was received (*paralambano*) when He ascended into heaven; 1 Thessalonians 4:17, where Paul taught that the saints remaining are caught up (seized); and Genesis 19:12–16 describing Lot and his family being seized by angels. All these Scriptures lend credence to interpreting verses 40–41 as the rapture of saints when Christ returns to reveal His kingdom—after the great tribulation.

Day Four: Be Ready

Today, we look at another parable in conjunction with Christ's timeline. It follows the fig tree parable where Jesus said, "When you see all these things, recognize that He is near, right at the door" (Matthew 24:33). How do we know when the coming of Jesus is near? What signs did He say we would see? The beginning of birth pangs in verses 1–14, Daniel's abomination of desolation in verses 15–26, and, finally, the heavens being shaken in verses 29–31. Jesus provided specific signs of His coming for our benefit. Specific signs! Yet only God the Father knows the exact timing. "Of that day and hour no one knows, not even the angels of heaven, nor the Son, but the Father alone."

Jesus also compared the day of His coming to the days of Noah. And Lot (Luke 17:28–30). People were eating, drinking, and marrying but without a right understanding of God. The same will be true when Jesus returns. Have we lost a right understanding of God today (Psa. 94:8–11)? Consider this: How many people believe Jesus Christ is returning to judge against the unrighteousness of humanity? How many Christians willingly sin as if it is inconsequential and there is no accountability? How many pulpits even mention Jesus returning or are actively preparing their congregations for the great tribulation or any tribulation at all?

After His fig tree illustration, Jesus compared two servants: one faithful and the other evil. Please look at Matthew 24:42–51 on your second Week Seven Worksheet at the end of this week, filling in the blanks on the right side. Let's finish strong today and tomorrow! Are you ready? I am.

1. **"Therefore" evokes a conclusion in verse 42. What is it?**

> alert *gregoreuo*: "watch, stay awake, be vigilant"

2. **What is the benefit of staying alert (vv. 43, 45)?**

We may not know the exact day or hour, but Jesus gave us specific signs and told us to stay "alert." As those signs transpire, the faithful slave should prepare the household entrusted to him or her by the master. The "master's household" refers to a church or family household, and the slave is the shepherd of either one. This parable is directed toward those in leadership positions tasked with staying alert for the sake of those placed in their care by Jesus.

The timeline of Christ is an invaluable resource recorded in the New Testament for the benefit of the elect. God did not leave us in the dark. We have Jesus, the timeline of His return, and the Holy Spirit residing within us—all provisional graces lavished upon the kingdom for purposes of salvation and sanctification as we await Christ's return. Recognize and fully invest yourself in these graces.

While the "coming of Shiloh" has been eclipsed today by other kingdom topics, the truth is the return of Jesus Christ is an unmatched, pinnacle event that will supersede anything humanity has witnessed or is capable of experiencing. All of God's creation will be dramatically altered (Acts 3:20–21). Our spiritual rebirth will be realized in the blink of an eye (Gen. 49:8–12, 1 Cor. 13:12). Emmanuel will descend as the light of heaven's glory! The Son of God, along with His saints, will then be revealed. Heaven and earth will be renewed, revamped—recreated. These are exciting promises! If we disregard the opportunity to study and know the signs of Christ's coming, then we are missing the significance of their revelatory purpose. We will find ourselves stumbling and unable to "feed" or sustain those under our care at the "proper time."

3. Which slave pays attention to the signs of His master's coming?

4. How is the faithful slave blessed?

Remember yesterday's lesson regarding the faithfulness of Noah? Hebrews 11:6–7 says, "And without faith it is impossible to please *Him*, for he who comes to God must believe that He is and *that* He is a rewarder of those who seek Him. By faith Noah, being warned *by God* about things not yet seen, in reverence prepared an ark for the salvation of his household, by which he condemned the world, and became an heir of the righteousness which is according to faith."

5. From Hebrews 11:6–7 above, what was the outcome of Noah's faith?

The beginning of birth pangs, as Christ described them, such as wars, famine, earthquakes, and persecution, have been occurring for ages. These preparatory pains are like Braxton Hicks contractions, reminding us of a forthcoming birth while soliciting our readiness. Think about how long the earth waited for the first coming of Jesus following God's Genesis 3:15 covenant promise. When He finally did come, God's people had endured four hundred years of silence after Malachi prophesied, "I am going to send you Elijah the prophet before the coming of the great and terrible day of the Lord" (Malachi 4:5). Whose voice ended the four hundred years of silence? John the Baptist in the spirit of Elijah (Matt. 11:14). By divine appointment, the day and hour for Jesus to come—came. Was anyone still actively watching, and waiting in anticipation of the Messiah?

On April 8, 1966, *Time* Magazine startled America with their cover: "Is God Dead?" It was perceived that God was indifferent or incapable of intervening in the sufferings of humanity. Those perceptions led to the disparaging question, "Is God dead?" The author claimed there was no longer evidence of God's presence, so he concluded that the earth had been abandoned. Is that how Israel felt during their four hundred years of silence? Perhaps. They too might have wondered, "Where is God? Why hasn't He saved us? Is He dead?"

6. In Luke 2:25–26, who looked for the Messiah and redemption of Israel?

7. In Luke 2:36–38, who else?

8. What about those in regions beyond the temple? See Matthew 2:1–2.

A representation of Jewish males, females, and even Eastern astrologers continued to believe in God's prophetic promises, watching and waiting for their fulfillment. Undoubtedly, both Joseph and Mary anticipated the reception of the Messiah as well. This lengthy period of waiting is again reminiscent of the storm the disciples encountered with Jesus in their boat. They yelled, "Lord, do you not care that we are perishing?" Jesus countered with a question of His own, "Where is your faith?"

9. Describe the thinking of the evil slave in verse 48.

If the head of a house knew when a thief was coming, he would have fortified his home. Those alert to the signs will be prepared and able to prepare others. "But you, brethren, are not in darkness, that the day would overtake you like a thief" (1 Thessalonians 5:4). Too many families today only have one faithful believer committed to the home front. Tragically, many more have none at all.

10. According to the definition of *evil*, what pursuits characterize the life of this servant?

> evil *kakos*: "worthless, inwardly foul"

11. How does Luke 21:34–36 describe alertness?

How do we steward and feed our families? Allow me to make a few suggestions. These have proven track records that may or may not fit into your family schedules. If they don't, pray for God to guide you otherwise. The idea is to instill into your family a willingness to exalt Christ by separating from ungodliness in preparation for His coming.

➤ Design a family altar time (Deut. 6:4–7). If your children don't readily sit still, then keep prayer and Bible reading short and sweet. Lead the family gently into a grace-loving relationship with Christ. Christ is both gentle and humble, never forcing His way into our lives but guiding us when we willingly receive Him (Matt. 11:29). Christianity becomes merely a religion when we lose sight of the relationships we are to nurture and develop.

Family altar time is an opportunity to share how Jesus has affected your life. Read the Bible with your children and allow God's Word to teach them rightly, then bear witness to the credibility of His truth by your example. Even if your children refuse to listen, they will be influenced by your testimony of faith. Ideally, the head of the home will take the lead in this effort. But whether it is the husband or the wife who is faithful, the children should be taught the ways of the Lord. Christ commissioned all of us to go and make disciples (Matt. 28:19–20). That challenge begins at home as an edict for both parents.

➤ Listen to one another and be sensitive to the obstacles that your children are facing. This generation is being force-fed a barrage of ungodly messages and struggling to decipher truth from error. Listen to their struggles. Build relationships by spending time together, unplugged from the consuming circuitry of electronic devices. Camp, sing, hike, play games, read good books together, etc. Hug them. Ask questions. They need you!

➤ Operate in the realm of grace and truth. Knowledge and a conviction of truth are the fabrics of a good judge, and the saints of God will one day judge the nations alongside Jesus Christ. Stand by kingdom truth without condemning. We don't know the heart or pain of another, so forgiveness and grace should commandeer every encounter rather than harsh judgments unless biblical exceptions apply. Judgment is ultimately God's responsibility, and He will rightly take that lead in the day of the Lord.

➤ Involve your family in Kingdom service. This is one of the best ways to participate in the Great Commission and keep life's pursuits in a proper perspective. Go to church together and begin to discover and develop everyone's spiritual gifting.

➢ Pray with your family regularly. Relationships are dependent upon open dialogue and meaningful communication. If your children see you talk to God, they will too. They will learn what it means to be in a real relationship with God. Got a problem? Let's pray. Need some direction? Let's pray. Excited about an achievement? Let's thank God for the success.

Application

No two families are the same, so please don't compare yours to others. Each family carries its own DNA blueprint with its own distinct struggles and experiences. Our backgrounds, handicaps, and strengths all differ. Access to educational and financial support varies profusely. Comparisons will only open the door for assumptions and jealousies that hinder us from focusing on the will of God for our particular family. My friends, raising a family is not a competition. It is a journey, a spiritual quest that requires resilient courage and raw faith in our heavenly Father to lead us individually.

When you experience a storm on the home front—and we all will—plant your feet in the center of that turbulence with your faith dependent solely upon God. The eye of a storm is a provisional place of quiet rest despite the fiercest winds circulating the perimeter. Stand before His throne and intercede for your family, one by one, day after day, until victory is secured through your Advocate (1 John 2:1). Storms do pass. In the interim, ask for guidance through these home-front battles because assistance is available. If you are the only Christian in your family—male or female, young or old—then you are the intercessor appointed by God to be there. Don't see that position as isolating and hopeless but one of God's anointing (1 Cor. 7:12–15). God's desire is for all to come to repentance (2 Pet. 3:9). Pray for your Heavenly Father to reveal His Son to each and every member of your family. Then stand back and watch the salvation of the Lord, "For nothing will be impossible with God" (Luke 1:37)!

> This is the confidence which we have before Him, that, if we ask anything according to His will, He hears us. And if we know that He hears us in whatever we ask, we know that we have the requests which we have asked from Him. (1 John 5:14–15)

We are in the last days, my friend. "In these last days [God] has spoken to us in His Son, whom He appointed heir of all things, through whom also He made the world" (Hebrews 1:2). There are differing opinions as to when Jesus will return and what our responsibilities are in the interim. Regardless of where you land, we should all desire to be found faithful when He comes. Maybe those around you lack the commitment to live a life that truly honors Christ, but I hope and pray it matters to you.

"He has told you, O man, what is good; and what does the LORD require of you but to do justice, to love kindness, and to walk humbly with your God?" (Micah 6:8). What are your thoughts about practicing justice and kindness and walking humbly with God? These fruits of the spirit are evidence of the Holy Spirit abiding within and directing your steps. Do you possess them? Today's culture promotes cheating, lying, and stealing as acceptable avenues for success. Would those traits be characteristic of an evil or faithful servant of God? Circle your answer:

Evil   Faithful

Application

Why do we need to hear that the return of Jesus is "imminent" for us to be motivated to readiness? Are we not more faithful than that? Are we not willing to endure trials and tribulations with steady hearts and steadfast minds in pursuit of Christ, even if we must wait hundreds of years for His return? Listen, Jesus could call you home today. Are you ready for that imminent encounter? Too many of us, it seems, must be reassured of escaping the great tribulation before feeling secure in God's hands. Why is that? Ask yourself where your faith is. Is it in the sufficiency of Jesus Christ to lead and provide? We are sealed and secure once saved. Do you believe that? If you cannot answer these questions affirmatively, then pray and trust the Holy Spirit to strengthen your faith for the stormy days ahead. You can rest assured that He will. Noah built an ark for the preservation of his family. God provided Jesus Christ as the ark for you. Inside His ark, we are protected. Inside the ark, we are safe and secure (Rom. 8:35–39). Kept for Jesus Christ (Jude 1:1).

> I have given them Your word; and the world has hated them, because they are not of the world, even as I am not of the world. I do not ask You to take them out of the world, but to keep them from the evil *one*. They are not of the world, even as I am not of the world. (John 17:14–16)

> I do not ask on behalf of these alone, but for those also who believe in Me through their word; that they may all be one; even as You, Father, *are* in Me and I in You, that they also may be in Us, so that the world may believe that You sent Me. (John 17:20–21)

Day Four Summary

Jesus shared a parable contrasting two servants, describing one as faithful and the other as evil. One stays alert and prepares his household for the return of his master. The other neglects his. Stay alert and prepare your family as Noah did, discerning and explaining the signs Jesus said to watch for. Whether we are the generation to see His return, or not, we should prepare our hearts and fortify our lives as if we will—after the great tribulation. Be ready. Stay alert. Know the signs of His coming.

Day Five: The Wedding

Jewish feasts aren't the only festivals integrated into Israel's culture that foreshadow the advents of Christ (Col. 2:16–17). Their ancient marriage customs do as well. Today is our last day together. I hope *Just Like the Days of Noah* has not been too overwhelming, and pray you find encouragement and blessing in this final lesson. What I have studied over the last twenty years, you have gleaned in just seven weeks—seven full weeks. It has been quite a journey together! We conclude today with Christ's parable of the ten virgins in Matthew 25:1–13. This is an extension of His timeline sermon in Matthew 24. Jesus will "come forth" for the salvation of His anointed (Hab. 3:13). Why would He? Because He is fully devoted to His chosen bride!

> Then the kingdom of heaven will be comparable to ten virgins, who took their lamps and went out to meet the bridegroom. Five of them were foolish, and five were prudent. For when the foolish took their lamps, they took no oil with them, but the prudent took oil in flasks along with their lamps. (Matthew 25:1–4)

1. What distinguished the prudent from the foolish?

In verses 1–4, a contrast is made between five prudent and five foolish virgins or bridesmaids. All went out to meet the bridegroom, but only five were prepared and ready. That is the crux of this parable. Verses 5–13 provide details of the backstory:

> Now while the bridegroom was delaying, they all got drowsy and *began* to sleep. But at midnight there was a shout, "Behold, the bridegroom! Come out to meet *him*." Then all those virgins rose and trimmed their lamps. The foolish said to the prudent, "Give us some of your oil, for our lamps are going out." But the prudent answered, "No, there will not be enough for us and you *too*; go instead to the dealers and buy *some* for yourselves." And while they were going away to make the purchase, the bridegroom came, and **those who were ready** went in with him to the wedding feast; and the door was shut. Later the other virgins also came, saying, "Lord, lord, open up for us." But he answered, "Truly I say to you, I do not know you." Be on the alert then, for you do not know the day nor the hour (Matthew 25:5–13).

2. How do the prudent illustrate both readiness and endurance?

3. Who went into the wedding feast with the bridegroom?

Parable points:

- All ten bridesmaids became drowsy.
- Five prudent bridesmaids were adequately prepared to sustain the wait.
- There was a shout at midnight, "Behold the bridegroom!"
- Those who were ready entered the wedding feast.
- Those who were not, could not. The door was shut.

Now, we all like stories with happy endings, and this wedding parable has one but only for half of the bridesmaids. The shout of the bridegroom's arrival came late at midnight, which explains why all ten bridesmaids became drowsy. When He did come, five were ready. They might not have been privy to the exact day and hour, but they did know: 1) he was coming, and 2) they were to prepare with a willingness to endure. Just like the previous parable of the faithful servant—being ready and alert is to be prepared (Matt. 24:42–51). Nahum 1:7 says, "The Lord is good, a stronghold in the day of trouble, and **He knows those** who take refuge in Him."

God the Father has gone to great lengths to script the history of Israel and integrate celebratory feasts that proclaim the glory and ministry of His Son. Just imagine what the full revelation and marriage supper will be like! The phases of a Jewish marriage explain the developing relationship between Christ and His bride. Let's look at them briefly. And again, think about this—Only God could orchestrate these celebrations as foreshadows of the first and second comings of Jesus Christ.

In this supernatural relationship, we are united together with God. Jesus expounded on that when He prayed, "I do not ask on behalf of these alone, but for those also who believe in Me through their word; **that they may all be one**; even as You, Father, *are* in Me and I in You, that they also may be in Us, so that the world may believe that You sent Me The glory which You have given Me I have given to them, **that they may be one, just as We are one**; I in them and You in Me, that they may be perfected in unity" (John 17:20–23). We have been united by the Father, Son and Holy Spirit—where love is freely bestowed upon all who are His. This phenomenal love is illustrated through the institution of marriage, more specifically, the three phases of a traditional Jewish marriage ceremony (Messianic.bible.com/Ancient Jewish Wedding Customs).

Matchmaking and mutual commitment (shiddukhin pronounced—shi-du-ken)

The first phase of a Jewish marriage is called **shiddukhin** when a couple is matched by a "shadkhan" or matchmaker. Traditionally, the groom's father was the one who selected his son's bride. Do you remember Abraham's search and qualifications for Isaac's wife (Gen. 24:1–4)? After Rebekah was selected, she was also extended the opportunity to reject or accept Abraham's offer to join Isaac in marriage. She accepted (Gen. 24:58).

4. **What does John 6:44 say about the Father's role in choosing Christ's bride?**

"You did not choose Me but I chose you and appointed you that you would go and bear fruit, and that your fruit would remain…" (John 15:16). Prior to the second phase of Jewish marriage, the couple is immersed in water as a declaration of cleansing and commitment to one another. Jesus insisted John baptize him in the Jordan River, saying, "Permit *it* at this time; for in this way it is fitting for us to fulfill all righteousness" (Matthew 3:15). Jesus was expressing an unwavering devotion for His bride. We do the same when we are baptized, setting ourselves apart unto Christ, just as He did for us.

The betrothal or engagement (erusin pronounced—arrusin)

After their baptism, the engagement phase or **erusin,** begins as the first of a two-part ceremony. The couple is legally married but not yet living together. A betrothal contract will be presented to the bride, specifying the terms and price that the bridegroom is willing to pay. If the she accepts, then the erusin contract is sealed by both parties who drink from a cup of wine together, acknowledging the blessings of marriage. Neither drink of the fruit of the vine again until they are reunited and their marriage is consummated.

5. **How did Jesus illustrate *erusin* in Matthew 26:27–29?**

Both parties enter into this erusin contract under a marriage canopy (chuppah), which is symbolic of building a new home together. The bridegroom guarantees the consummation of their marriage with gifts for his bride (Gen. 24:53). The parallel here is in the gift of the Holy Spirit, "given as a pledge of our inheritance," with a view to our redemption (Eph. 1:13–14). This erusin betrothal typically lasts for a year while the bridegroom prepares their dwelling and the bride prepares for his return. He cannot return for her until his father assesses their new home to be ready.

6. **What did Jesus promise His disciples in John 14:3?**

7. How does Matthew 24:36 concur with the *erusin* marriage phase?

During the erusin phase, the bride also selects her bridesmaids (church evangelism). Her bridesmaids keep their oil lamps ready in anticipation of the bridegroom coming who is announced with a shout and the blast of a shofar. Sound familiar? "For the LORD Himself will descend from heaven with a shout, with the voice of the archangel and with the trumpet of God" (1 Thessalonians 4:16). The bridesmaids who accompany the bride are to be ready as well.

> "Let us rejoice and be glad and give the glory to Him, for the marriage of the Lamb has come and His bride has made herself ready." It was given to her to clothe herself in fine linen, bright *and* clean; for the fine linen is the righteous acts of the saints. Then he said to me, "Write, Blessed are those who are invited to the marriage supper of the Lamb." And he said to me, "These are true words of God." (Revelation 19:7–9)

8. How is the bride dressed?

In these parables and throughout the New Testament, real faith is accompanied by a commitment to Christ, which is characterized by a separation from sin and participation in righteous deeds. Action rather than inaction. "Even so faith, if it has no works, is dead, *being* by itself. But someone may *well* say, 'You have faith and I have works; show me your faith without the works, and I will show you my faith by my works'" (James 2:17–18). Will sedentary saints be ready for the return of Jesus Christ, equipped with sufficient oil to endure the wait? The five foolish bridesmaids were not.

> **The marriage ceremony and consummation** (nissuin pronounced—ni-shoe-un)

Nissuin encompasses the third marriage phase and second of two ceremonies. Nissuin, meaning "**to take**," is a word that comes from *naso*, to "**lift up**." Luke 21:28 quoted Christ saying, "But when these things begin to take place (the signs we are to watch for), straighten up and **lift up** your heads, because your redemption is drawing near." Look again at Matthew 24:38-41:

For as in those days before the flood they were eating and drinking, marrying and giving in marriage, until the day that Noah entered the ark, and they did not understand until the flood came and took them all away; **so will the coming of the Son of Man be**. Then there will be two men in the field; one will be **taken** and one will be left. Two women *will be* grinding at the mill; one will be **taken** and one will be left.

When the Father's "day and hour" has arrived, Jesus Christ will return for His bride. The righteous dead will be resurrected (1 Thess. 4:16) on the last day (John 6:39–40, 43, 54). Then those who remain alive will be caught up to meet the Lord in the air. The marriage consummation occurs when the saints are transfigured. "Beloved, now we are children of God, and it has not appeared as yet what we will be. We know that when He appears, we will be like Him, because we will see Him just as He is" (1 John 3:2). United with God (John 17:21). Our joy is made full (John 17:13). This happens in a fraction of a second. "Behold, I tell you a mystery; we will not all sleep, but we will all be changed, in a moment, in the twinkling of an eye, **at the last trumpet**; for the trumpet will sound, and **the dead will be raised imperishable**, and we will be changed" (1 Corinthians 15:51–52). The last trumpet, or Revelation's seventh trumpet, announces the kingdom of Jesus Christ.

Christ's return for His church is disclosed in the final chapters of Revelation as a sneak preview. Remember that both Christ's timeline and His Revelation complement one another. His timeline specifies the order of future events; His Revelation expounds the details of those events. While foreshadows have been previously cast, those historical events did not fulfill the remaining prophetic Scriptures. Look around you. Has Jesus descended in glory on a white horse to reinstate peace and remove evil? Have the dead been resurrected or the saints raptured? Is there a new heaven and earth? Has Satan been bound or is Christ reigning from Jerusalem? Some attempt to dismiss and downgrade the day of the Lord to be mere allegory. Yet Jesus Himself told us to be ready and alert. Would that be for a symbolic fulfillment of prophecy? Hardly. All Bible prophecies fulfilled by Jesus when He first came were fulfilled literally and in the days of the corresponding Jewish feasts. Why would the remaining prophecies be fulfilled any differently?

- In Revelation 19:1–6, a unique four-fold Hallelujah chorus resounds in heaven. A grand event is about to be commence—one worthy of celebration and praise.

- In Revelation 19:7–9 we read, "'Let us rejoice and be glad and give the glory to Him, **for the marriage of the Lamb has come** and His bride has made herself ready.' It was given to her to clothe herself in fine linen, bright *and* clean; for the fine linen is the righteous acts of the saints. Then he said to me, 'Write, Blessed are those who are invited to **the marriage supper of the Lamb**.' And he said to me, 'These are true words of God.'"

The bride is ready!

- In Revelation 19:11–16, the glorious return of Christ is depicted. Nothing less than His glorious second coming is ever mentioned by any writer in Scripture. Jesus is joined by an army clothed in fine linen, which according to verse 8, refers to the saints. The saints are overcomers who have fought battles of faith as earthly pilgrims, forged into an alliance with God through multiple furnace fires. "Blessed be the Lord, my rock, who trains my hands for war, *and* my fingers for battle" (Psalm 144:1). Thus, the people of the Prince will be revealed "as He is," an army of overcomers. We will be gathered "into the freedom" of the glory of God (Ro. 8:21); shining forth as the stars of heaven (Dan. 12:3); released from the flesh and unfettered by pain (Rev. 21:4). The saints in this scene are not fighting. It is the sword from the mouth of Christ that judges and makes war. Jesus is the One who treads the wine press of the fierce wrath of God, the Almighty in the day of the Lord.

- In Revelation 19:17–18, the great supper of God is described as a feast for the birds of the air. Not a typical menu selection for a wedding feast yet satisfying nonetheless because justice is being served. The first Hallelujah chorus in Revelation 19:2 proclaims, "After these things I heard something like a loud voice of a great multitude in heaven, saying, 'Hallelujah! Salvation and glory and power belong to our God; because His judgments are true and righteous; for He has judged the great harlot who was corrupting the earth with her immorality, and **He has avenged the blood of His bond-servants** on her'" (Deut. 32:35; Rom.12:19). Justice is the first menu entrée enjoyed at the marriage feast of the Lamb.

- In Revelation 19:19–21, the beast with his army comes against Jesus Christ and His. Once again, a battle is not fought. The beast and false prophet are simply thrown into the lake of fire, and their militia "marked by the beast," slain by the Word of God.

- In Revelation 20:1–6, Satan is bound for 1,000 years while the saints rule alongside Christ. This era is typified in the Feast of Tabernacles which follows the Feast of Trumpets (see appendix "Seven Jewish Feasts"). It is in Jerusalem that the festive marriage feast will take place. Isaiah 25:6–7 says, "The Lord of hosts will prepare a lavish banquet for all peoples on this mountain; a banquet of aged wine, choice pieces with marrow, *and* refined, aged wine. And on this mountain He will swallow up the covering which is over all peoples, even the veil which is stretched over all nations." A marriage feast that lasts for a millennium!

Revelation 19 succeeds the great tribulation period, coinciding with the timeline of Christ in Matthew 24. In 2 Thessalonians 2:1–4, Paul stated that Jesus returns after the antichrist is revealed, writing the same congregation he addressed regarding the resurrection and rapture. Daniel's dream also revealed the coming of Christ to be after the great tribulation (Dan. 7). In Revelation 1:7, Jesus quoted Daniel in reference to His glorious coming while standing amidst seven church candlesticks (Dan. 7:13). Jesus was not referring to a silent return when He addressed those churches. And if all that is not sufficient evidence of a post-tribulation return, we also read in Acts 3:20-21 that God will send Jesus "the Christ appointed for you, whom heaven must receive **until *the* period of restoration of all things** about which God spoke by the mouth of His holy prophets from ancient time. Jesus returns when it is time to resurrect, renew and restore all things. Not before.

Jesus began the parable of ten virgins by stating, "Then the kingdom of heaven will be comparable to ten virgins who took their lamps and went out to meet the bridegroom" (Matthew 25:1). When Jesus returns, the wheat and chaff will be separated—the wheat taken or "caught up" while those left will incur the wrath of God. The great marriage supper of God then begins for those who are found ready (Eph. 3:4–6, Hosea 2:14–23).

My earnest prayer is that the timeline of Christ be acknowledged for what it truly is—a chronological sequence of signs preceding His Second Coming. It is a timeline for His Church, both Jew and Gentile. Jesus provided this information to prepare and fortify His redeemed with an understanding of what is happening when those signs unfold. Undoubtedly, they will usher in a time of chaos for those living in darkness or subsisting on the peripherals of Christianity like the five foolish virgins. In Luke's recording of Christ's timeline, he wrote that "there will be terrors and great signs from heaven" (Luke 21:11). The Greek word for "terrors" utilized by Luke is not found anywhere else in Scripture. It is *phobetra,* meaning "terrible sights, with an emphasis on its terrifying impact." This is why the kingdom of God is to walk in the light of Scripture by His Spirit—ready and alert.

Has this study been beneficial for you? If so, how? (Don't forget to go back to Day One of Weeks One and Week Three to see if your questions have been answered.)

Day Five Summary

The parable of the ten virgins relates to the importance of preparation and readiness. It also beckons us to consider the Jewish wedding customs and their foreshadowing of our coming Christ. The three phases of a Jewish marriage are (1) shiddukhin, or matchmaking; (2) erusin or the betrothal; and (3) nissuin, which is the marriage consummation. Revelation 19-20 is a confirmation of nissuin, the marriage consummation. All things will be made new (2 Pet. 3:10-14) and the glory of the Lord will fill the earth (Hab. 2:14)! Amen.

Week Seven Synopsis

> Be ready for His return and alert to the signs of His coming.

And behold, I am coming quickly.
(Revelation 22:7)

Week Seven Worksheet

Matthew 24:32–41

Now learn the parable from the fig tree: when its branch has already become tender and puts forth its leaves, you know that summer is near; so, you too, when you see all these things, recognize that He is near, right at the door.

Truly I say to you, this generation will not pass away until all these things take place. Heaven and earth will pass away, but My words will not pass away. But of that day and hour no one knows, not even the angels of heaven, nor the Son, but the Father alone.

For the coming of the Son of Man will be just like the days of Noah.

For as in those days before the flood they were eating and drinking, marrying and giving in marriage, until the day that Noah entered the ark, and they did not understand until the flood came and took them all away; so will the coming of the Son of Man be.

Then there will be two men in the field; one will be taken and one will be left.
Two women will be grinding at the mill; one will be taken and one will be left.

Observations

Jesus is right at the door when ...

- You see all these things.

What things?

The coming of the Son of Man will be just like ...

Then there will be two men in the field ...

One _____ and one _____

Two women grinding at the mill ...

One _____ and one _____

Antichrist/Israel Covenant		Abomination of Desolation		Jesus Returns
Dan. 9:27	3 1/2 years	great tribulation	3 1/2 years	1,000-year reign

WEEK SEVEN WORKSHEET

Matthew 24:42–51

Therefore … be on the alert, for you do not know which day your Lord is coming. But be sure of this, that if the head of the house had known at what time of the night the thief was coming, he would have been on the alert and would not have allowed his house to be broken into.

For this reason you also must be ready; for the Son of Man is coming at an hour when you do not think He will.

Who then is the faithful and sensible slave whom his master put in charge of his household to give them their food at the proper time?

Blessed is that slave whom his master finds so doing when he comes. Truly I say to you that he will put him in charge of all his possessions. But if that evil slave says in his heart, "My master is not coming for a long time," and begins to beat his fellow slaves and eat and drink with drunkards; the master of that slave will come on a day when he does not expect him and at an hour which he does not know, and will cut him in pieces and assign him a place with the hypocrites; in that place there will be weeping and gnashing of teeth.

And what I say to you I say to all …
Be on the alert!

Observations

Be on the alert …

- You do not know which _____

_____

If the head of the house knew what time of the night the thief was coming, he would

_____and would not

_____.

So be ready because …

- The Son of Man is coming at an hour when you do not think He will.

The faithful slave in charge of His master's household will _____

_____

Blessed …

- Is that slave whom his master finds so doing when he comes.

Truly, I say to you …

- The master will put him in charge of

_____

The evil slave says in his heart _____

_____

_____ and

will be assigned a place with the hypocrites, a place of weeping and gnashing of teeth.

Postscript

Just Like the Days of Noah has been an unbelievable expedition that you have now shared with me. Studying the timeline of Christ and related prophecies required a trek through Scripture from Genesis to Revelation. Thus, our journey could not have been brief nor easy. It has been like an archeological excavation, a digging of truth that required time and labor from all of us. By the Spirit and grace of God, we did it. Together!

I encourage you to continue examining the prophetic Scriptures, allowing the overarching counsel of His Word to guide you—unmuzzled, without censorship or human bias. Dedicate yourself to a patient pursuit of truth because it does take time. Do not spend most of it reading the plethora of books on apocalyptic topics or bouncing from speaker to speaker to collect data. Study what the Bible says about the return of Christ first. Then, sift through the studies of others. You will be better equipped and more inclined to recognize potential errors.

Theologians do not agree on how to correlate Daniel's dreams with John's visions and whether to interpret them literally or figuratively. Neither do they agree on the timing of Christ's return or the rapture of the saints. This does not mean God's truth is elusive. It means there are different systems of analysis being utilized. Covenant theologians use God's covenants as their schematic to interpret and explain His overall plan. Dispensational theologians use John Darby's framework. *Just Like the Days of Noah* embraces covenant theology as a dependable plumbline for interpretation. That was not the original intent but the chartered path determined by Scripture.

Some even pursue an extremely chaotic approach in the interpretation and application of Scripture, dismissing the contents as inerrantly inspired by the Holy Spirit. 2 Timothy 3:16–17 says, "All Scripture is inspired by God and profitable for teaching, for reproof, for correction, for training in righteousness; so that the man of God may be adequate, equipped for every good work." All Scripture. I'm not sure why these consider themselves to be Bible students or scholars when, in reality, they are denying the ability of God to reveal truth. This group should be avoided entirely. "Know this first of all, that in the last days mockers will come with their mocking, following after their own lusts (2 Peter 3:3). It would be more beneficial for the saints to allow the Word of God to speak freely as a miraculous revelation penned by men, anointed by ink from the well of the Holy Spirit.

> How blessed is the man who does not walk in the counsel of the wicked, nor stand in the path of sinners, nor sit in the seat of scoffers! But his delight is in the law of the LORD, and in His law he meditates day and night. He will be like a tree *firmly* planted by streams of water, which yields its fruit in its season and its leaf does not wither and in whatever he does, he prospers. (Psalm 1:1–3)

God's first covenant promise, found in Genesis 3:15, declares the day of the Lord and Satan's defeat. Through the saints such as Noah, Abraham, Moses, David and prophets from Israel, more covenant promises and prophecies came forth. Jesus fulfilled hundreds of those prophecies in His first coming, clearly identifying Him to be the Messiah. In the day of the Lord, the remaining prophecies will be fulfilled when He returns. We now wait for this glorious day! Old Testament prophets described and predicted it; New Testament writers encouraged us to be ready—not for the rapture but for the return of Christ and the day of the Lord. God called one man, Abraham, to father a nation to bring forth the Redeemer for all nations. One Gospel for all the world that once received, brings us into a union with God and one another. The Scriptures never reveal that once united, we are ever separated for any reason. God's overcomers are in it to win it—together!

Disseminating the great tribulation and rise of the Antichrist has been a flaming, red hot potato for Bible scholars through the centuries—difficult to handle. Opinions have evolved and devolved, as society and cultures demanded. For the layperson who cannot commit to years of dedicated study, the only recourse has been to depend upon the studies of those who could. Thus, we inadvertently place our faith in man rather than the Word of God. Foreseeing this dilemma, Jesus provided us with an anchor against the storm of confusing, contradictory interpretations. I am speaking of Christ's timeline, disclosed for both scholar and layperson but currently cloaked by proposals and penchant preferences. When we allow the timeline of Christ to lead the way, the task of deciphering all remaining prophecies and the varied interpretations, becomes simplified.

Today's escalating global, national, regional, and even personal skirmishes are preparatory faith conflicts purposed by God to prepare us for the day of the Lord and great tribulation—the final contest of the saints. Enduring the visual rise of the Antichrist and a great falling away from the faith in the latter days will require that we be alert and ready, living holy lives and committed to Christ today. Jesus shared two primary, preparatory directives: (1) see to it that no one misleads you, and (2) see that you are not frightened (Matt. 24:4–6). If you want to faithfully stand in these final days, commit yourself to the Word of God, not man. Face your fears. Don't run from them or they will relentlessly chase you. Take every anxious thought before His throne. Trust His heart. Trust His plan. Trusting God through trials and conflicts of faith is analogous to trusting Christ to redeem and resurrect you on that last day. John 6:29 says, "This is the work of God, that you believe in Him whom He has sent." Through thick or thin. To God be the glory!

> For the vision is yet for the appointed time; it hastens toward the goal and it will not fail. Though it tarries, wait for it; for it will certainly come, it will not delay. (Habakkuk 2:3)

Week One   See to it that neither deception or fear defines you.

Week Two   The righteous are resurrected and raptured at the seventh and last trumpet.

Week Three   The church of Jesus Christ is a union of Jews and Gentiles—God's elect, who endure the great tribulation together.

Week Four   Jesus returns to establish His kingdom in the days of the ten kings after the abomination of desolation and man of lawlessness is revealed.

Week Five   The Antichrist reigns for three and a half years prior to Jesus returning and visibly establishing His kingdom on earth.

Week Six   Scripture presents one return of Jesus Christ, one day of the Lord, one resurrection of the righteous, and one gathering of the elect.

Week Seven   Be ready for His return and alert to the signs of His coming.

Final Review of Matthew 24
Draw a line to match the following:

Matthew 24:1–14	Just like the days of Noah
Matthew 24:15–28	Being faithful
Matthew 24:29–31	Beginning of birth pangs
Matthew 24:32–41	Abomination of desolation
Matthew 24:42–51	Heavens are shaken.

Well done!
Faithful to the end.

Appendix

RAPTURE

1 Thessalonians 4:13–18

There are three different views on the timing of being caught up with Christ:

1. Pre-tribulation rapture—Jesus returns before the seven-year tribulation period.
2. Mid-tribulation rapture—Jesus returns after the Antichrist appears but before the great tribulation.
3. Post-tribulation rapture—Jesus returns after the seven-year tribulation period.

Pre-trib Rapture (Ro. 11:25)	Mid-trib Rapture (2 Thess. 2:3)	Post-trib Rapture (Mt. 24:29-30, Rev. 19)
Antichrist/Israel covenant	great tribulation	1,000-year reign

After studying Matthew 24 and the correlating Scriptures, one might ask, "Why are different timelines proposed and a pre-tribulation rapture presented so fervently in America today? And by some of our most notable evangelical pastors and pastors! Why aren't they teaching the timeline of Christ regarding His return?" Those would be excellent questions.

I did some digging. You can too. The answer is explained by researching the view of dispensational theology. Dispensationalists divide Scripture into eras of time: the dispensation of innocence, conscience, human government, promise, law, grace, and, finally, Christ's millennial kingdom. They propose that each dispensation ends before the next one begins, therefore the dispensation of grace or "church age" ends before the tribulation period and the church will be removed. In contrast, covenant theology interprets God's plan through His successive framework of pledges and promises made through Adam, Noah, Abraham, His land covenant, Moses, and David. These covenants were all mediated by the sacrifice of Christ into a new covenant of grace (Heb. 9:15), which will extend during the tribulation period as believers join the body of Christ. God's covenants build and progress from the first messianic promise in Genesis 3:15 to the revelation of the "seed" (Jesus Christ).

Now, for a history synopsis.

Dispensational theology emerged through Jonathan Edwards in the mid-1700s. The church age dispensation and theory of a pre-tribulation rapture were popularized through John Darby in the mid-1800s. Charles Scofield incorporated the church age dispensation into his Bible study notes in the early 1900s. The proposal gained momentum and found passage through notable evangelists like Dwight L. Moody, Charles Ryrie, and John Walvoord, who were influential in seminaries such as Dallas Theological Seminary. Tim LaHaye, author of the Left Behind series, contributed to its appeal through apocalyptic fictional literature. Please understand I am not interested in discrediting anyone, especially the family of faith in the body of Christ. But it is disconcerting that a theoretical view is being presented as biblically clear when it is not, and why would so many evangelicals support theological dispensations over covenant certainties?

The dispensations are theoretical. God's covenants are pillars of truth. Jesus left us a clear timeline that simplifies prophecy, taking us to the books of Daniel and Revelation, explaining what is coming, when, and how to prepare. Christ's timeline reveals a post-tribulation timing and even alludes to "one being taken and one left" when He returns. Regardless of our preference or persuasion, we should study and be fully acquainted with the entire timeline that Jesus revealed. He is the one who will come again. He knows the signs of His returning. While the Son of God may not know the specific "day or hour," everything else He knows! "For I am God … declaring the end from the beginning" (Isaiah 46:9-10).

SEVEN JEWISH FEASTS

Colossians 2:16–17

 Four Spring/Summer Feasts (Fulfilled in Christ's first coming)

*Passover (A lamb without blemish is sacrificed – Ex. 12:1-6)
 Jesus was crucified as the Passover Lamb – 1 Cor. 5:7–8.
 Celebrates God's redemption – Deut. 16:6.

Unleavened Bread (Bread eaten without yeast during Passover – Ex. 12:15)
 Jesus, the Bread of Life, was without sin – John 6:51.
 Celebrates God's righteousness – Deut. 16:3.

Firstfruits (One sheaf from the harvest is waved before the Lord for acceptance – Lev. 23:9–14)
 Jesus was resurrected as the first one to overcome death – 1 Cor. 15:20–23).
 Celebrates life, His harvest, and the rain (Holy Spirit).

*Pentecost (Two sheaves are waved, Jew and Gentile – Lev. 23:15–17)
 A new offering is waved seven weeks after the Feast of Firstfruits.
 Jesus sent the Holy Spirit to baptize and unite all believers with God – Acts 2:1–4.

 An interval between the spring and fall feasts allows opportunity for the Gospel to be preached around the world – Acts 1:8, Rom. 11:25.

 Three Fall Feasts (To be fulfilled in Christ's second coming)

Trumpets (First of the High Holy Days—ten days of repentance and renewal)
 Rosh Hashanah – Lev. 23:23–25. Announced by the blast of the shofar or ram's horn.
 The last trumpet announces Christ's return – 1 Thess. 4:13–18; 1 Cor. 15:52.

Atonement (Highest of Holy Days—judgment and forgiveness)
 Yom Kippur – Lev. 23:26–32. "Kippur" in Hebrew means "to cover"– Ps. 78:38.
 Those covered by the blood of Jesus are forgiven and sealed for life – Eph. 4:30.

*Tabernacles (Seventh Festival – Exod. 23:16, Lev. 23:33–44)

The harvest is complete and celebrated. Jesus gathers, dwells, and rules with His elect on earth for 1,000 years – Micah 4:1–7, Rev. 20:4.

---

*3 Pilgrim Feasts (Passover, Pentecost, and Tabernacles)

In Bible times, Jewish men traveled to Jerusalem to celebrate three primary feasts (Deut. 16:16–17). These pilgrim feasts comprise the three elements of God's prophetic plan regarding redemption. The Passover Feast was fulfilled in the sacrifice of Jesus Christ; the Feast of Pentecost in the uniting of Jews and Gentiles by the Holy Spirit; and the Feast of Tabernacles will be fulfilled when Jesus returns to reign with His elect in His millennium kingdom. The bride will "tabernacle" with her king!

THE SIXTH SEAL

During His earthly ministry, Jesus shared a timeline of events preceding His return (Mt. 24). From heaven Jesus sent visions to John to prepare His church—His bride (Rev. 1:4, 19:7, 22:16). These prophetic disclosures confirm and complement each other; they do not contradict one another. Dispensationalists interpret the scroll seals in Revelation as events that will happen when they are broken—before the scroll is even opened. Thus, the shaking of the heavens and wrath of the Lamb, revealed by the sixth of seven seals, is viewed as occurring at the onset of the tribulation period. That interpretation is used to undergird a pre-tribulation rapture since the redeemed are not subject to God's wrath (1 Thess. 1:10).

Read the description of the sixth seal:

> I looked when He broke the sixth seal, and there was a great earthquake; and **the sun became black as sackcloth** *made* **of hair, and the whole moon became like blood; and the stars of the sky fell to the earth,** as a fig tree casts its unripe figs when shaken by a great wind. The sky was split apart like a scroll when it is rolled up, and every mountain and island were moved out of their places. Then the kings of the earth and the great men and the commanders and the rich and the strong and every slave and free man hid themselves in the caves and among the rocks of the mountains; and they said to the mountains and to the rocks, "Fall on us and hide us from the presence of Him who sits on the throne, and from the wrath of the Lamb; for the **great day of their wrath has come**, and who is able to stand?" (Revelation 6:12–17)

Note the placement of this event on Christ's timeline:

> But immediately after the tribulation of those days **the sun will be darkened, and the moon will not give its light, and the stars will fall from the sky, and the powers of the heavens will be shaken.** And then the sign of the Son of Man will appear in the sky, and then all the tribes of the earth will mourn, and they will see **the Son of Man coming on the clouds of the sky with power and great glory.** (Matthew 24:29–30)

Since Jesus designated the shaking of the heavens to be immediately after the great tribulation in Matthew 24:29, we also have the timing of the sixth seal disclosure. It does not occur prior to the tribulation period but afterward. There is a cataclysmic failure of heaven's luminaries right before the Light of the world returns!

In Revelation 5:1–5, Jesus is the only one worthy to break the seals and open the scroll. Ancient scrolls were sealed typically by three to seven seals that either identified the document, the owner, or both. For an inheritance to be enacted, the seals were broken by the heir at the proper time in the presence of witnesses. This scroll in Revelation 5 can only be opened by the Lamb who will inherit the earth at the sanctioned "day and hour" before the throne of God.

The first four seals on the scroll depict four apocalyptic horses and riders: (1) on a white horse, Antichrist(s); (2) on a red horse, wars; (3) on a black horse, famine; and (4) on an ashen horse, death. The conditions described by these four horses and their riders align with the "beginning of birth pangs" on Christ's timeline in Matthew 24:4–8. In Zechariah 1:8–10, horses such as these patrol the earth, reporting conditions to the Lord. It follows that the four apocalyptic horsemen do the same. They depict the state of earth during the tribulation.

The fifth seal discloses what Jesus describes in Matthew 24:9–10. Birth pangs will intensify through persecution and martyrdom. Once again, the seals align with the timeline of Christ.

The sixth seal is an unmistakable fulfillment of numerous Old Testament prophecies regarding the day of the Lord. The shaking of the heavens announces the day of the Lord which Paul connects to the return of Christ (2 Thess. 2:1–2); after the abomination of desolation (2 Thess. 2:3–8); and at the last trumpet (1 Cor. 15:50–52).

Another problem with the sixth seal occurring before the scroll is even opened is in the mention of the "wrath of the Lamb." According to Revelation 11:15–18, God's wrath follows the seventh and last trumpet. And the trumpets sound off during the tribulation. More importantly, the saints escape God's wrath yet Scripture reveals His elect are on earth during the tribulation period (Matt. 24:21–22; Rev. 7:14, 12:17, 13:10; Dan. 7:21).

Because dispensationalists believe God's wrath is unleashed prior to the scroll's opening, they also believe the trumpets to be instruments of wrath. But since the Jewish fall feasts foreshadow the Second Coming of Christ, we should consider the purpose of the Feast of Trumpets. This feast observes a time of reflection and repentance prior to the Feast of Yom Kippur (Judgment Day). *L'shana Tova Tikateuv* or "May you be inscribed and sealed in the Book of life," is the theme of the festival. Thus, the trumpets warn of His wrath but they are not God's wrath. After the seventh and last trumpet, God's wrath comes forth from seven bowls (1 Cor. 15:52; Rev. 11:18).

When we let Christ's timeline determine the timing of the events depicted by the seals, they do not occur before the scroll is opened; instead, they reveal the contents of the scroll. They characterize the tribulation period as entailing the rise of the Antichrist and wars followed by their effects such as famine and death. Persecution escalates along with other outliers such as martyrdom. Then, at the close of the tribulation period, the powers of the heavens (sun, moon, stars) are shaken and the "sign" of the Son of Man appears—meaning Jesus is announced. It is pretty straight forward when utilizing Christ's timeline to interpret His Revelation. The Feast of Trumpets and the fact that the elect are on earth during the tribulation period align with Matthew 24.

Be silent, all flesh, before the Lord; for He is aroused from His holy habitation. (Zechariah 2:13)

When the seventh seal is broken, the scroll is then opened. "There is silence in heaven for about half an hour" (Revelation 8:1). Seven angels with seven trumpets position themselves to sound God's judgments upon the earth, similar to the signs and wonders in Egypt (Ex. 7:3–5). Isaiah 26:9 says, "For when the earth experiences Your judgments the inhabitants of the world learn righteousness."

Be silent before the Lord God! For the day of the Lord is near, for the Lord has prepared a sacrifice, He has consecrated His guests. (Zephaniah 1:7)